WITHDRAWN

The Ultimate 2000

Directory of Ethnic Organizations, Ethnic Media and Scholars for the Chicago Metropolitan Area

An
Illinois Ethnic Coalition
Publication

Edited by
Cynthia Linton

ISBN
09658445-2-8 (An Illinois Ethnic Coalition Publication)

Published by
The Illinois Ethnic Coalition
55 East Monroe, Suite 2930
Chicago, IL 60603
(312)368-1155; fax: (312)251-8815
www.medill.nwu.edu/IEC
iecchicago@aol.com

Book staff:
Executive Director: Jeryl Levin
Project Manager: Cynthia Linton, Adjunct Professor, Medill School of Journalism,
                              Northwestern University
Researcher: Michelle Kolak
Cover Design: Matthew Holzman

Also published by IEC: *The Ethnic Handbook: A Guide to the Cultures and Traditions of Chicago's Diverse Communities.*

The Illinois Ethnic Coalition is a not-for-profit organization dedicated to enhancing understanding of our region's diverse ethnic and racial communities and promoting cooperation between groups.

Contents

Introduction   P.   5

Organizations and agencies   P.   7

Media   P.   95

Consulates   P. 117

Ethnic studies programs & scholars   P. 123

Calendar   P. 139

Introduction

When the Illinois Ethnic Coalition released the first *Directory of Chicago Ethnic Organizations* in 1996, we wanted to provide the Chicago area with a comprehensive database of ethnic organizations serving the metropolitan area. Since its first incarnation, we have broadened and expanded this resource to include not only ethnic organizations, but ethnic media and experts that cover the metropolitan community.

In the 1980s and '90s, Chicago and its suburbs swelled with newcomers from literally all over the globe. They regenerated many of Chicago's neighborhoods and accounted for explosive growth in our suburbs. The newcomers continue to define America and, more to the point, our own communities. This growth is projected well into the year 2025 and it has national (and global) implications for everyone.

It is often said those who succeed in the 21st century will know how to cross boundaries and communicate effectively across cultures, especially when the broader American culture is defined by so many different groups.

The Chicago area is home to more than 100 language groups. For business and elected leaders, the civic institutions and media outlets that chronicle and mirror our lives, and the service providers and not-for-profits, casting a wider net has become increasingly important.

IEC is encouraged that so many have used this resource to tap into the wealth of diversity in our region.

In this edition of the *Ultimate,* you will find updated information on approximately 500 ethnic organizations serving immigrant, refugee and the native-born populations in Chicago and suburbs, as well 130 ethnic media and a wide array of ethnic scholars and experts.

New entries are designated +. You will also find updated information on e-mail addresses and Web sites.

If you do come across personnel changes or any other information you'd like us to know about, please call IEC at (312) 368-1155.

Here's hoping that this guide will help you cast a wider net into the year 2000 and beyond!

Sincerely,
Jeryl Levin, Director
The Illinois Ethnic Coalition
January 2000

Ethnic organizations and agencies
(in alphabetical order by ethnic group)

African

(see also Eritrean, Ethiopian, Ghanaian, Liberian, Nigerian, Senegalese)

United Africans Organization
1723 W. Wallen
Chicago, IL 60626
Phone: (773)761-3119
Evening/weekend: same
Chr.: Hayelom Ayele
No exec. dir., no office
Founded: 1988
Serves: The African community in Chicago and suburbs
Purpose: To provide an institutional vehicle for addressing common concerns and promote positive relations among Africans of diverse backgrounds as well as between Africans and all Chicagoans; to enhance service delivery capabilities of member organizations
Programs: Referrals, technical assistance, leadership development, advocacy and public awareness
Volunteers: Welcome

African American

Ada S. McKinley Community Services
725 S. Wells St., Suite 1-A
Chicago, IL 60607
Phone: (312)554-0600
Fax: (312)554-0292
e-mail: georgejones@iarf.org
Web: adasmckinley@adasmckinley.org
Exec. Dir.: George Jones, Jr.
Pres.: James P. Shoffner
Founded: 1919
Serves: Mostly African Americans, some Hispanics, whites, Native Americans, in metropolitan Chicago
Purpose: To serve individuals, families and people with disabilities who need help developing their abilities in order to lead healthy, productive and fulfilling lives
Programs: Residential housing, job training & placement for adults with disabilities, foster care & adoption services, educational services, Head Start, Upward Bound, talent search, tutoring, college placement, financial aid, early intervention, in-home counseling for troubled youth & families, juvenile delinquency intervention services, senior day programming and nutrition, food pantry, emergency assistance, drop-out programs, child care
Other locations: 100 E. 34th St., 11400 S. Edbrooke, 10530 S. Oglesby, 2647 E. 88th St., 8422 S. Damen, 8458 S. Mackinaw, 7939 S. Western, 7222 S. Exchange, 1938 E. 91st St. 219 S. Dearborn, 1112 E. 87th St., 6033 S. Wentworth, 6600 S. Stewart, 6701 S. Morgan, 4237 S. Indiana, 2961 S. Dearborn, 2907 S. Wabash, 2715 1/2 W. 63rd St., 4540 S. Michigan, 9135 S. Brandon, 10001 S. Woodlawn, 7640 S. Vincennes, 2659 W. 59th St., 230 S. Dearborn, 2452-54 W. 71st St., 1863 S. Wabash, 4543 S. Princeton, 2929 S. Wabash, 5401 S. Wentworth and 475 Blackhawk Dr., Ft. Sheridan
Volunteers: Welcome

African American Leadership Partnership, Inc.
1313 E. 60th St.
Chicago, IL 60637
Phone: (773)753-2470
Fax: (773)753-2480
Web: www.aalpinfo.org
Founded: 1979
Serves: African Americans on the West Side of Chicago (West Garfield Park)
Purpose: To help create a healthy, sustainable community of the West Side
Programs: Economic development, adult daycare, senior home repair, community safety, advocacy, housing, computer training and office skills, small business center, health care for mothers and children, in-home chore/homemaker services, family counseling, transitional shelter for homeless pregnant and parenting women, high school youth, WIC
Volunteers: Welcome

Black Contractors United
2860 E. 76ᵗʰ St., Suite 2-B
Chicago, IL 60649
Phone: (773)933-7950
Fax: (773)933-7957

Exec. Dir.: Paul King III
Pres.: Ernest Brown
Founded: 1979
Serves: African Americans in Chicago and surrounding suburbs and states
Purpose: To expand the base of minority contractors; to help them achieve parity in the free marketplace without the restriction of bias or prejudice; to increase the success potential of new or existing firms by providing quality professional, technical and managerial assistance; to help a selected number of firms reach higher levels of growth, development and profitability through focused assistance; to act as a liaison between minority and majority contracting communities to the benefit of both
Programs: Monthly informative meetings, affirmative action/consulting/monitoring, some technical, managerial and educational training to members, referral, membership assistance
Volunteers: Welcome

Black Ensemble Theater
4520 N. Beacon St.
Chicago, IL 60640
Phone: (773)769-4451
Evening/weekend: same
Fax: (312)769-4533
Exec. Dir. & Pres.: Jackie Taylor
Founded: 1976
Serves: African Americans and Hispanics in Chicago and Illinois
Purpose: To foster racial harmony by producing theater that attracts a diverse audience, involving them in a process that inspires interracial respect
Programs: Stages plays that have a positive statement, deliver a message across racial barriers, and educate as well as entertain; Outreach Program with schools; Little City Program that uses theater to increase cognitive, learning and developmental skills of participants; Community Access Program.
Volunteers: Welcome

Black on Black Love
1024 E. 87th St.
Chicago, IL 60619
Phone: (773)978-5055
Evening/weekend: (773)928-6269

Fax: (773)978-7620
Exec. Dir.: Frances Gutter
Pres.: Edward G. Gardner
Local chapter of national organization
Founded: 1983
Serves: Mostly African Americans, some Caucasians and Hispanics, in Chicago
Purpose: To fight crime by providing aftercare for female ex-offenders and services for low-income families
Programs: Arts, counseling, children, community center, community organizing, education, employment, family, prison outreach, referral, shelter, substance abuse
Volunteers: Welcome

Black United Fund of Illinois
1809 E. 71st St.
Chicago, IL 60649
Phone: (773)324-0494
Fax: (773)324-6678
e-mail: info@bufiorg
Web: www.buf.org
Pres.: Henry L. English
e-mail:english@bufi.org
VPs: Calvin Cook and Natalie Puryear
Admin. Asst.: Julie Houston
e-mail: Julie@bufi.org
Affiliate of national organization
Founded: 1986
Serves: Non-profit community organizations and programs in Illinois
Purpose: To encourage philanthropy for enhancement of the quality of life in African American communities and to help organizations reach self-sufficiency
Programs: Charitable payroll deduction campaigns, technical assistance, access to funding and grants
Volunteers: Welcome

Centers for New Horizons
4150 S. King Drive.
Chicago, IL 60653
Phone: (773)373-5700
Fax: (773)373-0063
e-mail: sokonik @cnh.org
Pres.: Sakoni Karanja
Chr.: Randall Hampton
Founded: 1971
Serves: African Americans in Greater Grand Boulevard neighborhood of Chicago

Purpose: To help families build self-reliance and contribute to the revitalization of their community
Programs: Day care, job referral, counseling (family and individual), community and economic development, housing
Volunteers: Welcome

Chicago Urban League
4510 S. Michigan Ave.
Chicago, IL 60653
Phone: (773)285-5800
Fax: (773)285-7772
e-mail: cul@igc.apc.org
Pres. & CEO: James W. Compton
Local chapter of National Urban League
Founded: 1916
Serves: African Americans in Chicago
Purpose: To bring about racial parity in every phase of American life
Programs: Education, economic development, advocacy and research, health services, community empowerment
Other facilities: 3424 S. State St.
Volunteers: Welcome

**Cosmopolitan Chamber
of Commerce**
1326 S Michigan Ave., Suite 100
Chicago, IL 60605
Phone: (312)786-0212
Fax: (312)786-9079
e-mail: Cchamber @ameritech.com
Pres.: Consuelo M. Pope
Founded: 1933
Serves: Mainly African Americans, some Latinos, Asians**Purpose:** To provide economic development, training and development for entrepreneurs
Programs: Advocacy, networking, counseling, economic development, education, mentoring, referral, technical assistance, electronic commerce training
Volunteers: Welcome

**DuSable Museum
of African American History**
740 E. 56th Place
Chicago, IL 60637
Phone: (773)947-0600
Fax: (773)947-0600
Web: www.dusablemuseum.org
Evening/weekend: same

Pres.: Antoinette D. Wright
Founded: 1961
Serves: All, with African-American focus in Chicago and suburbs
Purpose: To preserve the African American culture and history
Programs: Arts, culture, culture preservation, education, heritage/history, literacy, research
Volunteers: Welcome

Habilitative Systems, Inc.
415 S. Kilpatrick
Chicago, IL 60644
Phone: (773)261-2252
Evening/weekend: same
Fax: (773)854-8300
e-mail: dewhsi720 @aol.com
Web: www.habilitative.org
Pres. & CEO: Donald Dew
Founded: 1978
Serves: Mostly African Americans, some Hispanics, Native Americans, Asian Americans, European Americans, in Chicago
Purpose: To help people who are less able become more capable, independent and self-reliant
Programs: Day care, foster care, counseling, housing, shelter, vocational training, substance-abuse treatment, case management, employment, tutoring, translating, homeless, behavioral health services
Volunteers: Welcome

Howard Area Community Center
7648 N. Paulina
Chicago, IL 60626
Phone: (773)262-6622
Fax: (773)262-6645
Exec. Dir.: Roberta Buchanan
Pres.: Larry Rabyne
Founded: 1967
Serves: African Americans, Latinos, Caribbeans, in north Rogers Park
Purpose: To help low-income individuals and families to stabilize their lives and to develop social skills necessary to become effective community members
Programs: Social services, education, early childhood, infants and toddlers, translating,
Volunteers: Welcome

**Kenwood-Oakland
Community Organization**
1238 E. 46th St.
Chicago, IL 60653
Phone: (773)548-7500
Fax: (773)548-9264
Exec. Dir.: Robert Lucas
Founded: 1967
Serves: African Americans in Kenwood-Oakland
Purpose: To serve the Kenwood-Oakland community, devastated by poverty
Programs: Emergency food pantry, technical assistance to business groups, youth development, comprehensive earnfare, social services, H-Rail, family stability
Volunteers: Welcome

Lawndale Christian Health Center
3860 W. Ogden
Chicago, IL 60623
Phone: (773)843-3000
Evening/weekend: same
Fax: (773)521-2742
Exec. Dir.: Arthur Jones, MD
Pres.: Rev. Noel Castellanos
Founded: 1984
Serves: Mostly African Americans, also Hispanics, in North and South Lawndale
Purpose: To provide quality affordable health care
Programs: Primary health care, translating
Volunteers: Welcome

**Leadership Council
for Metropolitan Open Communities**
111 W. Jackson, 12th floor
Chicago, IL 60604-3502
Phone: (312)341-5678
Evening/weekend: same (voice mail)
Fax: (312)341-1958
Web: www.lcmoc.org
Pres.: Aurie A. Pennick
Chr.: Eve B. Lee
Founded: 1966
Serves: Mostly African American and Latino homeseekers, in Chicago and six collar counties
Purpose: To replace discrimination and segregation with an open housing market
Programs: Fair housing enforcement and litigation, housing counseling, education, advocacy, translating

Volunteers: Welcome, especially to test for housing discrimination

**Mid-South Planning
and Development Commission**
4309 S. King Drive
Chicago, IL 60653
Phone: (773)924-1330
Fax: (773)924-3151
e-mail: worthy30 @aol.com
Exec. Dir.: Thomas Worthy
Founded: 1990
Serves: African Americans and community residents in the Bronzville neighborhood of Chicago
Purpose: To improve the quality of life and preserve the cultural heritage of this predominantly African American community
Programs: Bronzeville Institute, Black Metropolis, family development, community organizing, culture preservation, economic development, education, employment, family, health care, heritage/history, housing, referral, technical assistance, entrepreneurial training
Volunteers: Welcome

NAACP -- Chicago Southside Branch
400 W. 76th St., Suite 200
Chicago, IL 60620
Phone: (773)224-7242
Evening/weekend: same
Fax: (773)224-7251
Exec. Dir.: Ginger Mance
Pres.: Dr. Joan Hill
Local chapter of national organization
Founded: 1910
Serves: Mostly African Americans, some others, on the South Side of Chicago
Purpose: To fight racial discrimination in the areas of education, housing, employment and police brutality
Programs: Legal referrals, job bank, holiday baskets for senior citizens, referrals to city and state service agencies, monitoring government agencies and programs affecting blacks and others, educating community about racial unrest and crime, following legislation affecting community
Volunteers: Welcome

**National Association of Black
Sales Professionals**
503 S. Oak Park Ave.
Oak Park, IL 60304
Phone: (708)445-1010
Fax: (708)848-6008
Web: www.jmrecruiter.com
Founded: 1994
Exec. Dir. & Pres.: Juan F. Menefee
No office, 1000+ members
Serves: Mostly African Americans and
Hispanics, some Asians and American
Indians, in Chicago metro area and
nationwide
Purpose: To foster growth potential for
minority sales professionals
Programs: Business/professional support,
counseling, economic development,
employment, mentoring, social/fraternal
Volunteers: Welcome

**National Council of Negro Women, Inc.,
Chicago/Midwest Section**
P.O. Box 4462
Chicago, IL 60680-4462
Phone: (312)409-6862
Evening/weekend: same (voice mail)
Pres.: Annetta Wilson
No exec. dir., no office, 200 members
Local chapter of national organization
Founded 1935
Serves: African Americans in Illinois
Purpose: To advance opportunities and the
quality of life for African American women,
their families and communities
Programs: Community empowerment,
heritage/history, family, leadership training,
career development, research and
assessment of support programs for women,
educational enrichment, substance-abuse
and dropout prevention, promotion of
excellence and equity in education, youth
counseling for transition from school to
work, support services for at-risk youth,
assistance for pregnant teens, senior
citizens, research on families, black family
reunions
Volunteers: Welcome

Near North Health Service Corp.
1276 N. Clybourn
Chicago, IL 60610
Phone: (312)337-1073
Evening/weekend: same

Fax: (312)337-7616
e-mail: bthomas@nmh.org
Exec. Dir.: Berneice Mills-Thomas
Chr.: William Moorehead
Founded: 1982
Serves: Mostly African Americans,
Hispanics, some others, in Near North,
Cabrini-Green, West Town and Humboldt
Park ; on South Side in Kenwood/Oakland,
Grand Boulevard, Douglas and Washington
Park.
Purpose: To provide quality,
comprehensive and primary health care to
the medically underserved
Programs: Primary health care, dental,
podiatry, ophthalmology, social services,
WIC, education, job referral, substance
abuse, infant-mortality reduction, translating
Other locations: 820 N. Orleans, 1276 N.
Clybourn, 923 N. Sedgwick, 1924 W.
Chicago Ave., 2750 W. North Ave., 4230 S.
Greenwood
Volunteers: Welcome

Near West Side Community Committee
1044 W. Taylor St.
Chicago, IL 60607
Phone: (312)666-8444
Evening/weekend: 243-6258
Fax: (312)666-3287
Pres. & Exec. Dir.: Emil J. Peluso
Affiliated with Chicago Area Project
Founded: 1946
Serves: Mostly African Americans, others
who live in area from Canal to Western and
Van Buren to Roosevelt
Purpose: To prevent and treat delinquency;
to provide drug-abuse information; to
provide guidance to those released from
Cook County, state and federal institutions
Programs: Neighborhood walk-ins,
neighborhood problems with U of I,
juveniles in trouble, counseling, anti-drug
abuse, civil rights
Volunteers: Welcome

No Dope Express Foundation
901 E. 104th St.
Chicago, IL 60628
Phone: (773)568-5600
Fax: (773)568-9812
e-mail: ndef1@accesschicago.com
Pres. & CEO: Earl King
V.P.: Darryll King

Founded: 1987
Serves: Mostly African Americans, some Hispanics, in Roseland and Pullman neighborhoods
Purpose: To offer positive alternatives to children and young adults in the ongoing struggle against gangs, drugs and violence
Programs: Job training, English and basic math tutorial, basketball and sports recreation, public speaking and self-esteem building,computer training
Volunteers: Welcome

Rainbow/PUSH Coalition
930 E. 50th St.
Chicago, IL 60615
Phone: (773)373-3366
Evening/weekend: same
Fax: (773)373-3571
Dep. Dir.: Axel Adams
Chr.: Rev. Willie Barrow
Founded: 1971
National organization based in Chicago
Serves: Mostly African Americans, some others, in the USA
Purpose: To provide a vehicle for social justice based on lasting values of spiritual regeneration, empowerment, parity and discipline
Programs: Weekly forum/community meeting, voter education, community services, youth oratorical and scholarship, community organizing, legal assistance, business development, research
Volunteers: Welcome

South Austin Coalition
Community Council
5071 W. Congress Parkway
Chicago, IL 60644
Phone: (773)287-4570
Evening/weekend: (773)287-4570
Fax: (773)378-3536
Exec. Dir.: Bob Vondrasek
Pres.: Edward Bailey
Serves: African Americans in South Austin
Purpose: To promote interests of residents in housing, safety, economic development, etc.
Programs: Community organizing, civil rights, economic development, education, housing, mentoring, referral, senior citizens, technical assistance, youth
Volunteers: Welcome

South Central Community Services (see Multi-ethnic)

South Side Help Center
10420 S. Halsted
Chicago, IL 60628
Phone: (773)445-5445
Fax: (773)445-9818
e-mail: sshc104@aol.com
Exec. Dir.: Betty Smith
Pres.: Eric Griggs
Founded: 1987
Serves: African Americans in Roseland, Pullman, West Pullman and Washington Heights neighborhoods
Purpose: To provide a comprehensive HIV/AIDS education and outreach program, along with prevention, education, cultural and social programs for youth
Programs: Youth self-enhancement; positive peer leadership; female and male mentoring; HIV/AIDS education, including outreach to shelters, CHA, street youth and public schools; school-based programs; emergency infant formula; free family clothing; HIV mental health support service;, HIV case management
Other locations: 11200 S. State St.
Volunteers: Welcome

Support Center
(See Multi-ethnic)

United Negro College Fund., Inc.
55 E. Monroe, Suite 1880
Chicago, IL 60603
Phone: (312)845-2200
Fax: (312)263-2751
Area Dev. Dir.: Morris Honore
Regional V.P.: Marquis Miller
Pres.: William H. Gray III
Founded: 1944
Serves: African Americans and others, in Illinois and Wisconsin
Purpose: General and operating funding for member colleges
Programs: Raise funds, to keep costs low and educational quality high
Volunteers: Welcome

West Englewood United Organization.
1650 W. 62nd St.
Chicago, IL 60620
Phone: (773)778-8855

Evening/weekend: (773)778-8854, -8861
Shelter: (773)778-8984
Fax: (773)778-8984
Exec. Dir.: Tempie Hampton
Pres.: Clara Kirk
Serves: All ethnic backgrounds
Purpose: To provide shelter for mothers and their children, help them build their self-esteem and get back into the work world
Programs: Shelter for homeless women and children, tutoring for children, counseling, housing, legal assistance, nutrition, budgeting
Volunteers: Welcome

2nd Stage Housing Program
Phone: (773)778-2811
Fax: (773)778-2884
Exec. Dir.: Sabrina Morgan
Purpose: For homeless and battered women and children to learn how to live independently
Programs: Tutoring for children, babysitting service, counseling, nutrition, budgeting, housing, job assistance
Volunteers: Welcome

Westside Assn. for Community Action
3600 W. Ogden
Chicago, IL 60623
Phone: (773)277-4400
Evening/weekend: same
Fax: (773)277-0270
Exec. Dir.: Gloria Jenkins
Pres.: Earlean Lindsey
Chr. & CEO: Ernest Jenkins
Founded: 1971
Serves: Mostly African Americans, Hispanics, in Near West Side, Lawndale, Little Village, Pilsen, Garfield, Austin, Brighton Park neighborhoods
Purpose: To strengthen family ties, enhance individual and group problem-solving skills, encourage leadership development and promote collaborative partnerships with other social service agencies, neighborhood groups, block clubs, business and local government to promote human and community growth and development of West Side communities
Programs: Multi-service community-based network of 35 groups and organizations and 135 individuals
Other location: 3525 W. Ogden

Volunteers: Welcome
Westside Health Authority
5437 W. Division St.
Chicago, IL 60651
Phone: (773)378-0233
Fax: (773)378-5035
e-mail: info@healthauthority.org
Exec. Dir.: Jacqueline Reed
Founded: 1988
Serves: African Americans in Austin, East and West Garfield Park, Lawndale and Near West Side neighborhoods
Purpose: To build community capacity for improving health, education and overall community life
Programs: Research, violence consortium, provider consortium, mentoring, health promotions, youth organizing, entrepreneurship in health care
Volunteers: Welcome

The Woodlawn Organization
6040 S. Harper
Chicago, IL 60637
Phone: (773)288-5840
Fax: (773)288-5796
Exec. Dir.: Orlando May
Chr.: Dr. Leon D. Finney, Jr.
Founded: 1960
Serves: African Americans in the Woodlawn neighborhood
Purpose: To ensure equal representation in local government where a leadership gap exists
Programs: Child care, adult skill training, social services, rehab facilities, community empowerment, Woodlawn Community Development Corp.
Volunteers: Welcome

Arab American

(see also Iranian, Iraqis, Palestinian)

American Arabian Ladies Society
8926 Oakdale
Orland Park, IL 60462
Phone: (708)460-3767
Pres.: Suraya Shalabi
No exec. dir., no office, 150 members
Founded: 1952
Serves: Arab Americans in Chicago and suburbs

Purpose: To promote culture, educational awareness, Islamic religion, Arab language
Programs: Community center, culture preservation, heritage/history, language, social, women's auxiliary, translating

Arab American Action Network
3148 W. 63rd. St.
Chicago, IL 60629
Phone: (773)436-6060
Fax: (773)436-6460
e-mail: aaan@aaan.org
bcostandi@earthlink.net
Exec. Dir.: Bishara T. Costandi
Founded: 1995
Serves: Arab immigrants and Arab Americans in Chicago metro area
Purpose: To improve the quality of life of Arab immigrants and Arab Americans by building our community's capacity to be an active agent for social change
Programs: Citizenship education, including ESL, civics classes, application assistance; youth programs, including after-school tutoring, mentoring, leadership development; life and parenting skills; breast cancer education; case management for individuals, families and children; Census 2000 and voter registration; Arab Arts Council
Volunteers: Welcome, especially if bilingual in Arabic and English

Arab American Bar Association
P.O. Box 81325
Chicago, IL 60681
Phone: (312)946-0110
Evening/weekend: same
Fax: (312)565-2070
Exec. Dir.: William J. Haddad
Founded: 1990
Serves: Americans of Arab descent in Chicago and Illinois
Purpose: To upgrade the image of this minority within the judiciary and the bar, networking
Programs: Judicial evaluation for the community, legal referral, professional counsel, informational programs
Volunteers: Welcome

+Arab-American Business and Professional Association
750 W. Lake Cook Road, Suite 155

Buffalo Grove, IL 60089
Phone: (847)459-1438
Evening/weekend: same (ans. Machine)
Fax: (847)459-1698
Pres.: Talat M. Othman
Founded: 1993
No office, 300 members
Serves: Arab-Americans and corporate America, in Illinois
Purpose: Networking, business, professional
Programs: Special business-interest seminars, dinners, luncheon speakers, business delegations to Middle East, receive business and government officials from Middle East, translation
Volunteers: Welcome

Arab Community Center
(same as Arab American Action Network)

Arab American Republican Federation
12231 W. Lady Bar Lane
Orland Park, IL 60462
Phone: (708)301-4269
Evening/weekend: same
e-mail: smsawalha@aol.com
Pres.: Dr. Shibli M. Sawalha
V.P.: Ziad Zeraikat
No exec. dir., no office, 400 members
Founded: 1984
Serves: Arab Americans in Chicago and suburbs and Illinois
Purpose: To train the Arab American community in civic involvement and empower them politically and professionally
Programs: Campaigning, voter registration, fund raising, election of local, state and national candidates, translating (sometimes)
Volunteers: Welcome

Arab Cultural Council of America
8120 W. 89th Place
Hickory Hills, IL 60457
Phone: (708)598-4724
Evening/weekend: same
Fax: same
Pres.: Dr. Hassan M. Abdallah
V.P.: Dr. Hassan Haddad
No exec. dir., no office 270 members
Founded: 1989
Serves: Mostly Arabs, and Muslims in general, in Chicago and suburbs
Purpose: To keep the Arab culture alive in Arab American youth; to educate the

American public about the standards, values and ethics of the culture
Programs: Arts, culture preservation, education, tutoring; translating (for a fee)

Iranian American Society
(see Iranian American)

Ramallah Club of Chicago
(see Palestinian American)

Asian American

(see also Burmese, Cambodian, Chinese, Hmong, Indian, Filipino, Japanese, Korean, Lao, Pakistani, Thai, Tibetan, Vietnamese)

Apna Ghar, Inc.
4753 N. Broadway, Room 518
Chicago, IL 60640
Phone: (773)334-0173
Evening/weekend: same
Fax: (773)334-0963
Hotline: (773)334-4663
e-mail: info@apnaghar.org
Web: www.apnaghar.org
Exec. Dir.: K. Sujata
Pres.: Hansa Sehgal
Founded: 1989
Serves: Mostly South Asian women and children
Purpose: To provide comprehensive multi-lingual, multi-cultural services to abused women and their children and supervised child visitation for court-mandated visits between non-custodial parents and their children
Programs: Shelter where clients stay for three months and where they have access to legal advocacy, counseling, art therapy, parenting classes and other life support services; supervised Child Visitation Center; 24-hour crisis line; community education on violence prevention
Volunteers: Welcome

Asian American Alliance/Asian Amer. Small Business Development Center
222 W. Cermak, Suite 302
Chicago, IL 60616-1986
Phone: (312)326-2200
Evening/weekend: same

Fax: (312)326-0399
e-mail: aasbdc@igcom.net
Exec. Dir.: Christine Takada
Pres.: Joseph Yi
Founded: 1995
Serves: Asian Americans in Chicago and suburbs
Purpose: To help Asian American entrepreneurs start and expand their businesses through educational, technical and direct services; to support services provided by chambers of commerce in the Asian American community
Programs: Business and professional support, economic development, technical assistance, advocacy, information resource
Volunteers: Welcome

Asian American Bar Association of the Greater Chicago Area
P.O. Box A3782
Chicago, IL 60690
Phone: (312)554-2044
Fax: (312)554-2054
e-mail: aaba-chi@ripco.com
Web: www.ripco.com:8080/-aaba-chi
Pres.: Rena M. Van Tine
V.P.: Asheesh Goel
Founded: 1987
No exec. dir., 300 members
Serves: Asian Americans in Chicago and suburbs
Purpose: To represent the interests of the Asian American community and attorneys; to foster the exchange of ideas and information among association members and with other members of the legal profession
Programs: Legal
Volunteers: Welcome

Asian American Educators Assn.
10 W. 35th St.
Chicago, IL 60615
Phone: (773)534-9082
Fax: (773)534-9090
Pres.: Edwin Lardizabal
V.P.: Merrylee M. Doden
No exec. dir., no office, 150 members
Founded: 1968
Serves: Asian Americans and others in Chicago and suburbs
Purpose: To advocate for Asian American students and educators

Programs: Advocacy, annual Asian American student talent show, education for community members and educators
Volunteers: Welcome

Asian American Institute
5415 N. Clark St.
Chicago, IL 60640
Phone: (773)271-0899
Fax: (773)271-1982
e-mail: AAIChicago@aol.com
Exec. Dir.: Tuyet Le
Pres.: Joanna Su
Founded: 1992
Serves: Pan-Asian community in Chicago, suburbs and Illinois
Purpose: To be the vehicle through which various ethnic Asian American communities can work together and benefit from joint actions in such areas as political empowerment, civic education, public-policy development, community service and employment opportunities.
Programs: Public policy research, public forums, lectures, film festival, advocacy

Asian Human Services, Inc.
4763 N. Broadway, Suite 700
Chicago, IL 60640
Phone: (773)728-2235
Fax: (773)728-4751
e-mail: services@ripco.com
Web: www.asianhumanservices.org
Exec. Dir.: Abha Pandya
Pres.: Michael Elliott
Founded: 1978
Serves: Asian Americans in Chicago's North Side neighborhoods and suburbs
Purpose: To provide quality and compassionate human services to Asian immigrant and refugee community of metro Chicago
Programs: Outpatient mental-health counseling, job placement, access to legal services, HIV/AIDS information, elderly services, case management, referral, ESL, youth counseling and mentoring, primary health care, education, training

Asian American Small Business Association of Chicago
5023 N. Broadway
Chicago, IL 60640
Phone: (773)728-1030

Exec. Dir.: Charlie Soo
Pres.: E. Cheng
Founded: 1978
Serves: Mostly Chinese Americans/Asians in the Argyle Street area of Uptown and rest of city
Purpose: To provide technical assistance to the small Asian businesses in the Argyle area and others, and to promote and enhance the Chinese business and cultural heritage through New Year celebrations, fests, seminars, etc.
Programs: Advocacy, economic development, business and professional, immigrant services

Asian/Pacific American Democratic Council of Illinois
1349 W. Winnemac Ave.
Chicago, IL 60640
Phone: (773)275-4988
Evening/weekend: same
Fax: (773)275-5774
Chr.: Ross Harano
Founded: 1988
No exec. dir., no office, 100 members
Serves: Asian Americans in Illinois
Purpose: To advocate for Asian American inclusion within the political process and to support Asian American Democratic candidates for public office
Programs: Political education and active support of Democratic candidates
Volunteers: Welcome

International Medical Council of Illinois (see Multi-ethnic)

Leadership Center for Asian Pacific Americans
P.O. Box 25465
Chicago, IL 60625
Phone: (312)409-9115
e-mail: LCAPA@aol.com
Web: http://users.aol.com/LCAPA
Chr.: Elvin Chan
Founded: 1995
Serves: The Asian American community and its organizations targeting high school students, college organizations and community organizations
Purpose: To build, develop and promote leadership among the Asian Pacific American community by strengthening

existing organizations and organizing Asian Pacific Americans around issues relevant to the community
Programs: They change. Check Web site for up-to-date information
Volunteers: Welcome

Nat. Asian Pacific Center on Aging Chicago, Senior Envir. Employ. Pgm.

122 S. Michigan Ave., Suite 1414
Chicago, IL 60603
Phone: (312)913-0979
Fax: (312)913-0982
e-mail: SyunLin@aol.com
Exec. Dir.: Clayton Fong
Pjct. Dir.: Mei Syun Lin
Local office of national organization .
Founded: 1979
Serves: Mostly Asian Pacific Islanders, some African Americans, Hispanics, American Indians, Alaskan natives and whites, in the Midwest
Purpose: To give workers age 55 and over the opportunity to use their skills in creative and meaningful jobs, to recognize talented older workers, to supplement EPA staff
Programs: Recruits, screens, hires and pays older workers, develops appropriate assignments in EPA offices, translating

National Association of Asian American Professionals -- Chicago

P.O. Box 81138
Chicago, IL 60681-1038
Phone: (773)918-2454
Evening/weekend: same
e-mail: naaap@naaap.org
Pres.: Wilbur Pan
V.P.: Sandra Wong-Darroch
No exec dir., no office, 350 members
Local chapter of national organization
Founded: 1987
Serves: Asian Americans in Chicago metro area
Purpose: To promote the personal and professional development of the Asian American community
Programs: Arts (culture), business and professional support, community volunteering, community organizing, education (seminars, workshops, speakers), college student mentoring, social, Illinois Annual Asian American Essay and Speech Contest

Volunteers: Welcome

South Asian Women's Society of America

P.O. Box 597544
Chicago, IL 60659
Phone: (847)933-1101
Evening/weekend: (773)248-5108
Fax: (847)675-1930
Pres.: Mohina Ahluwalia Sands
Founded: 1991
Serves: People from Bangladesh, Bhutan, Burma, India, Nepal, Pakistan and Sri Lanka in Chicago and suburbs
Purpose: To enhance the status of women through economic empowerment, education, volunteer services, social interaction and cultural awareness
Programs: Computer classes, literacy classes, career-oriented seminars, family counseling, immigrant adjustment, mentoring, senior citizens, vocational training, women-related programs, translating
Volunteers: Welcome

South-East Asia Center

1124/1134 W. Ainslie
Chicago, IL 60640
Phone: (773)989-6927
Evening/weekend: same
Fax: (773)989-4871
Exec. Dir.: Peter R. Porr
Pres.: José Nebrida
Founded: 1979
Serves: Mostly South-East Asians (Chinese, Vietnamese, Khmer, Lao) as well as some Korean, Russian and Filipino Americans in the Chicago metro area
Purpose: To build bridges among ethnic groups and promote understanding and cooperation between those of immigrant and American cultural backgrounds; to serve the needs of South-East Asian immigrants
Programs: Adult day care, business and professional support, counseling, child care, citizenship, civil rights, community center, community organizing, economic development, education, ESL, employment, family, health care, homework help, immigrant resettlement and adjustment, language, legal, literacy, tutoring,, lobbying, mental health, referral, research, senior citizens cross-cultural bridge building,,

summer school, translating, fraternal, technical assistance, youth, cross-cultural bridge-building, translating
Volunteers: Welcome

Assyrian American

Assyrian American Association
1618 W. Devon Ave.
Chicago, IL 60660
Phone: (773)338-3922
Fax: (773)338-7120
Exec. Dir.: Ben Benjamin
Pres.: Babel Gabriel
Founded: 1917
Serves: Assyrians in Chicago and suburbs
Purpose: To provide educational, cultural and social programs for Assyrian Americans
Programs: Social gatherings, education, cultural activities, translating
Volunteers: Welcome

Assyrian National Council of Illinois
2450 W. Peterson Ave.
Chicago, IL 60659
Phone: (773)262-5589
Fax: (773)262-0828
Exec. Dir.: Angel Kindo
Pres.: Sheba Mando
Founded: 1986
Serves: Mostly Assyrians, also some Jews, Hispanics and Russians, mostly in Rogers Park and Ravenswood
Purpose: To serve and support not only the Assyrian community, but other ethnic groups as well
Programs: Educational, welfare, cultural, health, youth job training, translating
Volunteers: Welcome

Assyrian Universal Alliance Foundation
7055 N. Clark St.
Chicago, IL 60626
Phone: (773)274-9262
Fax: (773)274-5866
e-mail: auaf@aol.com
Exec. Dir.: Homer Ashurian
Pres.: Helen J. Schwarten
Founded: 1978
Serves: Assyrian Americans in Chicago and suburbs

Purpose: To serve the Assyrian community, especially immigrants and refugees, through education, employment and counseling
Programs: English classes, employment, youth sports, refugee counseling, Ashurbanipal Library, Assyrian Historical Museum, lecture series, scholarships, translating
Volunteers: Welcome

Austrian American

Kaernter Klub Koschat
c/o G. Wax, 1906 Camp McDonald Rd.
Mt. Prospect, IL 60056
Phone: (773)973-3124
Evening/weekend: same
Fax: (773)973-2072
Pres.: Kurt Von Pasecky
Sec.-Treas.: Gertrude Wax
No exec. dir., no office, 100 members
Founded: 1917
Serves: Austrian Americans in Chicago and suburbs
Purpose: To encourage culture preservation and heritage
Programs: Culture preservation, social

Bangladeshi American

Bangladesh Association of Chicagoland
P.O. Box 59849
Chicago, IL 60659
Phone: (773)774-0401
Evening/weekend: same
Fax: same
Exec. Dir.: Mohammed Elahi
Pres.: Dr. Khairul Anam Zazi
Founded: 1980
No office, 400 members
Serves: Bangladeshi Americans in Illinois
Purpose: To promote the culture
Programs: Children, cultural, community organizing, immigration, political, picnic for elderly, translating (Bengali to English and English to Bengali)
Volunteers: Welcome

Barbadian American

Barbados Caribbean American Assn.
2857 W. 84th St.
Chicago, IL 60652
Phone: (773)476-2009
Fax: (773)434-0724
Pres.: Andrew Husbands
V.P.: Perry Boyce
No exec. dir., no office
Local chapter of national organization
Founded: 1994
Serves: Mainly Barbadians and descendants, some West Indians and Americans in Illinois
Purpose: To promote Barbadian heritage and culture; to act as a link between Barbados and Chicago and to be a support group in case of disaster
Programs: Cultural activities, contributions to charities in USA and Barbados, member support, disaster and emergency assistance
Volunteers: Welcome

Belizean American

Belizean Cultural Association Inc.
3950 N. Lake Shore Drive, #2017C
Chicago, IL 60613
Phone: (773)549-4341
Fax: (773)549-1991, Star 2
Exec. Dir.: Shelly Waight
Pres.: Birdy Haggerty Francis
Founded: 1987
Serves: Mostly Belizeans and Belizean Americans, some African Americans, in Chicago and suburbs
Purpose: To share and keep Belizean culture alive in America for those of Belizean heritage
Programs: Arts, community organizing, culture preservation, heritage/history, recreation
Volunteers: Welcome

+Belizean Day in the Park Committee
9405 S. Throop
Chicago, IL 60620
Phone: (773)881-0412
Evening/weekend: same
Pres. & Exec. Dir.: Sylvia Manderson
Founded: 1980
No office, 10 members
Serves: Belizeans and Americans of Belizean descent in Chicago and suburbs
Purpose: To sponsor, promote and organize an annual Belize Day in the Park and scholarship fund for students of Belizean descent
Programs: Culture preservation, education, heritage/history, recreation
Volunteers: Welcome

Belize Social Club
9405 S. Throop
Chicago, IL 60620
Phone: (773)881-0412
Bus. Mgr.: Sylvia Manderson
Pres.: Montique Belgrave
No office, 20 members
Founded: 1971
Serves: Belizeans and other Caribbean Americans in Chicago, Illinois and Belize
Purpose: To help Belizean American people in their time of need
Programs: Culture preservation, arts, financial aid, heritage/history, community organizing, citizenship, social, health care
Volunteers: Welcome

Bielarusian American

Bielarusian Coordinating Committee of Chicago, Illinois
c/o Bielarusian Religious & Cultural Center
3107 W. Fullerton Ave.
Chicago, IL 60647-2809
Phone: (773)745-8216
Exec. Dir.: Nick Zyznieuski
Sec.: Vera Romuk
Advisor: Dr. Witold Romuk
Founded: 1973
Serves: Bielarusians in Illinois
Purpose: To be a cultural and social ethnic organization
Programs: Culture preservation, language and heritage, history, spokesman for Bielarusian causes in Bielarus and U.S., translating

Bosnian American

Bosnian-American Cultural Assn.
1810 N. Pfingsten Rd.
Northbrook, IL 60062
Phone: (847) 272-0319; (773)992-0808
Fax: (847)272-0348
Pres.: Saban Torlo
V.P.: Dr. Hasim Cosovic
Headquarters of national organization
Founded: 1906
Serves: Bosnians, also Montenegro, Sanjak in Chicago and suburbs
Purpose: To help its people, wherever they are; to preserve Bosnian language, customs and traditions; to provide humanitarian aid to Bosnia and help wounded children, adults, refugees
Programs: Education, financial aid, foreign humanitarian aid, social/fraternal, sponsorship of medical evacuees, funeral services
Volunteers: Welcome

Bosnian & Hercegovinian American Community Center
6574 N. Sheridan Road
Chicago, IL 60626
Phone: (773)274-0044
Fax: (773)274-6188
Coord.: Zumra Kusocic
Local chapter of national organization
Founded: 1994
Serves: Bosnians in Chicago
Purpose: To help Bosnian refugees
Programs: Community center, community organizing, education, adjustment, language, employment, mental health, arts, counseling, children's culture preservation, recreation, ESL, translating
Volunteers: Welcome

Burmese American

Synapses Inc.
1821 W. Cullerton
Chicago, IL 60608
Phone: (312)421-5513
Evening/weekend: (773)293-2178
Fax: (312)421-5513 (call first)
e-mail: synapses@igc.org
Pgm. Coord.: Don Erickson

Founded: 1981
Part of an international network that works for Burma; subsidiary Christian Peacemaker Teams
Serves: International concerns of Burmese community and negative effects of globalization in Third World countries
Purpose: To be a peace action network connecting people involved in long-term work for justice; to support the right to self-determination of communities around the globe and lessen obstacles that stand in the way of economic and human development; to support the democratic movement in Burma
Programs: Burma Project, Globalization Project
Volunteers: Welcome

Cambodian American

Cambodian Association of Illinois
2831 W. Lawrence Ave.
Chicago, IL 60625
Phone: (773)878-7090
Fax: (773)878-5299
Exec. Dir.: Kompha Seth
Pres.: Tung Kim Yap
Founded: 1976
Serves: Cambodians in Uptown and Albany Park neighborhoods of Chicago
Purpose: To serve the needs of a highly traumatized, limited-English speaking refugee group
Programs: Arts, counseling, children, citizenship, community center, community organizing, culture preservation, education, employment, family, immigrant resettlement and adjustment, literacy, referral, senior citizen, tutoring, women, youth, translating
Volunteers: Welcome

Chinese American

Chicago Chinatown Chamber of Commerce
2169B South Chicago Place
Chicago, IL 60616
Phone: (312)326-5320
Fax: (312)326-5668
Founded: 1982

Exec. Dir.: Myling Tang
Pres.: Sam Ma
Founded: 1982
Serves: Chinese Americans in Chicago's Chinatown
Purpose: To promote Chinatown business and serve Chinese businessmen
Programs: Business and professional support, community organizing, culture preservation, economic development, heritage/history, referral, technical assistance, Chinatown parking lot, translating, youth summer job program Satellite office -- Asian American Small Business Development Center
Volunteers: Welcome

Chicago Chinese Council
5023 N. Broadway
Chicago, IL 60640
Phone: (773)271-2644
Evening/weekend: (773)878-7843
Fax: (773)271-4247
Exec. Dir.: Raymond Tu
Pres.: Sammy Luk
Founded: 1978
Serves: Chinese Americans in Greater Chicago
Purpose: To help facilitate economic development among the Chinese people
Programs: Community organizing, economic development, fraternal, translation
Volunteers: Welcome

Chinese American Service League
310 W. 24th Place
Chicago, IL 60616
Phone: (312)791-0418
Fax: (312)791-0509
Exec. Dir.: Bernarda Wong
Pres.: Arthur Wong
Founded: 1978
Serves: Chinese in Chicago metro area
Purpose: To provide programs and services so Chinese can become self-sufficient; to aid youth, elderly and immigrants
Programs: Counseling, day care, employment and training, immigration, naturalization, youth center, family services, elderly services, translating
Volunteers: Yes

Chinese Consolidated Benevolent Association of Chicago
250 W. 22nd Place
Chicago, IL 60616
Phone: (312)225-6198
Fax: (312)225-1155
Pres.: Duc Huang
Sec.: Eddy Jeong
Founded: 1906
Serves: Mostly Chinese Americans and Asian Americans, in Chicago metro area
Purpose: To be a liaison to and work for the welfare of Chinese living in America
Programs: Golden Diners Club, volunteer home delivery of meals, free clinic, food sanitation program, Chinese cemetery, Chinese school, Confucius Center, special events such as Chinese New Year parade, summer fair and Double Ten parade.
Volunteers: Welcome

Chinese Fine Arts Society
4343 W. Norwood
Chicago, IL 60646
Phone: (312)409-7814
e-mail: Info@ChineseFineArts.org
Web: www.chinesefinearts.org
Pres.: Eric Suen
Hon. Pres.: Barbara Tiao
Founded: 1991
Serves: Chinese Americans and others in Chicago, suburbs and Midwest
Purpose: To discover Chinese music and its cultural significance, to develop interest and appreciation in Chinese music and arts, to foster discipline and determination in these cultural endeavors
Programs: Music/Ink painting competition, annual Chinese Music Concert, exhibitions on Chinese culture, music and arts, translating
Volunteers: Welcome

Chinese Mutual Aid Association
1016 W. Argyle St.
Chicago, IL 60640
Phone: (773)784-2900
Fax: (773)784-2984
Exec. Dir.: Grace B. Hou
e-mail: chinesemutualaid@ameritech.net
Founded: 1981
Serves: Mostly Chinese Americans, some other Asians and other immigrants and

refugees in Edgewater, Uptown, Albany Park neighborhoods
Purpose: To enhance the socioeconomic well-being of the ethnic Chinese in Chicago and encourage their participation and contribution to American society
Programs: Adjustment counseling, literacy, citizenship, education, Chinese culture and language classes, refugee adjustment, health, community safety, senior, youth, employment, literacy, social services, translating (for a fee)
Volunteers: Welcome

Croatian American

Croatian-American Association
3339 S. Halsted St.
Chicago, IL 60608
Phone: (773)890-1001
Evening/weekend: (630)314-8622 (pager)
Fax: (773)890-1146
e-mail: peraicalaw@aol.com
Exec. Dir.: Steve Zakic
Pres.: Anthony J. Peraica
Local chapter of national organization
Founded: 1990
Serves: Croatian Americans in Illinois
Purpose: To educate and inform, as well as lobby media and politicians on issues that affect Croatian Americans
Programs: Croatian Days on Capitol Hill is an annual event bringing about 200 Croatian Americans to Washington to meet with representatives; annual banquet in March before Illinois primary; fund-raisers and political gatherings, translating
Volunteers: Welcome

+Croatian Cultural Center
2845 W. Devon Ave.
Chicago, IL 60659
Phone: (773)338-3839
Evening/weekend: (773)338-3839
Fax: (773)338-3898
Pres. & Exec. Dir.: Ilija Vasilj
Founded: 1974
Serves: Croatians in Chicago and suburbs
Purpose: To be a charitable, social, cultural organization
Programs: Charitable, social, cultural
Volunteers: Welcome

Croatian Ethnic Institute
4851 S. Drexel Blvd.
Chicago, IL 60615
Phone: (773)373-4670
Evening/weekend: same
Fax: (773)373-4746
e-mail: croetljubo@aol.com
Exec. Dir.: Ljubo Krasic
Founded: 1975
Serves: Croatian Americans in the U.S. and Canada
Purpose: To maintain a central collection on Croatians and their descendants; to collect and preserve publications and artifacts relating to the ethnic heritage of 2.5 million people of Croatian descent in the U.S. and Canada; to promote and develop curricular materials for the study of ethnic heritage; to conduct research on the Croatian and other European migrations
Programs: Culture preservation, education, heritage/history, language, referral, research
Volunteers: Welcome

Croatian Women, Branch No. 1 Chicago
2241 N. Janssen
Chicago, IL 60614
Phone: (773)404-1530
Evening/weekend: (773)525-8571
Fax: (773)404-1530 (same as phone)
Pres. & Exec. Dir.: Nevenka Jurkovic
Treas.: Zdenka Barun
Local chapter of national organization
Founded: 1929
No office, 250 members
Serves: Croatians and Croatian Americans in Illinois
Purpose: Humanitarian and cultural
Programs: Art exhibits, citizenship, community organizing, culture, preservation, foreign aid, heritage/history, immigrant resettlement and adjustment, language, recreation, social, financial aid, translating
Volunteers: Welcome

Cuban American

Cuban American Chamber of Commerce
3330 N. Ashland Ave.
Chicago, IL 60657
Phone: (773)248-2400
Fax: (773)248-6437

Pres.: Jose A. Garcia
Sec.: Guillermo Bauta
Founded: 1968
Serves: Mostly Cubans, some other Hispanics and Anglos, in Chicago and suburbs
Purpose: To assist Cuban immigrants with a variety of concerns, including citizenship, credit, job placement and housing
Programs: Citizenship, economic development, technical assistance, business and professional support, housing, jobs, translating
Volunteers: Welcome

Czech American

Czechoslovak American Congress
122 W. 22nd St.
Oak Brook, IL 60523
Phone: (630)472-0500
Evening/weekend: (708)442-4444
Fax: (630))472-1100
Pres.: Vera A. Wilt
V.P.s: Marvin Lanzel, Gary Wilt
No exec. dir., no office
Founded: 1975
Serves: Czechs and Slovaks in Chicago and suburbs
Purpose: To coordinate activities and common interests of many groups in area
Programs: Annual commemorative events: Lidice Massacre in June, founding of Czechoslovakia Oct. 28; annual picnic in July

Czechoslovak Heritage Museum, Library and Archives
122 W. 22nd St.
Oak Brook, IL 60523
Phone: (630)472-0500
Fax: (630)472-1100
e-mail: lifecsa@aol.com
Exec. Dir.: Deborah Zeman
Pres.: Vera Wilt
Founded: 1974
Serves: Czechs, Moravians, Slovaks nationwide
Purpose: To preserve and promote the culture of the Czech, Slovak and Moravian people
Programs: Museum, archives, exhibits, history, rare books, photos, music, art

Volunteers: Welcome

Czechoslovak National Council of America
2137 Lombard Ave.
Cicero, IL 60804-2037
Phone: (708)656-1117
Fax: (708)656-5611
Exec. Sec.: Olga Kovar
Pres.: John M. Richard
Founded: 1918
Serves: Czech and Slovak Americans, individuals and institutions interested in Czech and Slovak cultural heritage, resources and activities.
Purpose: To preserve ethnic artifacts and archives in the U.S.; inventory works of art by Czech and Slovak Americans, historical sites; help new immigrants and visiting travelers; maintain relations with social, cultural, educational institutions and authorities of the Czech Republic and Slovakia; advise members of Congress and executive departments on matters concerning relations with Slovakia and the Czech Republic; support all ethnic organizations that share our concerns.
Programs: Publish periodicals, books & pamphlets; present lectures, provide speakers, organize observance of events important to the ethnic community, commemorate historical events, social & cultural life promotion.

United Moravian Societies
2140 Wesley Ave.
Berwyn, IL 60402
Phone: (708)788-7856
Evening/weekend: (708)562-2307
Pres. & Exec. Dir.: Joseph Borysek
No office, 75 members
Founded: 1939
Serves: Mainly Czech Americans, some Poles, Slovaks, Croats in Illinois (performs elsewhere in the U.S. and Canada)
Purpose: To perpetuate and propagate Moravian folklore, heritage and traditions including, but not limited to, folk dancing, singing, cultural and benevolent work; to advocate among the members the value of American citizenship, which is enhanced by appreciation of a background of Moravian culture

Programs: Dancing lessons for youth, adult singing group, Czech language classes, translating, museum dedicated to Moravian culture, community center, education, heritage/history
Volunteers: Welcome

Dutch American

Dutch Heritage Center
6601 W. College Drive
Palos Heights, IL 60463
Phone: (708)597-3000, ext. 4930
Fax: (708)385-5665
Curator: none at present
Founded: 1982
Serves: Dutch Americans in Chicago metro area
Purpose: To preserve the archives of Dutch accomplishments
Programs: Cultural preservation, education, heritage/history

Eritrean American

Association of Eritrean Community in Chicago
c/o Anghesom Atsbaha
Truman College
1145 W. Wilson Ave.
Chicago, IL 60640
Phone: (773)907-4067
Pres.: Anghesom Atsbaha
V.P.: Zerzghi Iyassu
Founded: 1994
Serves: Eritreans in Chicago and suburbs
Purpose: To build a constructive sense of united Eritrean community and cultural identity and to better use combined resources for a peaceful and prosperous life
Programs: Social, cultural, education, employment, legal advice, summer child and youth programs, heritage/history, language, literacy, translating

Ethiopian American

Ethiopian Community Association
4750 N. Sheridan Rd.
Chicago, IL 60640
Phone: (773)728-0303
Fax: (773)728-0571
e-mail: eyimer@aol.com
Exec. Dir.: Erku Yimer
Pres.: Yittayih Zelalem
Founded: 1984
Serves: Ethiopians and other Africans in Chicago and suburbs
Purpose: To address the socioeconomic needs and interests of its constituency
Programs: Counseling, employment, youth and children, health outreach, ESL, citizenship, tutoring, referral, technical assistance translating
Volunteers: Welcome

Filipino American

Filipino American Council of Chicago
1332 W. Irving Park Road
Chicago, IL 60613
Phone: (773)281-1210
Fax: (773)281-9586
Pres.: Rey Sapnu
Founded: 1965
Serves: Filipino Americans on the North Side of Chicago and in the suburbs
Purpose: Social, charity, civic
Programs: Nutrition for seniors, free food distribution, medical referral, free legal advice, translating
Volunteers: Welcome

Filipino American Historical Society of Chicago
5472 S. Dorchester Ave.
Chicago, IL 60615-5309
Phone: (773)947-8696
Fax: (773)955-3635
e-mail: ealamar@aol.com
Pres.: Estrella R. Alamar
V.P.s: Willi Buhay, Hercules Auza, Romeo Munoz
Founded: 1986
Serves: Filipino Americans in Chicago and suburbs
Purpose: To provide a record and photographic history of Chicago's Filipino Americans; to preserve artifacts and documents; to promote public interest in the history of Chicago's Filipino Americans
Programs: Culture preservation, education, heritage/history, language, research, archives depository, translating

Other locations: : New museum at 3952 N. Ashland Ave., Chicago 60613
Volunteers: Welcome

+Filipino American Law Center
1332 W. Irving Park Road
Chicago, IL 60613
Phone: (773)404-8445
Fax: (773)281-9586
e-mail: AlBascos@msn.com
Exec. Dir.: Alfonso S. Bascos
Founded: 1996
Serves: Mostly Filipino Americans on North Side and suburbs
Purpose: To provide free legal consultation
Programs: Free legal advice to seniors, low-income individuals and newly arriving immigrants; translating
Volunteers: Welcome

Filipino American Political Assn.
1332 W. Irving Park Rd.
Chicago, IL 60613
Phone: (773)445-3230
Exec. Dir.: Rudy Figueroa
Pres.: Gerry Reyes
Local chapter of national organization
Founded: 1976
Serves: Filipino Americans in Chicago and suburbs
Purpose: To provide political education and empowerment for Filipinos in the Chicago area
Programs: Political education
Volunteers: Welcome

Philippine Chamber of Commerce of Chicago
2457 W. Peterson Ave., #3
Chicago, IL 60659
Phone: (773)271-8008
Fax: (773)271-8058
E-mail: PhCCChgo@aol.com
Exec. Dir.: Luis Bautista
Pres.: Gerry Alcantara
Founded: 1984
Serves: Filipino Americans in Chicago and suburbs
Purpose: Chamber of commerce
Programs: Economic development

Finnish American

+Finnish American Society of the Midwest and Finlandia Foundation Chapter
407 South 6th Ave.
St. Charles, IL 60174-2935
Phone: (630)584-1684, (815)756-9564
e-mail: snkoivula@aol.com
oforsman@niu.edu
Sec.: Steve Koivula
Pres.: Oscar Forsman
Founded: 1977
No office, 200 members
Local chapter of Finlandia Foundation
Serves: Finnish people and others in Chicago metro area, Illinois and several other states
Purpose: To promote Finnish American culture, adult education and community outreach
Programs: Arts, workshops, lectures, adult learning, culture preservation, heritage/history, honorary consul, citizenship, legal issues, scholarships for children's language study, translation
Volunteers: Welcome

German American

American Aid Society of German Descendants
6540 N. Milwaukee Ave.
Chicago, IL 60631
Phone: (773)763-1323
Evening/weekend: same
No exec. dir., no office, 500 members
Pres.: Hans Gebavi
V.P.: Walter Scheffrahn
Founded: 1944
Serves: Mainly Donau Schwaben (German) and other German and Austrian Americans in Chicago and suburbs
Purpose: Started as aid society, expanded to cultural functions
Programs: Children, culture preservation, heritage/history, immigrant, language, museum, senior citizen, social service, youth
Volunteers: Welcome

**German American
Chamber of Commerce of the Midwest**
401 N. Michigan Ave., Suite 2525
Chicago, IL 60611-4212
Phone: (312)644-2662
Fax: (312)644-0738
e-mail: gaccom@techinter.com
Pres.: Christian J. Roehr
Local office of national organization
Founded: 1963
Serves: Germans and Americans in the
Midwest
Purpose: To heighten Americans'
awareness of opportunities for business in
Germany and vice versa
Programs: Trade promotion, membership
organization, database access, credit-report
checks

German American National Congress
4740 N. Western Ave.
Chicago, IL 60625
Phone: (773)275-1100
Fax: (773)275-4010
e-mail: dankorg@mail.megsinet.net
Pres.: Ernst Ott
Founded: 1959
Serves: Mostly German Americans, some
Austrians, nationwide
Purpose: To cultivate German-American
heritage
Programs: Cultural, social, German-
language schools
Volunteers: Welcome

German American Police Association
4740 N. Western Ave.
Chicago, IL 60625
Phone: (312)979-5000
Evening/weekend: same
Chr.: Anthony Menzyk
Pres.: Roger J. Haas
Founded: 1975
Local chapter of national organization
Serves: German Americans in Chicago,
suburbs and Illinois
Purpose: To provide members with
functions to meet and associate with others
of same heritage and job interests
Programs: Fraternal, charitable gifts to
Altenheim Retirement Center and children
of deceased members

Hamburg Chicago Club
25 W. 256 Plamondon Rd.
Wheaton, IL 60187
Phone: (630)462-6943, -9370
Evening/weekend: same
Fax: (630)462-0143
Pres.: Renate Bonde
V.P.: Bert Lachner
No office, no exec. dir., 55 members
Founded: 1993
Serves: German Americans in Chicago and
suburbs
Purpose: Getting together with other people
from Germany
Programs: Strictly social

Rheinischer Verein Inc.
7139 Days Terrace
Niles, IL 60714
Phone (847)647-1922
Evening/weekend: same
Fax: same
Exec. Dir. & Pres.: Josef Matuschka
1st V.P.: Emil Wehrle
Founded: 1890
Serves: Mostly German Americans in
Chicago and suburbs
Purpose: To organize Mardi Gras functions,
maintain tradition of Karneval and preserve
the German language
Programs: Mardi Gras, Narrensitsung,
Amazonen Dancing Group, Fanfaren Drum
and Bugle Corps
Other locations: Club House, 4265 N.
Elston, Chicago

**Steuben Society of America,
Christopher Ludwick Unit #30**
1205 W. Sherwin, Suite 103
Chicago, IL 60626-2287
Phone (773)761-4488
Evening/weekend: same
Fax: (773)743-0771 Attn. Harold Kekstadt
e-mail: kekstadt@sprynet.com
Web: www.steubensociety.org
Chr.: Harold Kekstadt
Founded: 1919
Unit of national organization
Serves: The nearly 60 million Americans of
Germanic Descent
Purpose: Civic fraternal organization to
promote good citizenship for German
immigrants and descendants, to preserve a
sense of pride in the heritage of the German

American community and provide a voice before our local, state and federal governments
Programs: Public affairs, lobbying in D.C., assisting with German American parade, scholarships, encouraging excellence in the study of German language

United German American Societies of Greater Chicago
26WO31 Birch
Wheaton, IL 60187
Phone: (630)653-1716
Evening/weekend: same
Pres.: Erich Himmel
Sec.: Helga Zettl
Founded: 1920
Serves: German Americans in Chicago and suburbs
Purpose: To be the parent organization for approximately 60 German clubs, including social, choral, dance and educational groups
Programs: Culture preservation, education, heritage/history

Ghanaian American

Ghana National Council
P.O. Box 7123
Chicago, IL 60680-7123
Phone: (773)288-2325
Evening/weekend: same
Sec. Gen.: Nana Owusu-Bempah
No exec. dir., no office, 5000 members
Umbrella organization of 9 associations
Founded: 1984
Serves: Mostly Ghanaians, some other Africans, in Chicago metro area
Purpose: To unite Ghanaians in the metropolitan area, to promote the general welfare and unity of all Ghanaians, to establish and maintain friendly relationships with other organizations
Programs: Immigration, job referral, baptism, funerals, cultural shows to promote co-existence, financial assistance, counseling, translating
Volunteers: Welcome

Greek American

Chicago Council on Justice for Cyprus
P.O. Box 268500
Chicago, IL 60626
Phone: (773)274-7850
Evening/weekend: same
Fax: (773)338-4550
e-mail: ChicagoCyprus@aol.com
Pres.: James Chiakulas
No exec. dir., no office
Local chapter of international organization
Founded: 1955
Serves: Greek Americans in Chicago, suburbs and Illinois
Purpose: To inform the public about the Cyprus/Turkey dispute
Programs: Political action, public relations, informative events

Enosis of Hellenic American Organization of Illinois
2155 W. 80th St.
Chicago, IL 60620
Phone: (773)994-2222
Fax: (773)994-4682, -5037
e-mail: tgshanc@aol.com
Web: www.hellasusa.com/hanc
Pres.: Theodor G. Spyropoulos
V.P.: Mike Mastorakis
Founded: 1978
Serves: Greek Americans in Illinois
Purpose: Political action and cultural
Programs: Arts, culture preservation, education, heritage/history, citizenship, civil rights
Additional location: 5941 N. Milwaukee
Volunteers: Welcome

Greek-American Community Services
3940 N. Pulaski Road
Chicago, IL 60641
Phone: (773)545-0303
Fax: (773)545-0388
Exec. Dir.: John Psiharis
Pres.: Costa Zografopoulos
Founded: 1983
Serves: Mostly Greek Americans, others in need, in Chicago and suburbs and Illinois
Purpose: To address social service needs of the community, and provide cultural programs

Programs: Adult day care, cultural and arts, in-home services for the elderly, information and referral, translation, low-income home-energy assistance, benefits, culture preservation, translating
Volunteers: Welcome

Greek-American Library Association
5026 N. Lincoln Ave.
Chicago, IL 60625
Phone: (773)784-6662
Evening/weekend: same
Pres.: Aris F. Yanibas
Founded: 1986
Serves: Greeks throughout the world and others
Purpose: To collect and preserve the books, periodicals and other materials of the entire Greek civilization, especially the Greek American experience
Programs: Library, lectures
Volunteers: Welcome

Greek Orthodox Ladies
Philoptochos Society
40 E. Burton Place
Chicago, IL 60610
Phone: (312)337-4130
Fax: (312)337-9391
Pres.: Mary Ann Bissias
Diocese division of national organization
Founded: 1931
Serves: Greek Americans in six Midwest states
Purpose: To be the philanthropic arm of the Greek Orthodox Church
Programs: Philanthropy fund, food for the hungry, scholarships, Hellenic Heart Program

Hellenic Bar Association of Illinois
11 S. LaSalle St., Suite 1020
Chicago, IL 60603
Phone: (312)368-1222
Web: www.members.aol.com/hbaofill
Pres.: Angelo Leventis
No exec. dir., no office, 175 members
Founded: 1952
Serves: Greek Americans in Chicago and suburbs
Purpose: To establish and maintain the honor and dignity of the legal profession; to advance and improve the administration of justice; to protect the interests of the public,

especially those of Hellenic descent; to furnish legal aid to the indigent; to advocate the equal rights of all; to cultivate social interaction among the members of the association
Programs: Professional support, education, legal, referral, social/fraternal, scholarships
Volunteers: Welcome

Hellenic Family and Community Services
(Hellenic Foundation)
6251 W. Touhy
Chicago, IL 60646
Phone: (773)631-5222
Evening/weekend: same
Fax: (773)631-2835
Dir.: Angelike Mounianis
Exec. Dir.: Lea C. Ames
Pres.: James Gatsiolis
Founded: 1975
Serves: Greek Americans and their spouses in Chicago and suburbs and Illinois, Northwest Indiana and Milwaukee
Purpose: To meet the social-service needs of Greek Americans through bilingual and bicultural outreach, education, intervention and prevention
Programs: Counseling, children, citizenship, community organizing, education, family, immigrant resettlement and adjustment, literacy, senior citizen, substance abuse, youth, translating
Additional location: 10150 S. Roberts Road, Palos Hills, IL 60465
Volunteers: Welcome

Hellenic Foundation
5700 N. Sheridan Road
Chicago, IL 60660
Phone: (773)728-2603
Evening/weekend: same
Fax: (773)728-1718
Exec. Dir.: Lea C. Ames
Pres.: James J. Gatziolis
Founded: 1953
Serves: Greek Americans in Chicago metro area, Illinois, Northwest Indiana and Milwaukee
Purpose: To identify and address the social service needs of individuals and families of Greek descent
Programs: Counseling, advocacy, citizenship, community organizing, employment, housing for elderly, immigrant

resettlement, literacy, referral, research, substance abuse, technical assistance, vocational training, children, youth, family, senior citizens. Has three agencies under its auspices: Hellenic Family & Community Services, Hollywood House and Hellenic Golden Circle.
Additional locations: 6251 W. Touhy, and 10150 S. Roberts Road, Palos Hills, IL 60465
Volunteers: Welcome

Hellenic Museum and Cultural Center
168 N. Michigan, 4th floor
Chicago, IL 60601-7509
Phone: (312)726-1234
Evening/weekend: same
Fax: (312)726-8539
e-mail: Hellenicmu@aol.com
Admin.: Marina Tanzer
Pres.: Dino Armiros
Founded: 1981
Serves: Greek Americans and the general public on the Near North Side and throughout the Midwest and USA
Purpose: To preserve and perpetuate the heritage of the Greek culture and showcase
Programs: Art -- exhibits and lectures; culture preservation -- archives and exhibits; children -- workshops, exhibit at Children's International Fest at Navy Pier, outreach for schools; education; family; heritage/history

Hellenic Society of Constantinople
2500 N. Sheridan Road
Evanston, IL 60201
Phone: (847)475-0044
Evening/weekend: same
Pres.: Vina Lukidis
No exec. dir., no office, 100 members
Founded: 1939
Serves: Mostly Greek Americans in Chicago and suburbs
Purpose: To raise funds for philanthropic organizations in Greece, the USA and the ecumenical Patriarch of Constantinople
Programs: Philanthropic, culture preservation, heritage/history, social, educational, immigrant, scholarships
Volunteers: Welcome

Hollywood House
5700 N. Sheridan Rd.
Chicago, IL 60660

Phone: (773)728-2600
Evening/weekend: same
Fax: (773)728-1718
Prop. Mgr.: Stavros Papadakis
Pres.: James J. Gatziolis
Founded: 1973
Serves: Mostly Greek Americans, others, in Illinois, Northwest Indiana and Milwaukee
Purpose: To provide affordable and dignified housing to Greek and non-Greek elderly
Programs: Senior citizens housing, financial assistance to low-income elderly, homemaker services, physician and dental offices, beauty services, laundry services, round-the-clock security, social and recreational

Macedonian Society of Greater Chicago
8350 N. Lincoln Ave.
Skokie, IL 60077
Phone: (847)673-3112
Evening/weekend: (847)259-4145 or (847)681-0668
Pres.: Marcus A. Templar
Sec.: Pitsa Panagiotopoulos
Local chapter of national organization
Founded: 1974
Serves: Mainly Greek Americans, in Chicago and suburbs
Purpose: To preserve the Greek heritage and promote social and cultural Greek-American relations
Programs: Arts, community center, culture preservation, heritage/history, women, youth, dance troupe
Volunteers: Welcome

Order of AHEPA - American Hellenic Educational Progressive Assn.
3838 Grace Lane
Glenview, IL 60025
Phone: (847)724-6529
Fax: (847)724-1422
e-mail: PZM@flash.net
Dist. Gov.: Peter Margetis
13th District of national organization
Founded: 1922
Serves: Greek Americans in Illinois and Wisconsin
Purpose: To promote Hellenism, education, philanthropy, civic responsibility, and family and individual excellence

Programs: Fraternal, the Ahepa family consists of Daughters of Penelope, Sons of Pericles and Maids of Athena; culture preservation, scholarships, heritage/history, public policy, senior housing, civil rights

Pan-Messinian Federation of USA and Canada
360 N. Michigan Ave., Suite 710
Chicago, IL 60601
Phone: (312)357-6432
Fax: (312)357-0527
e-mail: hellenes@panmessenian.org
Web: www.panmessinian.org
Pres.: Chris Tomaras
National organization
Founded: 1945
Serves: Greek Americans from Messinia province, in Greece, USA and Canada
Purpose: To preserve the Hellenic culture among Greek Americans
Programs: Culture/preservation, social events, translation
Volunteers: Welcome

Society Kalavrytinon "Agia Lavra"
650 Graceland Ave.
Des Plaines, IL 60016
Phone: (847)824-4017
Evening/weekend: (708)453-1240
Fax: (847)824-4018
Pres.: Dimitrios Mitropoulos
Sec.: Helen Koufis
Founded: 1928
Serves: Greek Americans in Illinois
Purpose: Philanthropic
Programs: Counseling, citizenship, civil rights, community services, education, culture preservation, foreign aid, heritage/history, immigrant settlement, language, legal, fraternal
Volunteers: Welcome

United Hellenic American Congress
75 E. Wacker Drive, Suite 500
Chicago, IL 60601
Phone: (312)345-1000
Fax: (312)345-1015
e-mail: uhacnational@uhac.org
Nat. Chr.: Andrew A. Athens
V. Chr.: John L. Marks
National organization
Founded: 1974

Serves: Hellenic Americans in Chicago, metro area and USA
Purpose: To preserve and promote our ethno-religious heritage and to respond to ethnic and religious concerns of the community
Programs: Involved with Hellenic Heritage events such as Hellenic-American parade, Greek Orthodox Diocese of Chicago, Hellenic Foundation and Hellenic Museum and Cultural Center
Volunteers: Welcome

United Hellenic Voters of America
525 W. Lake St.
Addison, IL 60107
Phone: (630)628-1721
Evening/weekend: same
Fax: (630)543-7001
Exec. Dir.: Dr. Dimitrios Kyriazopoulos
Pres.: Dr. Dimitrios Kyriazopoulos
Founded: 1974
Serves: Mainly Greek Americans in Chicago and the USA
Purpose: To get broader representation in government
Programs: Civic lectures, voter registration, translating
Volunteers: Welcome

Guatemalan American

Casa Guatemala
3731 N. Ravenswood Ave.
Chicago, IL 60613
Phone: (773)348-8979
Evening/weekend: same
Phone/fax: (773)348-8980
e-mail: casaguate@aol.com
Web: http://members.aol.com/casaguate/
Exec. Dir.: José L. Oliva
Pres.: Maria Del Rosario Paz
Founded: 1983
Serves: Mostly Guatemalan Mayans and descendants, other Latin Americans, in Chicago and suburbs
Purpose: Multi-purpose
Programs: Health promotion, ESL and Spanish literacy, Spanish as a Second Language, immigration information and support, Mayan culture preservation, community assistance, community

organizing, human rights advocacy, youth, translating
Volunteers: Welcome

**Organization in Solidarity
with the People of Guatemala**
P.O. Box 25333
Chicago, IL 60652
Phone: (773)281-7954
Fax: (773)296-2345
e-mail: pbondy@worldnet.att.net
Co-ords.: Lucrecia Oliva, Pamela Bondy
Local chapter of national organization
Founded: 1981
Serves: Guatemalans and others in the Chicago metro area and Midwest
Purpose: To educate people in the U.S. about the current political, economic and social situation in Guatemala
Programs: Culture preservation; education about Guatemala's current political, social and economic situation; U.S. tours for Guatemalan leaders of grassroots organizations, especially with human rights focus; fund raising for Guatemalan grassroots organizations

Haitian American

Haitian American Community Assn.
1619 W. Morse Ave.
Chicago, IL 60626
Phone: (773)764-2209
Evening/weekend: same
Fax: (773)764-2669
Exec. Dir.: Carmel Lafontant
Pres.: Marie Lynn Toussaint
Reinstated: 1992
Serves: Mostly Haitian Americans, some Belizean, Panamanian, Jamaican and African Americans and Hispanics, in Rogers Park, Uptown, West Ridge and elsewhere in Chicago and suburbs
Purpose: To help Haitian Americans access social services and overcome language and cultural barriers
Programs: Food pantry, shelter, clothing, crisis and family intervention, referral for legal, health and dental, after-school program, translation/interpretation
Volunteers: Welcome

**Midwest Association
of Haitian American Women**
P.O. Box 87477
Chicago, IL 60680-0477
Phone: (847)882-5848
Evening/weekend: (312)842-2475
Fax: (312)225-9586
e-mail: mahaw@aol.com
Pres.: Monique Germain
Founded: 1995
No exec. dir., no office, 30 members
Serves: Haitian and Haitian American Women in Chicago and suburbs
Purpose: To provide service to the Haitian community
Programs: Health fair, literacy, financial information, arts, social, translators (French and Creole)
Volunteers: Welcome

Hispanic/Latino

(see also Cuban, Guatemalan, Mexican, Nicaraguan, Puerto Rican)

Alivio Medical Center
2355 S. Western Ave.
Chicago, IL 60608
Phone: (773)650-1202
Evening/weekend: same
Fax: (773)650-1226
Exec. Dir.: Carmen Velasquez
Pres.: Peter Martinez
Founded: 1989
Serves: Latinos (mostly Mexicans) in Pilsen, Little Village, Back of the Yards and Heart of Chicago neighborhoods
Purpose: To provide health care and health education for the uninsured and under-insured
Programs: Pregnancy care, social services, community outreach, advocacy, care for children, WIC, nutrition, parenting classes, counseling, Ounce of Prevention, PTS, midwifery services and home births
Volunteers: Welcome

Alliance of Latinos and Jews
P.O. Box 10644
Chicago, IL 60610-0644
Phone: (312)409-8737
e-mail: alliance@ameritech.net
Co-chrs.: Jesse Jimenez, Fred Siegman

Founded: 1994
Serves: Latinos and Jews in Chicago and
suburbs
Purpose: To build new and enhance
existing relations between the Jewish and
Latino communities
Programs: Business and economic
development, culture, social, education,
immigration; co-sponsors events with other
organizations.

Asi
2619 W. Armitage Ave.
Chicago, IL 60647
Phone: (773)278-5130
Fax: (773)278-1380
Exec. Dir.: Rebecca Cruz
Pres.: Raymond G. Massie
Founded: 1975
Serves: People of all backgrounds, with
special emphasis on Hispanics
Purpose: To serve the growing population
of people who need home care to stay out of
institutions
Programs: Home-care services to seniors
and people with disabilities, training and
employment for those wanting to work in
the home-care field, translating
Volunteers: Welcome

Aspira Inc. of Illinois
2435 N. Western Ave.
Chicago, IL 60647
Phone: (773)252-0970
Fax: (773)252-0994
e-mail: aspira_il@hotmail.com
Chr.: Sonia Sanchez
Pres. & CEO: Jose Rodriguez
Founded: 1968
Serves: Puerto Ricans, Mexican Americans
and other Latinos in West Town, Logan
Square, Humboldt Park neighborhoods and
metro area
Purpose: To develop leadership skills of
Latino youth
Programs: Leadership Development
Institute, Health Careers Program, Drug
Prevention Program, Public Policy Program,
Aspira Parents for Educational Excellence,
math and science, alternative
high school, college counseling, financial
aid, heritage/history, literacy, mentoring,
tutoring, translating
Volunteers: Welcome

Association House of Chicago
1116 N. Kedzie Ave.
Chicago, IL 60651
Phone: (773)772-7170
Sat.: same
Fax: (773)384-0560
Exec. Dir.: Harriet Sadauskas
Pres.: David C. DeBauche
Founded: 1899
Serves: Mostly Latinos, also African
Americans and all in need in West
Town/Humboldt Park
Purpose: To provide social services to
families, children, adolescents, adults and
seniors
Programs: Counseling, citizenship,
community center, education, employment,
language, literacy, mental health, child
welfare, mentoring, referral, senior outreach,
substance abuse, tutoring, community
organizing,, vocational training, translating
Volunteers: Welcome

Boys & Girls Clubs of Chicago --
Little Village
2801 S. Ridgeway
Chicago, IL 60623
Phone: (773)277-1800
Evening/weekend: (773)277-1800
Fax: (773)277-4777
Exec. Dir.: Robert Cepeda
Pres.: Robert Hassin
Local chapter of national organization
Founded: 1908
Serves: Mostly Mexican, some others, in
South Lawndale and Little Village
Purpose: To help young people grow up to
be responsible, caring adults
Programs: Leadership development,
education, physical ed, cultural enrichment,
environmental education, social
development, HIV education, job training,
college preparation, computer education

CALOR (a division of Anixter Center)
3220 W. Armitage Ave.
Chicago, IL 60647
Phone: (773)235-3161
Fax: (773)772-0484
e-mail: olopez8315@aol.com
Exec. Dir.: Omar N. Lopez
Pres.: Stuart G. Ferst
Founded: 1992

Serves: Latinos in West Town, Logan Square, Humboldt Park
Purpose: To provide services to Latinos impacted by HIV/AIDS and other disabilities
Programs: HIV/AIDS prevention for gay Latino men, women of color, sex-industry workers,; vocational services for Latinos with disabilities; substance-abuse counseling for Latinos with HIV; translating
Volunteers: Welcome

Casa Aztlan
1831 S. Racine
Chicago, IL 60608
Phone: (312)666-5508
Fax: (312)666-7829
Exec. Dir.: Carlos Arango
Pres.: Guillermo Gomez
Founded: 1970
Serves: Latinos in Pilsen/Little Village
Purpose: To support heritage and culture; to offer assistance to underprivileged Latinos
Programs: Arts, counseling, citizenship, education, literacy, community center, youth after-school, translating .
Volunteers: Welcome

Casa Central
1343 N. California
Chicago, IL 60622
Phone: (773)465-2300
Fax: (773)645-2475
Pres.: Ann R. Alvarez
Founded: 1954
Serves: Latinos and others in the Chicago metro area, using bilingual bicultural approach
Purpose: To stabilize and empower families, encourage self-sufficiency and promote health, family and community functioning
Programs: Skilled nursing home, transitional housing for homeless families, day care, after-school programs, counseling, literacy and pre-employment training, Certified Nurses Aide training, adult day care, child welfare, domestic violence, foster grandparents, over-55 employment, Homemakers, nutrition
Additional locations: 1335 N. California, 1343 N. California 1349 N. California, 1320 N. Kedzie, 1901 N. Kedzie, 2222 N. Kedzie
Volunteers: Welcome

Centro de Información
62 S. Grove Ave.
Elgin, IL 60120
Phone: (847)695-9050
Fax: (847)931-7991
Exec. Dir.: Audrey Reed
Pres.: Sonny Garza
Founded: 1972
Serves: Mostly Hispanics, in Kane and McHenry counties and western Cook County
Purpose: To encourage and help Hispanics to participate fully in the life of the community
Programs: Counseling, immigration, citizenship, education, employment, family, health care, housing, legal, mental health, youth program, referral, translating
Other offices: Centro de Informacion Y Progreso Neighborhood Resource Center, 2380 Glendale Terr. #5, Hanover Park, IL 60103
Volunteers: Welcome

Centro Para Desarrollo Comunitario y Liderato
4720 W. Diversey
Chicago, IL 60639
Phone: (773)286-9590
Fax: (773)286-9592
Exec. Dir.: Raphael Morales
Pres.: Dr. Jose D. Rodriguez
Founded: 1981
Serves: Mostly Latinos, some African Americans, in West Town, Humboldt Park, Hermosa and Logan Square neighborhoods
Purpose: To do ecumenical advocacy work with Latinos and develop leadership
Programs: Civil rights, community center, technical assistance, community empowerment, community organizing, education reform, food pantries, HIV/AIDS education and prevention, youth outreach
Volunteers: Welcome

Centro Romero
6216 N. Clark St.
Chicago, IL 60660
Phone: (773)508-5300
Evening/weekend: (773)262-8739
Fax: (773)508-5399
Exec. Dir.: Daysi J. Funes
Pres.: Charles H. Wintersteen
Founded: 1984

Serves: Hispanics on Chicago's Northeast Side

Purpose: Multi-service community center for economically and educationally disadvantaged.

Programs: Adult ed, counseling, violence reduction, youth programs, crisis intervention, legal

Volunteers: Welcome

**Centro Sin Fronteras
(see Mexican American)**

**Chicago Association of
Hispanic Journalists**
Michael Martinez
c/o Chicago Tribune
435 N. Michigan Ave.
Chicago, IL 60611
Phone: (312)409-0602
e-mail: mjmartinez@tribune.com
Exec. Dir.: Frank Diaz
Interim Pres.: Ana Mendieta
Contact: Mike Martinez
Founded: 1986
Serves: Latino journalists and students, in Chicago and suburbs
Purpose: To promote and encourage Latinos in journalism
Programs: Professional support, counseling, culture preservation, education, employment, heritage/history, language, mentoring, referral, research, translating (on request)
Volunteers: Welcome

Chicago Latino Cinema
c/o Columbia College
600 S. Michigan Ave.
Chicago, IL 60605
Phone: (312)431-1330
Fax: (312)344-8030
Exec. Dir.: Pepe Vargas
Chr.: Isidro Lucas
Founded: 1987
Serves: Mostly Latinos, and others, in the Chicago area, Illinois and USA
Purpose: To promote Latino culture and create greater awareness of Latinos' contributions
Programs: Arts, heritage/history, children, education, Chicago Latino Film Festival, translating
Volunteers: Welcome

**Chicago Religious Leadership Network
on Latin America**
59 E. Van Buren, #1400
Chicago, IL 60605
Phone: (312)939-3271
Evening/weekend: same (voice mail)
Fax: (312)939-3272
e-mail: crln2cmsa@igc.apc.org
Exec. Dir.: Gary L. Cozette
Founded: 1990
Serves: Latinos, and religious and community leaders concerned with Latin American issues. This is a joint project of the Chicago Metropolitan Sanctuary Alliance, Committee in Solidarity with the People of El Salvador, Organization in Solidarity with the People of Guatemala, Nicaragua Solidarity Committee, Witness for Peace, and Chicago Cuba Coalition
Purpose: To provide educational opportunities about Latin America (mainly Central America, Cuba and Mexico) through delegations and speaking events; to advocate for just U.S. policies toward Latin America
Programs: Speakers regarding human rights, economics, political atmosphere of a specific country, delegations to Latin America, lobbying in Washington, D.C.

**Coalicion de Ministros
Latino-Americanos**
1116 N. Kedzie, Suite 5W
Chicago, IL 60651
Phone: (773)489-7212
Fax: (773)489-6981
Exec. Dir.: Rev. Daniel Matos-Real
Pres.: same
Founded: 1995
Serves: Mostly Hispanics, in Chicago
Purpose: Advocacy and technical assistance to churches providing social services
Programs: After-school tutoring, technical assistance, community organizing
Volunteers: Welcome

Cordi-Marian Settlement & Day Care
1100 South May Street
Chicago, IL 60607
Phone: (312)666-3787
Evening/weekend: Same
Fax: (312)666-3562
Exec. Dir.: Mary Moore
President: the Rev. Michael Boland
Founded: 1936

Serves: Hispanics, some African Americans and Asian Americans on Near West Side and in Pilsen, 26th Street, UIC and Tri-Taylor areas
Purpose: To provide social services, day care and settlement house programs
Programs: Children, citizenship, social services, translating
Volunteers: Welcome

**Division Street Business
Development Association**
2502 W. Division St.
Chicago, IL 60622
Phone: (773)782-0454
Evening/weekend: same
Fax: (773)278-0635
Exec. Dir.: Eduardo Arocho
Pres.: Bill Farhan
Founded: 1985
Serves: Humboldt Park and West Town
Purpose: To improve and revitalize the business community on Division Street
Programs: Economic development, technical assistance
Volunteers: Welcome

East Village Youth Program
1943 W. Division St.
Chicago, IL 60622
Phone: (773)489-9088
Fax: (773)489-1565
e-mail: evyp@chicagonet.net
Exec. Dir.: Jeannie Balanda
Pres.: Jess Levine
Founded: 1989
Serves: Mostly Latinos, a variety of others, grades 6 through college, in West Town
Purpose: To encourage and prepare disadvantaged youth in West Town for a college education
Programs: Arts, education, financial aid, mentoring, recreation, tutoring, youth
Volunteers: Welcome

Healthcare Alternative Systems, Inc.
2755 W. Armitage
Chicago, IL 60647
Phone: (773)252-3100
Fax: (773)252-8945
e-mail: hascares@aol.com
Web: www.hascares.org
Exec. Dir.: Marco E. Jacome
Founded: 1974

Serves: Mostly Latinos, also African Americans and Anglos in Humboldt Park, Wicker Park and Logan Square
Purpose: To provide behavioral health services to the community
Programs: Alcohol and drug prevention, parenting classes, support groups, leadership training, intensive outpatient counseling, family case management for pregnant women and women with infants, domestic violence prevention, counseling, court advocacy and referrals, residential drug treatment center, translating
Other locations: 4534 N. Western, women's program 1942 N. California, residential program 1949 N. Humboldt, prevention 1736 W. 47th St.
Volunteers: Welcome

**Hispanic Alliance
for Career Enhancement**
14 E. Jackson Blvd., Suite 1310
Chicago, IL 60604
Phone: (312)435-0498
Fax: (312)435-1494
e-mail: haceorg@enteract.com
Web: www.hace-usa.org
Exec. Dir.: Jose Gomez
Pres.: Ray Arias
Founded: 1982
Serves: Hispanics in Chicago metro area and Midwest
Purpose: To empower Hispanics to occupy economic leadership positions, thus benefiting Hispanic community
Programs: Professional candidate referral and placement, annual career conference, career development seminars, Future Professionals Program of scholarships, internships, seminars
Volunteers: Welcome

**Hispanic American
Construction Industry Association**
542 S. Dearborn, Suite 610
Chicago, IL 60605
Phone: (312)786-0101
Fax: (312)786-0104
Exec. Dir.: Rafael Hernandez
Pres.: Dominic Delgado
Founded: 1979
Serves: Not only Hispanics but also all minorities and women in the Chicago metro area and Illinois

Purpose: To advocate on behalf of minority- and women-owned businesses, and ensure equitable participation of its members in the Chicago area construction industry; as well as to promote growth, professionalism, integrity and quality of work

Programs: Economic development; business support; membership services such as contract opportunities and referrals, marketing assistance, MBE certification assistance, business workshops, conflict resolution assistance; employment services, such as referrals, specialized training, and educational assistance to enhance employment

Volunteers: Welcome

Hispanic Council
1204 W. Irving Park
Bensenville, IL 60106
Phone: (630)595-7400
Fax: (630)595-7480
e-mail: poliudg@aol.com
Exec. Dir.: Juan Matus-Carreno
Pres.: Luis E. Pelayo
Founded: 1987
Serves: Mostly Latinos, in Midwest
Purpose: To assist and educate the community in order to improve its standard of living
Programs: Civil rights, community center, community organizing, culture preservation, immigrant resettlement and adjustment, language, legal, literacy, translating
Volunteers: Welcome

Hispanic Housing Development Corp.
205 W. Wacker Dr., Suite 2300
Chicago, IL 60606
Phone: (312)443-1360
Fax: (312)443-1058
Pres.: Hipolito Roldan
Founded: 1975
Serves: Mostly Latinos, some others, in Latino neighborhoods of Chicago and suburbs
Purpose: To provide quality, affordable housing for Latino neighborhoods and spur economic development
Programs: Quality affordable housing for low-moderate income residents, serving elderly, handicapped, multi-family and

single occupancies; assistance with referrals to community agencies
Volunteers: Welcome

Hispanic Institute of Law Enforcement
30 East Lake St.
Chicago, IL 60601
Phone: (312)641-5756
Exec. Dir.: Teresita Diaz-Lewis
Pres.: José L. Urteaga
Founded: 1982
Serves: Mostly Hispanics, in Chicago
Purpose: To improve ties between the criminal justice system and Hispanic community
Programs: Education, community service, career development, recruitment, relations between police and Hispanic community, tutorial for law enforcement exams, legal seminars for police officers, translating
Volunteers: Welcome

Hispanic Lawyers Scholarship Fund
130 E. Randolph Dr., Suite 3200
Chicago, IL 60601
Phone: (312)861-6632
Fax: (312)861-2899
e-mail: Martin.R.Castro@bakernet.com
Chr.: Martin Castro
Founded: 1997
Serves: Hispanics in Illinois
Purpose: To provide scholarships and fellowships for Hispanic law students
Programs: Scholarships, fellowships, grammar school essay contest, annual reception and dinner
Volunteers: Welcome

Hispanocare, Inc.
836 W. Wellington
Chicago, IL 60657
Phone: (773)296-7157
Fax: (773)327-8208
CEO: Lucy Robles-Aquino
Founded: 1988
Serves: Hispanics and some others in Chicago
Purpose: To provide quality, user-friendly, culturally sensitive health care to Hispanics
Programs: Health care, education
Volunteers: Welcome

**Illinois Association of Hispanic
State Employees**
P.O. Box 641526
Chicago, IL 60664-1526
Phone: (312)814-8942
Evening/weekend: (773)227-2380
Fax: (312)814-8942
Pres.: Hilda Lopez
V.P.: Peter F. Viña
Founded: 1987
Serves: Mostly Hispanics, some whites and
African Americans, in Illinois
Purpose: To increase Hispanic employment
at the state level and develop services to
help the Hispanic community and Hispanics
in government
Programs: Education, in conjunction with
state universities; communication skills and
conferences; career development; general
meetings several times a year
Volunteers: Welcome

Illinois Migrant Council
28 E. Jackson Blvd. #1600
Chicago, IL 60604
Phone: (312)663-1522
Fax: (312)663-1994
Exec. Dir.: Eloy Salazar
Pres.: Guadalupe Cordova
Founded: 1966
Serves: Mostly Hispanics, also African
Americans and all other farm workers in
Illinois
Purpose: To aid migrant and seasonal farm
workers, who face many obstacles to
attaining economic self-sufficiency
Programs: Emergency food and shelter, job
training, social services, job counseling, job
development and placement, ESL classes,
migrant education/coordination outreach,
translation/interpretation, crisis intervention,
family counseling, referrals
Other offices: Momence, Peoria,
Champaign, Cairo, Woodstock, Hoopston
Volunteers: Welcome

**Illinois Migrant
Legal Assistance Project**
111 W. Jackson, 3rd Floor
Chicago, IL 60604
Phone: (312)347-8394
Evening/weekend: Same
Fax: (312)341-1041
e-mail: vbeckman@lapchicago.com

Dir.: Vincent H. Beckman
Pres.: James D. Wascher
Founded: 1972
Serves: Mostly Hispanics, all migrant
farmworkers in Illinois
Purpose: To provide legal assistance to
migrant farmworkers
Programs: Legal services and community
legal education
Volunteers: Welcome

Instituto del Progreso Latino
2570 S. Blue Island Ave.
Chicago, IL 60608
Phone: (773)890-0055
Evening/weekend: same
Fax: (773)890-1537
Exec. Dir.: Maria T. Ayala
Pres.: Juan Salgado
Founded: 1975
Serves: Hispanics in near South Side Latino
communities
Purpose: To provide better educational
services to the community
Programs: Primarily educational; some
social services, immigrant, advocacy
Volunteers: Welcome

Latin American Chamber of Commerce
3512 W. Fullerton Ave.
Chicago, IL 60647
Phone: (773)252-5211
Evening/weekend: same (voice mail)
Fax: (773)252-7065
e-mail: sbdclacc@ix.netcom.com
 Web: www.lac1.com
Chr.: D. Lorenzo Padron
Pres.: Antonio R. Guillen
Founded: 1976
Serves: Hispanic and other minority
businesses in Chicago and suburbs
Purpose: To organize all Hispanic
businesses as one economic group; to foster
growth and development among members
by providing professional and technical
assistance and management
education/training; to facilitate business
transactions between members; to increase
level of employment of local residents
through entrepreneurship
Programs: Financial consulting,
government contracting, business insurance,
general business consulting
Volunteers: Welcome

Latin American Police Association
P.O. Box 4551
Chicago, IL 60680-4551
Phone: (773)927-5058
Evenings/weekends: same
Fax: (312)666-2981
e-mail: lapa1961@hotmail.com
Web: www.lapa1961.cjb.net
Pres.: Tony Naverette
No office, no exec. dir., 450 members
Founded: 1961
Serves: Latin Americans in Chicago
metro area
Purpose: To assist Hispanics in the field of
law enforcement, promote professionalism
and advancement, and encourage
understanding and cooperation between
Hispanic community, Chicago Police and
other law enforcement agencies
Programs: Networking and education.
Founded Hispanic Institute of Law
Enforcement (see listing above)

**Latin United Community
Housing Association**
2750 W. North Ave.
Chicago, IL 60647
Phone: (773)276-5338
Fax: (773)276-5358
Exec. Dir.: Juan B. Rivera
Pres.: Myrna Rodriguez
Founded: 1982
Serves: Hispanics and other residents of
West Town , Humboldt Park and Logan
Square
Purpose: To fight for community housing
interests
Programs: Technical assistance
(tenant/landlord rights), loans to home
buyers, insurance help, home repair and
housing development
Volunteers: Welcome

**Latino Counseling Service
(Counseling Center of Lake View)**
3225 N. Sheffield
Chicago, IL 60657
Phone: (773)549-5886
Fax: (773)549-3265
Exec. Dir.: Norman Groetzinger
Pgm. Dir.: Gelsys Rubio
Founded: 1975

Serves: Spanish-speaking residents on the
North Side of Chicago, with emphasis on
Lake View
Purpose: To provide for mental health
needs of Spanish-speaking population
Programs: Individual, family and group
counseling of adults, children and
adolescents; specialty in family violence and
psychiatric/psychological consultation when
needed

Latino Firefighters Association
P.O. Box 38-8281
Chicago, IL 60638
Phone: (773)229-0926
Evening/weekend: same
Fax: (773)229-0933
e-mail: 1hoses1@aol.com
Pres.: Charles Vazquez Sr.
V.P.: Eduardo Aviles
No exec. dir., no office
Founded: 1975
Serves: Hispanics in Chicago
Purpose: To protect the interests of
Hispanic firefighters in the Chicago Fire
Dept.
Programs: Free fire detectors to needy, fire
prevention and awareness; fraternal
Volunteers: Welcome

Latino Treatment Center
2608 W. Peterson Ave.
Chicago, IL 60659
Phone: (773)465-1161
Fax: (773)465-1693
Exec. Dir.: Dr. Ernest Pujals
Pres.: George Irizarry
Founded: 1986
Serves: Hispanics on North Side and in
suburbs
Purpose: Provide alcohol/drug treatment to
underserved Hispanic population
Programs: Alcohol and drug treatment
Other facilities: Latino Treatment Center in
Elgin (see immediately below)
Volunteers: Welcome

Latino Treatment Center
54 S. Grove Ave.
Elgin, IL 60120
Phone: (847)695-9155
Fax: (847)695-9194
Exec. Dir.: Dr. Ernest Pujals
Pgm. Dir.: Marie Pujals

Founded: 1986
Serves: Hispanics in Kane, Cook, McHenry, Lake counties
Purpose: To help the Latino population
Programs: DUI evaluation and individual counseling; DUI remedial education with group and family counseling, DUI risk intervention program and adolescent treatment, outpatient treatment for dual diagnosis and chemical dependency problems, translating
Other offices: 2608 W. Peterson Ave., Chicago (see immediately above)
Volunteers: Welcome

Latino Youth, Inc.
2200 S. Marshall Blvd.
Chicago, IL 60623
Phone: (773)277-0400
Evening/weekend: same
Fax: (773)277-0401
Exec. Dir.: Carmen Aviles
Pres.: Jose Alatorre
Founded: 1974
Serves: Mostly Latinos, some African Americans, in Little Village and Pilsen
Purpose: To provide critical educational and social service to at-risk youth and their families on Chicago's lower West Side
Programs: Alternative high school, counseling, children, culture preservation, day care, education, family, literacy, temporary housing, substance abuse, gang prevention, vocational training, Youth for Unity, parenting skills
Volunteers: Welcome

Latinos Progresando
1624 W. 18th St.
Chicago, IL 60608
Phone: (312)850-0572
Evening/weekend: same
Fax: (312)850-0576
Exec. Dir.: Luis Gutierrez
Pres.: Antonio Gonzalez
Founded: 1997
Serves: Latinos in Pilsen and metro Chicago
Purpose: To help Latinos with any immigration case at a low cost
Programs: Citizenship classes/applications, referral, adjustment of status applications, family visa petitions, ESL classes, translating
Volunteers: Welcome

Little Village Chamber of Commerce
3610 W. 26th St., 2nd floor
Chicago, IL 60623
Phone: (773)521-5387
Fax: (773)521-5252
Exec. Dir.: Frank Aguilar
Pres.: Agustin Granja
Founded: 1965
Serves: Mostly Mexican Americans, other Latinos, some Korean Americans
Purpose: Economic development
Programs: Economic development, technical assistance, referral
Volunteers: Welcome

Little Village Community Council
3610 W. 26th St.
Chicago, IL 60623
Phone: (773)762-3468
Evening/weekend: same
Fax: (773)762-7200
Act. Dir. & Pres.: Eriberto Campos
Founded: 1967
Serves: Mostly Mexican Americans, some other Hispanics and Poles, in South Lawndale and Little Village
Purpose: To assist Mexican Americans and other members of the community with a variety of services and referrals to meet economic, legal and immigrant needs
Programs: Legal assistance, tax assistance, English classes, legal referral, employment referral, immigrant assistance, translating
Volunteers: Welcome

Logan Square Neighborhood Assn.
3321 W. Wrightwood Ave.
Chicago, IL 60647
Phone: (773)384-4370
Evening/weekend: same
Fax: (773)384-0624
e-mail: LSNA@one.org
Exec. Dir.: Nancy Aardema
Founded: 1962
Serves: Mostly Hispanics, others in Logan Square neighborhood
Purpose: To strengthen families in the community by bringing people together to work on issues regarding their common self-interest in areas of housing, education, employment and crime prevention
Programs: Community organizing, home ownership for low-income people, tenants rights workshop/aid, landlord information,

parent involvement in schools, block club organizing, school community learning centers
Volunteers: Welcome

Logan Square YMCA
3600 W. Fullerton Ave.
Chicago, IL 60647
Phone: (773)235-5150
Fax: (773)235-4489
Exec. Dir.: Rey Colón
Pres.: Lynn S. Crawford
Local chapter of national YMCA
Founded: 1854
Serves: A diverse, predominantly Latino population in Humboldt Park and Logan Square
Purpose: To support the physical, mental and spiritual well-being of individuals and families and aid in the development of Christian values
Programs: Aquatics, early-childhood development, fun clubs, sports, leagues, dance, self-defense, after-school child care, teen leaders, adult health, fitness, and family nights
Volunteers: Welcome

LULAC National Educational Services Center
4355 W. 26th St.
Chicago, IL 60623
Phone: (773)277-2513
Fax: (773)277-3930
Dir.: Gabriel Hernandez
Local chapter of national organization
Founded: 1973
Serves: Mostly Hispanics, some others, in Little Village, Pilsen, Brighten Park and South Chicago neighborhoods
Purpose: To inform and help students pursue a post-secondary education
Programs: Scholarships, mentorships, leadership development, literacy, academic and career counseling, financial-aid counseling
Volunteers: Welcome

Mexican American Legal Defense & Educational Fund (MALDEF)
188 W. Randolph St.
Chicago, IL 60601
Phone: (312)782-1422
Fax: (312)782-1428

Reg. Counsel: Patricia Mendoza
Pres. & Gen. Counsel: Antonia Hernandez
Local chapter of national organization
Founded: 1968
Serves: All Latinos in Chicago, suburbs, Illinois and the Midwest
Purpose: To protect the civil rights of Latinos
Programs: Class-action cases in areas of education, voting rights, immigrant rights, employment discrimination, and public resource equity

Mexican American Chamber of Commerce, Mexican American Police Organization, Mexican Civic Committee, Mexican Civic Society of Illinois, Mexican Community Committee, Mexican Fine Arts Center Museum (see Mexican American)

Midwest Hispanic AIDS Coalition
1753 N. Damen Ave.
Chicago, IL 60647
Phone: (773)772-8195
Evening/weekend: e-mail
e-mail: mhac@techinter.com
Exec. Dir.: Cathy Lins
Pres.: Nancy Rivera
Founded: 1988
Serves: Latinos in the Midwest
Purpose: To reduce HIV among Latinos by helping human services organizations involved in prevention with training and information; to empower Latino communities in the Midwest by providing a centralized forum for integration, coordination and networking
Programs: Technical assistance, training, resource center, Latino Provider Network
Volunteers: Welcome

Mujeres Latinas En Accion (Latin Women in Action)
1823 W. 17th St.
Chicago, IL 60608
Phone: (312)226-1544
Fax: (312)226-2720
e-mail: mujereslat@aol.com
Exec. Dir.: Norma Seledón
Pres.: Doris Salomón
Founded: 1973
Serves: Latinos in Chicago and suburbs

Purpose: To serve monolingual Spanish-speaking women; to advocate for linguistically and culturally sensitive services in all areas, including courts, police and social service agencies
Programs: Domestic violence and sexual-assault prevention and counseling, Latina leadership training, homelessness prevention, parent support groups, after-school tutoring and recreation for children 6-12, youth crisis intervention
Volunteers: Welcome

National Comm. to Free Puerto Rican Prisoners of War and Political Prisoners (see Puerto Rican)

National Council of La Raza, Midwest Regional Office
203 N. Wabash, Suite 918
Chicago, IL 60601
Phone (312)269-9250
Fax: (312)269-9260
e-mail: jhinojosa@nclr.org
Dir.: Jorge Hinojosa
. Nat. Pres.: Raul Yzaguirre
Regional chapter of national organization
Founded: 1968
Serves: Latinos in the Midwest
Purpose: To empower Hispanics, from the grassroots up, and build a community-based constituency predicated on mutual respect and credibility
Programs: Advocacy, assistance in management, program operations and resource development for community-based organizations; applied research and policy analysis; public information; special and international projects
Volunteers: Welcome

Pilsen Little Village Community Mental Health Clinic, Inc.
2319 S. Damen
Chicago, IL 60608
Phone: (773)579-0832
Fax: (773)579-0762
V.P.: Luis Ortiz
Founded: 1967
Serves: Mostly Latinos, some African Americans, in Pilsen and Little Village neighborhoods of Chicago
Purpose: To be a comprehensive mental health organization

Programs: Mental health, substance abuse, transitional housing, vocational rehabilitation, AIDS education, outreach, counseling, children
Volunteers: Welcome

Pilsen Neighbors Community Council
2026 S. Blue Island
Chicago, IL 60608
Phone: (312)666-2663
Fax: (312)666-4661
e-mail: Pilsenncc@aol.com,
ReyLC@aol.com
Exec. Dir.: Juan Soto
Pres.: Teresa Fraga
Bus. Dir.: Rey Lopez Calderon
Founded: 1954
Serves: Latinos in Pilsen area
Purpose: To develop effective leaders and improve educational opportunities
Programs: Leadership development, mentoring, tutoring, job placement, professional business training, scholarships, Fiesta del Sol

Pilsen YMCA
1608 W. 21st Place
Chicago, IL 60608
Phone: (312)738-0282
Fax: (312)738-1915
e-mail: PilsenY@uic.edu
Exec. Dir.: Michael Lozano
Pres.: (YMCA Metro Chicago) Tino Mantella
Founded: 1981
Serves: Mostly Hispanics, some non-Hispanic whites and African Americans, in Pilsen and Little Village neighborhoods of Chicago
Purpose: To provide vitally needed programs at affordable rates to people in Pilsen and Little Village
Programs: After-school child care, summer day camp, Head Start, teen leaders club, youth basketball, Summer Youth Employment Program, adult ESL and citizenship classes
Volunteers: Welcome

Project VIDA
2659 S. Kedvale Ave.
Chicago, IL 60623
Phone: (773)522-4570
Fax: (773)522-4573

e-mail: ProjVida@aol.com
Exec. Dir.: Luule Vess
Pres.: Pedro Lopez
Founded: 1992
Serves: Latinos and African Americans in South and North Lawndale and citywide
Purpose: HIV prevention and risk reduction for youth; direct services to PWHIV/AIDS
Programs: Outreach, school programs, alternative therapies, mental health counseling, food pantry for PWAs, girls groups, gay/lesbian/bi support groups, on-site HIV/syphilis testing and counseling
Volunteers: Welcome

Puerto Rican Chamber of Commerce, Puerto Rican Cultural Center, Puertorriquenos Unidos De Chicago (see Puerto Rican)

Resurrection Project (see Mexican American)

El Rincon Community Clinic (see Puerto Rican)

Segundo Ruiz Belvis Cultural Center
1632 N. Milwaukee Ave.
Chicago, IL 60647
Phone: (773)235-3988
Evening/weekend: same
Fax: (773)235-8080
Exec Dir.: America Sorrentini
Founded: 1971
Serves: Latinos in the greater Humboldt Park-Wicker Park area of Chicago
Purpose: To offer community empowerment, revitalization through culture, and other self-development services
Programs: Counseling, art, cultural, music, dance, GED classes, literacy, ESL
Volunteers: Welcome

North-West Latino Community Center
3411 W. Diversey Ave., Suites 6 & 7
Chicago, IL 60647-1125
Phone: (773)278-8345, -4021
Fax: (773)278-4023
Pres.: Walter Urroz
Founded: 1999
Serves: The community in general and Latinos in particular, on the North and West side s of Chicago and surrounding areas

Purpose: To provide services to our community for its empowerment, to obtain government aid for their development, and to direct resources to those in need
Programs: Community organizing, adult education, culture preservation, citizenship, translating, political education, job referral
Volunteers: Welcome

Spanish Action Committee of Chicago (see Puerto Rican)

Spanish Coalition for Housing
4035 W. North Ave.
Chicago, IL 60639
Phone: (773)342-7575
Fax: (773)342-8528
Exec. Dir.: Ofelia Navarro
Pres.: Carlos DeJesus
Founded: 1966
Serves: Mostly Hispanics, some African Americans and Anglos, in Chicago and suburbs
Purpose: To supply housing information to homeowners, potential homeowners, renters and people seeking affordable housing
Programs: Pre-purchase, foreclosure-prevention and post-purchase counseling; pre-rental and post-rental counseling; referrals, CHA and Section 8 applications, translation
Volunteers: Welcome

Spanish Coalition for Jobs, Inc.
2011 W. Pershing Road
Chicago, IL 60609
Phone: (773)247-0707
Fax: (773)247-4975
e-mail: SCJ@ameritech.net
Pres. & CEO: Mary Gonzalez-Koenig
Founded: 1972
Serves: Most Latinos, some African Americans and non-Latino whites, in Chicago and suburbs
Purpose: To enhance the quality of life of Latinos through educational, vocational and employment services, thus enabling them to achieve economic independence
Programs: Economic development, counseling, education, employment, community organizing, vocational training, welfare-to-work
Other offices: 1737 W. 18th St.

**Union League Barreto
Boys and Girls Club**
2713 W. Crystal
Chicago, IL 60622
Phone: (773)235-0870
Fax: (773)235-8244
Exec. Dir.: Mariano Acevedo
Pgm. Dir.: Kenneth Soohov
Local chapter of national organization
Founded: 1967
Serves: Mostly Hispanics, also African
Americans and non-Hispanic whites, in area
west of Damen to Kedzie and from Chicago
Ave. to Fullerton
Purpose: To promote the social, physical,
moral and educational development of boys
and girls in the Chicago area
Programs: Arts, education, recreation,
sports, social, tutoring
Other locations: 65 W. Jackson Blvd.
Volunteers: Welcome

**The United Neighborhood Organization
of Chicago (UNO)**
954 W. Washington Blvd.
Chicago, IL 60607
Phone: (312)432-6301
Evening/weekend: (312)432-6300
Fax: (312)432-0077
Exec. Dir., Pres.: Juan Rangel
Founded: 1980
Serves: Mostly Latinos, other immigrants in
Chicago and suburbs
Purpose: To empower communities and
revitalize ethnic neighborhoods; to address
issues that affect quality of life through a
comprehensive strategy
Programs: Education, economic
development, home ownership, citizenship,
safety, gang reduction, other neighborhood
issues.
Other offices: 3066 E. 92nd St.
Volunteers: Welcome

**United Network for Immigrant
& Refugee Rights**
1620 W. 18th St., 2nd Floor
Chicago, IL 60608
Phone: (312)563-0002
Evening/weekend: same
Fax: (312)563-9864
e-mail: unirjaguar@aol.com
Exec. Dir.: Oscar Tellez
Pres.: Carlos Arango

Founded: 1989
Serves: Mostly Latinos, some Eastern
Europeans, Asians, Middle Easterners, in
Chicago and suburbs
Purpose: To advocate for civil and human
rights for immigrants
Programs: Citizenship, civil rights, labor
rights, immigration, education, visa
processing, referral, translation
Volunteers: Welcome

Universidad Popular
1510 N. Rockwell St.
Chicago, IL 60622
Phone: (773)772-0836
Evening/weekend: same
Fax: (773)772-0837
Exec. Dir.: Olivia Flores-Godinez
Pres.: Irene Damota
Founded: 1972
Serves: Mostly Latin Americans, some
Arab, Polish and African Americans, in
Chicago
Purpose: Community empowerment
Programs: Adult education, ESL,
translating
Volunteers: Welcome

El Valor Corp.
1850 W. 21st St.
Chicago, IL 60608
Phone: (312)666-4511
Fax: (312)666-6677
e-mail: allocco@mcs.com
Exec. Dir.: Dr. Vincent A. Allocco
Founded: 1973
Serves: Mostly Hispanics, some African
Americans, Caucasians, in Pilsen, South
East Chicago, Little Village neighborhoods
of Chicago
Purpose: To set a new standard for the
education of inner-city communities and to
promote inclusion of people with disabilities
into all aspects of community life
Programs: Vocational training and job
placement, community housing, family
support and respite, early intervention,
prevention, Head Start, advanced-degree
education
Other locations: Programs at several
locations: 1951 W. 19th St., 1931 W. 19th
St., 3012 E. 92nd St., 2624 S. Hamlin, 2658
S. Drake, 2711 W. 23rd St., 2425 S.
California and in Cicero

Volunteers: Welcome

**Viva Family Center
(Children's Home & Aid Society)**
2516 W. Division St.
Chicago, IL 60622
Phone: (773)252-6313
Evening/weekend: same
Fax: (773)252-6866
Exec. Dir.: vacant
Mgr.: Linda Brinker
Founded: 1980
Serves: Mostly Hispanics/Latinos, some African Americans, in Chicago
Purpose: To offer programs to increase the mental and physical well-being of members of the Hispanic community, as well as various other ethnic groups, translating
Programs: Day care, pre-school (3-5), youth counseling, recreation
Additional location: Day care at 1279 N. Milwaukee (773)862-5999
Volunteers: Welcome

Westtown Concerned Citizens Coalition
3501 W. Armitage Ave.
Chicago, IL 60647
Phone: (773)235-2144
Fax: (773)235-2159
Exec. Dir.: Tito Vargas
Pres.: Ephraim Ramirez
Founded: 1978
Serves: Mostly Hispanics, some African Americans, in Logan Square neighborhood
Purpose: Provide needed community services
Programs: Crime, drug and gang prevention; workshops and seminars for youth, parents; economic development, housing, adult education GED, ESL, citizenship, advocacy, immigrant counseling, referral, translating
Volunteers: Welcome

Youth Service Project, Inc.
3942 W. North Ave.
Chicago, IL 60647
Phone: (773)772-6270
Fax: (773)772-8755
e-mail: youserve@condor.depaul.edu
Web: www.depaul.edu/~youserve
Exec. Dir.: G. Sequane Lawrence
Pres.: Sherman West
Founded: 1975

Serves: Latinos and African Americans, in greater Humboldt Park
Purpose: To assist youth to realize their potential and create more meaningful lives
Programs: Counseling, community organizing, youth employment and readiness training, substance abuse, HIV/AIDS prevention, literacy and GED, delinquency prevention, college scholarships, 24-hour crisis intervention
Volunteers: Welcome

Hmong American

**+Hmong International
Human Rights Watch**
4631 N. Kenmore Ave.
Chicago, IL 60640
Phone: (773)334-4443
Evening/weekend: same
e-mail: HIHRW@usa.net
Web: www.geocities.com/ Capitol Hill/ Congress/8725
Exec. Dir.: Xiong Chuhu
Founded: 1997
Serves: Hmong community internationally
Purpose: To bring human rights to the Hmong people all over the world
Programs: Protecting Hmong human rights as described under the U.N. Declaration of Human Rights, mainly Hmong problems in Laos and Thailand; help with asylum cases and information on deportation for Hmong in the U.S.
Volunteers: Welcome

Indian American

Alliance of Midwest India Associations
642 N. Ashbury Ave.
Bolingbrook, IL 60440-1164
Phone: (630)739-7089
Evening/weekend: same
Fax: (630)739-3650
Exec. Dir.: Prem T. Lalvani
Pres.: Avtar Bhandari
Founded: 1987
Serves: Asian Indians and others, in Illinois
Purpose: To promote good will and welfare of the society and lead our community to participate in the affairs of mainstream America; to provide services to the society

we live in while enhancing Indo-American identity and developing understanding and closer ties with others
Programs: Indian Republic Day celebration, Asian American Coalition banquet, health fair, Asian American Coalition parade, Thanksgiving dinner open to all, assistance for discrimination on the job and in the community
Volunteers: Welcome

Association of Indians in America
2629 W. Devon Ave.
Chicago, IL 60659
Phone: (773)973-2995
Evening/weekend: same
Fax: (773)973-1299
Pres.: L.R. Madan
No office, 250 members
Local chapter of national organization
Founded: 1967
Serves: Indian Americans in Illinois
Purpose: To support migrants' assimilation into the mainstream
Programs: Business seminars, culture preservation, economic development, health care, legal support, sports participation, translating
Volunteers: Welcome

Bihari Cultural Association
5809 N. Napoleon
Chicago, IL 60631
Phone: (773)763-9050
Evening/weekend: same
e-mail: moonshanu@yahoo.com
Pres.: Moin "Moon" Khan
Founded: 1990
Serves: Asian Americans in the Midwest
Purpose: To keep and strengthen ties among those from the state of Bihari
Programs: Folk music and dances, receptions for visitors from India, picnics, community service awards, cultural programs arts, culture preservation, heritage/history, social/fraternal, translating (Hindi and Urdu)
Volunteers: Welcome

Federation of India Association
8301 Parkside
Morton Grove, IL 60053
Phone: (847)967-6784
Evening/weekend: same

Fax: (847)967-6786
Pres.: Ramesh Goyal
Sec.: Moin "Moon" Khan
Founded: 1965
Chapter of national organization
In Chicago, 138 organizations
Serves: Asian Indians in Illinois and USA
Purpose: To be an umbrella organization of more than 790 organizations
Programs: Community organizing, culture preservation, family, heritage/history, language
Volunteers: Welcome

Federation of Indo American Christians of Greater Chicago
410 Potter Rd.
Des Plaines, IL 60016
Phone: (847)296-3803
e-mail: PallekondaJ@hotmail.com
Pres.: Dr. Jayachand Pallekonda
V.P.: Mohan Katta
No exec. dir., no office, 300-400 members
Founded: 1978
Serves: Mostly Indians, some other Asian Americans in North America
Purpose: To serve the community needs of the Indo American Christians in North America
Programs: Fund raising for the needy, particularly in a natural disaster, general assistance, support services, community organizing, cultural/music, translating. helping Christians being prosecuted in India
Volunteers: Welcome

Illinois Malayali Association
4900 W. Howard St.
Skokie, IL 60077
Phone: (847)674-7694
Evening/weekend: same
Fax: (630)238-0305
e-mail: anilpillai@juno.com
or karambhan@aol.com
Exec. Dir.: Anil Kumar Pillai
Pres.: Sam George
Founded: 1990
Serves: Asian Indians in Illinois
Purpose: To promote culture, education and job placement
Programs: Educational classes, youth, cultural activities and interaction
Volunteers: Welcome

India Development Service
P.O. Box 980
Chicago, IL 60690
Phone: (630)655-3880
Fax: (708)524-2058
Dir.: Dr. Nila Vora
Pres.: Mahender Vasandani
No office, 400 members
Founded: 1974
Serves: Indians in India
Purpose: To aid social/economic
development of disadvantaged people
Programs: Economic development,
education, health care, literacy, vocational
training, women
Volunteers: Welcome

India Medical Association
17 W. 300 22nd St., Suite 250
Oak Brook Terrace, IL 60181-4490
Phone: (630)530-2277
Fax: (630)530-2475
Pres.: Vijay Kumar
Founded: 1981
Serves: Indian Americans in Northern
Illinois and Northwest Indiana
Purpose: Advocacy and philanthropy
Programs: Professional support,
government affairs, community service,
charity
Volunteers: Welcome

Indo American Democratic Organization
P.O. Box 597649
Chicago, IL 60659
Phone: (773)743-1109
e-mail: a-kalayil@uchicago.edu
Exec. Dir.: Kuriakose Mathew
Pres.: Ann Kalayil
Founded: 1981
Serves: Asian Indians in Illinois
Purpose: To encourage Asian Indian
participation and leadership in the political
process
Programs: Advisory referendum, lobbying,
voter registration, political education
Volunteers: Welcome

Indo-American Center
6328 N. California Ave.
Chicago, IL 60659
Phone: (773)973-4444
Fax: (773)973-0157
e-mail: iac@indoamerican.org

Exec. Dir.: Manoj Sanghvi
Pres.: Larry Dsouza
Founded: 1990
Serves: Primarily Asians, also Russians,
Ukrainians, Middle Easterners, Hispanics,
African Americans in metro Chicago
Purpose: To serve unmet needs in the
community
Programs: Immigration, citizenship, ESL
tutoring, referral, research, health care,
education, culture preservation
Volunteers: Welcome

Iranian American

Iranian American Society
P.O. Box 578567
Chicago, IL 60657
Phone: (312)281-7028
Fax: same
e-mail: babapour@megsinet.net
Exec. Dir.: Dr. Afra Shekarloo
Pres.: Shuhla Forutan
No office, 250 members
Founded: 1990
Serves: Iranian Americans in Chicago and
suburbs
Purpose: To address matters of concern to
Iranian Americans and their families
Programs: Arts, counseling, civil rights,
community center, culture preservation,
education, family, heritage/history,
immigration resettlement and adjustment,
legal, mentoring, referral, social/fraternal,
youth, literary, translating
Volunteers: Welcome

Iraqi American

+Al-Bayt Al-Iraqi (Iraqi House)
3334 W. Lawrence, Suite 301
Chicago, IL 60625
Phone: (773)583-1755
Evening/weekend: (773)583-1839
e-mail: albaytiraq@aol.com
Local coords: Basim Alkhafaji, Kifah
Alsharfi
Founded: 1998
Sponsored by The Iraq Foundation,
Washington, D.C.
Serves: Iraqis, other Arabic-speaking people,
and others

Purpose: Assist Iraqi refugees and newcomers to improve their living conditions and adjust to life here in the U.S.
Programs: Translation and follow-up services, help with filling out INS application, ESL, computer training, children's programs, community organizing, women's programs, cross-cultural education, referral and mentoring
Volunteers: Welcome

Irish American

Irish American Alliance
11134 S. Western Ave.
Chicago, IL 60655
Phone: (773) 233-5040, 229-8800
Fax: (773)239-9030, 229-0768
Exec. Dir.: Ann Bourke
Pres.: John Brogan
Founded: 1990
Serves: Irish Americans in Chicago and suburbs
Purpose: To provide social and charitable activities and to establish a retirement home
Programs: Social, charitable, heritage/history, culture, job network, scholarship program
Volunteers: Welcome

Irish American Heritage Center
4626 N. Knox Ave.
Chicago, IL 60630
Phone: (773)282-7035
Evening/weekend: same
Fax: (773)282-0380
Op. Mgr.: Conor O'Keeffe
Pres.: Michael Hammon
Founded: 1976
Serves: Irish American in Chicago, suburbs and Illinois
Purpose: To promote and preserve the Irish culture, language and arts
Programs: Arts, culture, dance, music, theater, museum, social activities, children's programs, seniors group, language classes, immigration assistance, genealogy, library, translating
Volunteers: Welcome

Young Irish Fellowship Club of Chicago
P.O. Box 2363
Chicago, IL 60690
Phone: (312)902-1943
Evening/weekend: same
Pres.: Robert E. Ryan Jr.
Founded: 1975
Serves: Irish Americans ages 21-35 in Chicago and suburbs
Purpose: To be a social/charitable organization that donates money to Chicago charities
Programs: Provide cultural programs to enhance awareness of heritage, participate in job fairs for Irish immigrants, promote friendship and good times through events that raise about $60,000 a year for charity
Volunteers: Welcome

Italian American

Amerital Unico Club of Chicago
8524 W. Lawrence
Norridge, IL 60706
Phone: (312)829-2460
Fax: (312)829-4715
Exec. Dir.: Anthony Fornelli
Pres.: Angelo Del Guidice
Local chapter of national organization
Founded: 1946
Serves: Mostly Italian Americans, in Chicago and suburbs
Purpose: To foster community awareness and to provide a positive attitude toward Italian Americans
Programs: Sponsors Festa Italiana, an ethnic festival showcasing arts and culture of Italian Americans
Volunteers: Welcome

Arcolian Dental Arts Society
1220 Roosevelt Rd.
Glen Ellyn, IL 60137
Phone: ((708)456-0800
Fax: (708)456-0352
Pres.: Sal Storniolo, DDS
No exec. dir., no office, 100 members
Founded: 1935
Serves: Italian Americans in Chicago and suburbs
Purpose: To foster and perpetuate a fraternal/social organization of dentists of

Italian lineage to create a spirit of
friendliness
Programs: Social/fraternal,
business/professional

Calabresi in America Organization
6501 W. Roosevelt Rd.
Berwyn, IL 60402
Phone: (708)788-9220
Evening/weekend: (312)726-6951
Fax: (773)869-6560
Exec. Dir.: Renato "Ron" Turano
Pres.: Silvana Turano
Local chapter of national organization
Founded: 1987
Serves: Italians from the region of Calabria,
in Chicago metro area
Purpose: To retain culture and way of life
Programs: Heritage/history, fraternal,
translating

**+Chicagoland Italian American
Charitable Organization**
P.O. Box 27
Bloomingdale, IL 60108
Phone: (847)619-8400
Fax: (847)619-5533
Pres.: Sam Tornatore
No exec. dir., no office, 145 members
Founded: 1998
Serves: Italian Americans in Chicago and
suburbs
Purpose: To raise money for scholar ship
and charitable purposes
Programs: Civic, educational,
philanthropic, heritage/history
Volunteers: Welcome

Columbian Club of Chicago
c/o Law Offices of John Peter Curielli
126 S. Northwest Highway
Barrington, IL 60010-4608
Phone: (847)381-7555
Fax: (847)381-7578
Pres.: Vincent P. Morreale
1st V.P.: Frank J. Lucchese
No exec. dir., no office, 100 members
Founded: 1935
Serves: Italian Americans in the Chicago
metro area
Purpose: To provide a variety of social,
business and charitable events

Programs: Civic welfare, social, business
and professional standards, preservation of
Italian ethnicity

The Etruscans
195 N. Harbor Dr., Suite 1002
Chicago, IL 60601
Phone: (312)540-0669
Fax: (312)540-9738
Pres.: Theresa M. Petrone
No exec. dir., no office, 60 members
Founded: 1976
Serves: Italian Americans in Chicago and
suburbs
Purpose: To further the study of the Italian
contribution to world civilization
Programs: Culture preservation, sponsor
travel and study programs to Italy

The Gregorians
902 W. Wildwood
Prospect Heights, IL 60070
Phone: (847)459-3642
Evening/weekend: same
Chr.: James Dever
No exec. dir., no office, 84 members
Founded: 1964
Serves: Italian American educators in
Chicago and suburbs.
Purpose: To promote professional growth,
engage in cultural pursuits and provide an
opportunity for members to socialize
Programs: Bimonthly dinner meetings,
Christmas parties, Saint Joseph's Table,
summer outdoor events
Volunteers: Welcome

**Harlem Avenue Italian and American
Business Association**
P.O. Box 594
River Grove, IL 60171
Phone: (708)867-9500
Pres.: Frank Di Piero
V.P.: Tom Bucaro
No exec. dir., no office, 100 members
Founded: 1990
Serves: Italian Americans on Harlem
Avenue (Chicago's Little Italy)
Purpose: To promote business and culture
in the area
Programs: Business mixers, Little Italy
banners on Harlem Ave.
Volunteers: Welcome

The Heart of Italy Association
2359 S. Western Ave.
Chicago, IL 60608
Phone: (773)254-6168
Fax: same
Exec. Dir.: Catherine Rondinelli
Pres.: Ilona Silvestri
Founded: 1993
Serves: Italian Americans and some
Hispanics in the neighborhood bounded by
23rd Place, Blue Island, Western Ave., and
Leavitt St.
Purpose: To assist neighborhood businesses
Programs: Business support and
development, economic development

Italian American Chamber of Commerce
30 S. Michigan Ave., Suite 504
Chicago, IL 60603
Phone: (312)553-9137
Fax: (312)553-9142
e-mail: info.chicago@italchambers.net
Web: www.italchambers.net/chicago
Exec. Dir.: Leonora LiPuma
Pres.: Dan Corrado
Founded: 1907
Serves: Italians and anyone in the Midwest
who wishes to do business with Italy
Purpose: To promote trade between Italy
and the USA and between its members
Programs: Business support, economic
development, information on Italian
companies, trade fairs in Italy, translating
Volunteers: Welcome

Italian American Labor Council
1919 S. Highland Ave., Suite 200-C
Lombard, IL 60148
Phone: (630)691-1031
Fax: (630)691-1152
Pres.: Joseph C. Serpico
1st V.P.: Joseph L. Martucci
Founded: 1966
Serves: Italian Americans in Chicago and
suburbs
Purpose: To provide activities that are
charitable, benevolent, civic, educational,
patriotic and social
Programs: Citizenship, culture
preservation, education, charitable,
heritage/history, social

Italian American Medical Association
7605 1/2 W. North
River Forest, IL 60305
Phone: (708)366-7200
Fax: (708)366-0710
Pres.: Dr. Bruno Cortis
No office, no exec. dir., 60 members
Founded: 1987
Serves: Italian Americans in Chicago and
suburbs
Purpose: To promote friendship, knowledge
and professional relationships among Italian
American doctors
Programs: Fraternal, educational, guest
speakers at four meetings per year
Volunteers: Welcome

Italian-American Police Association
6351 W. Montrose, Suite 210
Chicago, IL 60634-1563
Phone: (312)370-5176
Evening/weekend: same
e-mail: aipal@aol.com
Pres.: Ralph DeBartolo
Chr.: Robert Notini
No exec. dir., no office, 250 members
Founded: 1968
Serves: Mostly Italian Americans in
Northern Illinois, with some in other states
Purpose: To carry out an educational
program to improve the administration of
justice; to cultivate talents in suitable
candidates for various governmental law
agencies
Programs: Training seminars, legislative
alerts, fraternal cooperation, national/ethnic
pride
Volunteers: Welcome

Italian Cultural Center
1621 N. 39th Ave.
Stone Park, IL 60165
Phone: (708)345-3842
Fax: (708)345-3891
Visiting hours: 10-4, M-F
Exec. Dir.: Rev. Gino Dalpiaz
Pres.: Joe Bruno
Founded: 1970
Serves: Mostly Italian Americans, in
Chicago and suburbs
Purpose: To foster appreciation of cultural
and artistic endeavors through the
performing arts, painting, sculpture, music
and literature; to help Italian immigrants

preserve their ethnic background and culture; to foster religious life and help Italians and Italian Americans integrate into local parishes
Programs: Arts, counseling, children, culture preservation, heritage/history, vocal scholarships, religious program, Italian classes, social services, translating
Hours: M-F, 10 a.m. to 4 p.m.
Volunteers: Welcome

Italian Cultural Society
3649 E. 106th St., Suite 232
Chicago, IL 60617-6813
Phone: (312)409-2296
e-mail: Italian2@aol.com
Contact: Elia Storino
Founded: 1995
No office, 350 members
Serves: Italian Americans in Chicago and suburbs
Purpose: To provide an avenue for Italian Americans to express and share their culture and traditions
Programs: Culture preservation, education, heritage/history, language, social/fraternal, youth, translating
Volunteers: Welcome

Italian-Polish American Unity Organization
6730 W. Higgins Rd.
Chicago, IL 60656
Phone: (773)775-4400
Evening/weekend: same
Fax: same
Pres.: Zenon Golba
V.P.: Ross A. Pontarelli
Exec. Dir.: Zenon Golba
Founded: 1993
Serves: Italian Americans and Polish Americans in the U.S., as well as some Czechs, Slovaks, Ukrainians and Russians
Purpose: To promote and establish greater understanding among people of Italian and Polish descent, greater understanding about their cultures, access and involvement in political advancement, and expansion and development of business and industry
Programs: Legal, business and investment help and information, politics, culture, translating
Volunteers: Welcome

Italian Women's Prosperity Club
P.O. Box 183
Highwood, IL 60040
Phone: (847)432-3047
Evening/weekend: Same
Pres.: Rose Brugioni
V.P.: Donna Krol
No office, no exec. dir., 195 members
Founded: 1929
Serves: Italian Americans in Chicago and suburbs
Purpose: Philanthropic works
Programs: Community center, community organizing, cutter preservation, financial aid, heritage/history, senior citizen, women; baby showers for unwed mothers
Volunteers: Welcome

Italo American National Union Foundation
P.O. Box 812
Hillside, IL 60162
Phone: (708)343-9885
Fax: (708)343-9888
Exec. Dir.: Josephine R. Petitti
Pres.: Kenneth J. Kolnicki
Chr.: Pascal F. Naples
Founded: 1895
Serves: Italian Americans in the USA
Purpose: Originally to bring Sicilian immigrants together. Now Italians helping Italians and their friends
Programs: Scholarships, fraternal, culture

Joint Civic Committee of Italian Americans
500 N. Michigan Ave.
Chicago, IL 60611-3704
Phone: (312)828-0010
Evening/weekend: (773)252-8961
Fax: (312)828-9155
Exec. Sec.: Marie Palello
Pres.: Joseph Gagliardo
Founded: 1952
Serves: Italian Americans in Chicago
Purpose: To fight defamation against the Italian American community, promote Italian culture, support worthy causes and uphold good name of Italian Americans
Programs: Scholarships, social services, human relations, referral, translating; two women's divisions, young adult division
Volunteers: On occasion

Justinian Society of Lawyers
734 N. Wells St.
Chicago, IL 60610
Phone: (312)255-8550
Fax: (312)255-8551
Web: www.justinians.org
Exec. Asst.: Nina Albano Vidmer
Pres.: James J. Morici, Jr.
No exec. dir., no office, 800 members
Founded: 1921
Serves: Italian Americans in Cook County
Purpose: To promote the exchange of ideas
and the advancement of legal issues among
attorneys and judges of Italian descent
Programs: Monthly dinner meetings with
speakers, scholarships, golf outing,
Christmas dinner dance
Volunteers: Welcome

Lucchesi nel Mondo
3856 N. Odell Ave.
Chicago, IL 60634
Phone: (773)589-0730
Fax: (773)589-0731
Pres.: Rafaello Del Grande
No exec. dir., no office, 240 members
Local chapter of international organization
Founded: 1952
Serves: Italian Americans in Chicago and
suburbs
Purpose: To promote high business and
professional standards; to build a better
community by rendering altruistic service;
to further understanding between the USA
and Italy
Programs: Advocacy, civic/fraternal,
business and professional, philanthropic,
scholarships

Mola Foundation of Chicago
3838 Division St.
Stone Park, IL 60165
Phone: (708)450-1060
Fax: (708)450-9309
Pres.: Mario Ventrella
Founded: 1994
Serves: Italian Americans in Chicago,
suburbs and Illinois
Purpose: To promote education, preserve
the Italian culture, donate to charitable
organizations and build a community center
Programs: Culture preservation, education,
philanthropic
Volunteers: Welcome

National Italian American Foundation
30 W. 766 Woodewind
Naperville, IL 60563
Phone: (630)961-1957
Fax: (630)961-7530
Reg. V.P.: Joseph A. Consiglio
Regional chapter of international
organization
Founded: 1975
Serves: Italian Americans in Central Region
Purpose: To promote the good name of
Italian Americans, assist other organizations
in their ventures, promote good will, educate
and develop and to be the primary voice in
the nation for Italian Americans
Programs: Arts, business and professional
support, counseling, children, citizenship,
community center, community organizing,
culture preservation, economic
development, education, employment,
family, financial aid, foreign aid,
government, health care, heritage/history,
immigrant resettlement and adjustment,
language, law enforcement, legal, literacy,
mentoring, political, recreation, referral,
research, senior citizen, social/fraternal,
youth, technical assistance, tutoring,
veterans, women
Volunteers: Welcome

**Order of Sons of Italy in America,
Grand Lodge, State of Illinois**
7222 W. Cermak Road, Suite 220
North Riverside, IL 60546
Phone: (708)447-6304
Fax: (708)447-6255
Pres.: Giovanna Verdecchia
Local chapter of national organization
Founded: 1924
Serves: Italian Americans in Illinois
Purpose: To preserve cultural heritage,
promote the positive contributions of Italian
Americans, encourage participation in the
political and civic life of our communities
and raise money for national and
international charities and scholarships
Programs: Social/fraternal, culture
preservation, scholarships, charity

St. Anthony Chapter 13 IANU
8300 W. Lawrence
Norridge, IL 60656
Phone: (708)456-8300

Pres.: Philip Parker
Founder: Anthony Lupo
No office, no exec. dir., 100 members
Local chapter of national organization
Founded: 1980
Serves: Italian Americans in Chicago and
suburbs
Purpose: To provide charity and
scholarships
Programs: Fund raising for charities,
holiday food baskets for the needy,
scholarships
Volunteers: Welcome

Scalabrini League
c/o Villa Scalabrini
480 N. Wolf Rd.
Northlake, IL 60164
Phone: (312)828-0010
Evening/weekend: (773)252-8961
Pres.: currently vacant
1st V.P.: Rose Zoubi
Sec.: Marie Palello
No office, no exec. dir.
Founded: 1950
Serves: Italian Americans in Chicago and
suburbs
Purpose: To raise funds to benefit the
residents of Villa Scalabrini, the Italian
home for the aged
Programs: Volunteer services at events
sponsored by Villa Scalabrini, fund raising

Society S.S. Crocifisso
5425 N. Lincoln Ave.
Chicago, IL 60625
Phone: (773)334-3250
No office, 140 members
Exec. Dir. & Pres.: Frank Pavone
V.P.: Nick Lepore
Local chapter of national organization
Founded: 1981
Serves: Italian Americans in Chicago and
suburbs
Purpose: To bring together people from the
same town in Italy
Programs: Religious tradition, picnic,
meetings
Volunteers: Welcome

Unico National,
Greater Chicago Chapter
10 W. Chicago Ave.
Chicago, IL 60610

Phone: (312)654-8400
Fax: (312)654-8402
Pres.: Frank Nocita
No exec. dir., no office, 75 members
Local chapter of national organization
Founded: 1992
Serves: Italian Americans in Chicago and
suburbs
Purpose: To raise funds for charitable
organizations
Programs: Philanthropic
Volunteers: Welcome

Veneti Del Nord America
8318 W. Catherine Ave.
Chicago, IL 60656
Phone: (773)631-8242
Fax: same
Pres.: Attilio Scolaro
V.P.: Raymund Venzon
No exec. dir., no office, 90 members
Founded: 1990
Serves: Italian Americans from Venice
living in Chicago and suburbs
Purpose: To keep close ties with the culture
and provide a bridge between new and old
generations to instill their culture and
tradition
Programs: Work with Italian Cultural
Center, helping with banquets, selling
tickets, etc.; charity work helping Veneti
families in time of need

Japanese American

Chicago Japanese American
Citizens League
5415 N. Clark St.
Chicago, IL 60640
Phone: (773)728-7170
Fax: (773)728-7231
e-mail: midwest@jacl.org
Midwest Dir.: William Yoshino
Pres.: Lawrence Schectman
Founded: 1944
Serves: Mostly Japanese Americans, other
Asian Americans in Illinois
Purpose: To protect the welfare of the
Japanese American/Asian American
community
Programs: Civil rights, culture
preservation, education

Volunteers: Welcome

Chicago Japanese American Historical Society
745 Beaver Road
Glenview, IL 60025
Phone: (847)998-8101
Weekend/evening: same
e-mail: JMishima@aol.com
or A-Murata@neiu.edu
No exec. dir., no office, 33 members
Pres.: Jean M. Mishima
Sec.: Alice Murata
Founded: 1992
Serves: Japanese Americans and others in Chicago and suburbs
Purpose: To inform the public of the history of Japanese American people, especially in Chicago metro area
Programs: Culture preservation, education, heritage/history, research
Volunteers: Welcome

Japanese American Service Committee of Chicago
4427 N. Clark St.
Chicago, IL 60640
Phone: (773)275-7212
Fax: (773)275-0958
Exec. Dir.: Jean M. Fujiu
Pres.: Lisa Sakai
Founded: 1946
Serves: Mostly Japanese Americans, some Korean, Chinese, Filipino and Vietnamese Americans in Chicago and suburbs
Purpose: To meet the social and cultural needs of Japanese Americans in the Chicago area
Programs: Counseling, adult day care, health care, home help, cultural, arts & crafts, nutrition
Volunteers: Welcome

Japanese American Service Committee Housing Corp. (Heiwa Terrace)
920 W. Lawrence Ave.
Chicago, IL 60604
Phone: (773)989-7333
Fax: (773)989-8398
Mgr.: Keith Chase-Ziolek
Pres.: Mary Doi
Founded: 1976
Serves: Japanese American seniors and disabled

Purpose: To provide Sec. 8 HUD subsidized seniors independent living complex
Programs: Housing
Volunteers: Welcome

Japanese Mutual Aid Society of Chicago
1740 W. Balmoral Ave.
Chicago, IL 60640
Phone: (773)769-2226
Evening/weekend: same
Exec. Dirs.: Yutaka Kanemoto and George Izui
Pres.: Hiro Mayeda
Founded: 1934
Serves: Japanese Americans in metropolitan Chicago
Purpose: To serve those Japanese Americans interested in being laid to rest among other members of their culture
Programs: Co-sponsor annual Memorial Day services at Montrose Cemetery, provide final rites and burial for destitute, locate in Japan relatives of deceased
Volunteers: For special events

Jewish American

Alliance of Latinos and Jews
(see Hispanic/Latino)

American-Israel Chamber of Commerce Chicago
180 N. Michigan Ave.
Chicago, IL 60601
Phone: (312)641-2937
Evening/weekend: same (voice mail)
Fax: (312)641-2941
e-mail: aicci@interaccess.com
Web: www.investisrael.org
Chr.: Maurice P. Ralzes
Pres.: Marlene Greenberg
Local chapter of national organization
Founded: 1958
Serves: Business and professional people interested in bilateral trade and investment between the U.S. and Israel, with an emphasis on high-tech and biotech sectors
Purpose: To develop mutually beneficial and profitable commercial relationships between U.S. and Israeli firms
Programs: Trade, economic development, business exchanges

Volunteers: Experienced business
professionals welcome

American Jewish Committee
55 E. Monroe, Suite 2930
Chicago, IL 60603
Phone: (312)251-8800
Evening/weekend: (847)674-4419
Fax: (312)251-8815
e-mail: Chicago@ajc.org
Exec. Dir.: Jonathan Levine
Pres.: Julie Baskes
Local chapter of national organization
Founded: 1944
Serves: Jewish community and others in
Illinois, NW Indiana, Indianapolis and
Louisville
Purpose: To secure the religious and civil
rights of Jews and all groups; to encourage
support for Israel; to work toward
strengthening the vitality of the Jewish
community
Programs: Inter-ethnic, inter-racial and
inter-religious dialogues; prejudice-
reduction programs for high schools;
political advocacy; educational programs
Volunteers: Welcome

American Jewish Congress
22 W. Monroe, Suite 1900
Chicago, IL 60603
Phone: (312)332-7355
Fax: (312)332-2814
e-mail: chicago@ajcongress.org
Exec. Dir.: Joel L. Rubin
Pres.: Dr. Lya Dym Rosenblum
Local chapter of national organization
Founded: 1918
Serves: Mostly Jews, in Midwest region
Purpose: To promote religious liberty and
separation of church and state, and support
civil rights and liberties
Programs: Advocacy, legal services,
women, Jewish/Israeli-oriented culture
program, anti-handgun, separation of church
and state, joint projects with African
American and Latino communities,
translating Hebrew/English, English/Hebrew
and Russian/English
Volunteers: Welcome

**American Zionist Movement,
Chicago Region**
5050 Church St., #215
Skokie, IL 60077
Phone: (847)677-5949
Fax: (847)677-3750
e-mail: azmchi@2cc.com
Exec. Dir.: Linda Harth
Pres.: Dr. A. I. Weinzweig
Local chapter of national organization
Founded: 1972
Serves: Jewish Americans in the Chicago
metro area and Illinois
Purpose: To be an umbrella group for the
Zionist membership organizations and voice
of unified Zionism in the greater Chicago
area
Programs: Hebrew Ulpan, Zionist
resources and education, cultural events
related to Israel and Zionism, Israel
advocacy
Volunteers: Welcome

AMIT Women
3856 Oakton, Suite B
Skokie, IL 60076
Phone: (773)973-0688
Fax: (773)973-0057
e-mail: amitchgo@aol.com
Reg. Coord.: Beth Gottesman
Co-Pres.: Tirza Kahan & Rochelle
Rosenfeld
Midwest office of national organization
Founded: 1925
Serves: Jewish Americans in Chicago and
suburbs
Purpose: To support social services in
Israel, as well as educational needs
Programs: Funding for services in Israel
that include counseling, education,
vocational training
Volunteers: Welcome

Anti-Defamation League
309 W. Washington St., Suite 750
Chicago, IL 60606
Phone: (312)782-5080
Evenings/weekends: same
Fax: (312)782-1142
e-mail: chiadl@aol.com
Reg. Dir.: Richard S. Hirschhaut
Reg. Chr.: Sylvia R. Margolies
Regional office of national organization
Founded: 1913

Serves: Jews and others in Greater Chicago and Illinois, Wisconsin, Indiana, Minnesota, and North and South Dakota
Purpose: To combat anti-Semitism and all forms of hatred, prejudice and bigotry
Programs: Advocacy, education, civil rights and human relations

The Ark
6450 N. California
Chicago, IL 60645
Phone: (773)973-1000
Fax: (773)973-4362
Exec. Dir.: Miriam Weinberger
Pres.: Justin Gordon
Founded: 1971
Serves: Mostly Jewish Americans,.in Chicago and suburbs
Purpose: To serve the indigent in the target population
Programs: Food pantry, counseling, medical, legal, social, home-delivered meals, translating
Volunteers: Welcome

AZRA/World Union, North America
555 Skokie Blvd., #225
Northbrook, IL 60062
Phone: (847)509-0990
Evening/weekend: (847)677-4263
Fax: (847)509-0970
Exec. Dir.: Simone Lotven Sophian
Pres.: Isac Kapulski
Local chapter of national organization
Founded: 1977
Serves: Jewish Americans in Chicago metro area
Purpose: To provide knowledge about and support for Israel, support and advocacy of civil and religious rights in Israel, support of Reform Judaism in Israel and throughout the world
Programs: Education, civil rights, community organizing, culture preservation
Volunteers: Welcome

B'nai B'rith, Midwest Region
9933 Lawler, Suite 230
Skokie, IL 60077
Phone: (847)676-0011
Fax: (847)676-9414
e-mail: bbrith@aol.com
Reg. Dir.: Gerald Dicker
Reg. Pres.: Joseph A. Morris

Local chapter of international organization
Founded: 1843
Serves: Mostly Jewish Americans, in Illinois, Indiana and Wisconsin
Purpose: To provide community service for all, provide a platform for Jewish people's concerns, and be the voice of Jewry
Programs: Senior housing, Jewish education, culture preservation, community services, speakers, interfaith dialogues, promotion of democracy and world peace
Volunteers: Welcome

B'nai B'rith Youth Organization, Great Midwest Region
1901 Raymond Dr., Suite 14
Northbrook, IL 60062
Phone: (847)564-5802
Fax: (847)564-8285
e-mail: gmrbbyo@aol.com
Reg. Dir.: Rachel A. Charlip
Adult Bd. Chr.: Jay Swidler
Local chapter of national organization
Founded: 1924
Serves: Jewish high-school teens in Chicago metro area, Illinois and the tri-cities
Purpose: To develop leadership skills, build self-esteem and work toward a stronger Jewish community
Programs: Leadership training, social, recreational, community service
Volunteers: Adults welcome

Council on Jewish Workplace Issues
(was Bur. on Jewish Employment Problems)
618 S. Michigan Ave., Suite 703
Chicago, IL 60605
Phone: (312)663-9470
Fax: (312)663-3162
Exec. Dir.: Steven M. Lissner
Pres.: Robert G. Luskin
Founded: 1937
Serves: The Jewish community of metropolitan Chicago
Purpose: To offer innovative methods of recruitment to employers to reach the large pool of highly skilled and educated Jewish men and women , to educate corporate executives about Jewish issues of meeting schedules, holiday observances, recruiting and outreach to the Jewish community
Programs: Advocacy, education, corporate diversity training

Council for Jewish Elderly

3003 W. Touhy
Chicago, IL 60645
Phone: (773)508-1000
Fax: (773)508-1028
Web: www.cje.net
Exec. V.P.: Ronald Weismehl
Pres.: William I. Goldberg
Affiliate of Jewish Federation of
Metropolitan Chicago
Founded: 1972
Serves: Mainly Jewish Americans, in
Chicago metro area
Purpose: To provide essential and non-
essential services to help seniors maintain
their independence
Programs: Home-delivered meals, adult
day services, counseling, consultations,
health services, resource centers including a
housing resource center, community
education, specialized housing, translation
of Russian and Yiddish
Other locations: Lieberman Geriatric Health
Centre, Skokie; adult day services center,
Evanston; Weinberg Community for Senior
Living, Deerfield
Volunteers: Welcome

Decalogue Society of Lawyers

39 S. LaSalle St., Suite 410
Chicago, IL 60603
Phone: (312)263-6493
Fax: (312)263-6512
Exec. Dir.: Carol Straus
Pres.: Gerald Schur
Founded: 1934
Serves: Jews mainly in Illinois, but
throughout the USA and other countries
Purpose: To combine the attributes of
members' lives as attorneys and Jews to
accomplish public service and social action,
using the activities, goals and strengths of a
bar association
Programs: Free 30-session legal lecture
series open to public, human rights, civil
rights, culture preservation, financial aid,
community building with other ethnic and
non-ethnic bar associations, student
involvement, arrangements for legal aid,
mentoring, training, social publications,
community awards
Volunteers: Welcome

EZRA Multi-Service Center
(Jewish Community Centers)

4539 N. Sheridan Road
Chicago, IL 60640
Phone: (773)275-0866
Fax: (773)275-3917
Exec. Dir.: Anita Weinstein
Founded: 1984
Serves: Everyone (languages: Russian,
English, Spanish)
Purpose: To help disadvantaged people
obtain life's basic requirements: jobs,
housing, clothing, access to benefits and
food
Programs: Russian-English and Yiddish-
English translation services, Jewish cultural
programs, weekly religious observances,
community center, community organizing,
employment, family, housing, immigrant
adjustment, language, lobbying, mental
health, mentoring, seniors, veterans,
advocacy, emergency problem-solving,
information and referral
Volunteers: Welcome

Friends of Refugees of Eastern Europe

2935 W. Devon Ave.
Chicago, IL 60659
Phone: (773)274-5123
Evening/weekend: same
Fax: (773)274-3810
e-mail: f.r.e.e.@ix.netcom.com
Exec. Dir.: Rabbi Shmuel Notik
Pres.: Reitza Kosofsky
Local chapter of national organization
Founded: 1973
Serves: Russian Jews in Chicago and
suburbs
Purpose: To promote needed social services
and provide knowledge of Jewish heritage to
Russian immigrant Jews
Programs: Judaic lessons, ESL, Hebrew
Sunday School, bar/bat mitzvahs,
circumcision, traditional Jewish weddings,
counseling, citizenship, community center,
community organizing, culture preservation,
education, employment, family, language,
heritage/history, immigrant resettlement and
adjustment, recreation, referral, senior
citizens, technical assistance, tutoring,
women, youth, translating
Volunteers: Welcome

Hadassah
111 N. Wabash, Room 810
Chicago, IL 60602
Phone: (312)263-7473
Fax: (312)263-7481
e-mail: Hadassah@net56.net
Ofc. Mgr.: Karen Bell
Pres.: Esther Yelen Berman
Local chapter of national organization
Founded: 1912
Serves: Jewish Americans in Chicago and
suburbs
Purpose: To support two hospitals in Israel,
schools and social benefits here and in Israel
Programs: Charitable support for health
care, education and medical research
Volunteers: Welcome

Hebrew Immigrant Aid Society
One S. Franklin, Room 411
Chicago, IL 60606
Phone: (312)357-4666
Fax: (312)855-3291
Exec. Dir.: Suzanne Franklin
Pres.: Ralph Reubner
Local chapter of national organization
Founded: 1911
Serves: Mostly Jewish immigrants and
refugees in Chicago and suburbs
Purpose: To provide a full continuum of
immigration services to needy refugees and
immigrants
Programs: Refugee processing, citizenship,
immigrant petitions, asylum assistance,
green-card processing, location services,
indemnification
Volunteers: Welcome

The Hillels of Illinois
1 S. Franklin, Suite 704
Chicago, IL 60606
Phone: (312)444-2868
Evening/weekend: same
Fax: (312)855-2479
e-mail: psaiger@juf.org
Exec. Dir.: Rabbi Paul Z. Saiger
Pres.: Jerry Cohen
Regional operation of national organization
Founded: 1923
Serves: Jewish Americans in the Midwest
Purpose: To serve and represent Jewish
university students and young adults
Programs: Arts, counseling, community
organizing, culture preservation, education,

heritage/history, mentoring, recreation,
social/fraternal, tutoring, women, youth
Chapters at universities including UIC,
Loyola, DePaul, Northwestern, U of I,
U of C

**Holocaust Memorial Foundation
of Illinois**
4255 Main St.
Skokie, IL 60076-2063
Phone: (847)677-4640
Fax: (847)677-4684
e-mail: holmemil@flash.net
Exec. Dir.: Lillian Polus Gerstner
Pres.: Lisa Derman
Founded: 1981
Serves: All people in Illinois and the
Midwest
Purpose: To provide educational training
and resources about the Holocaust to
teachers, students and the community at
large
Programs: Graduate-level courses,
museum, library and resource center,
speakers' bureau, video rental, monthly
community programs, translating
Volunteers: Welcome

Jewish Big Sisters
1316 W. Fargo
Chicago, IL 60626
Phone: (773)764-4759
Fax: (773)764-7567
Evening/weekend: same
Pres.: Louise Franks
V.P.: Ruth Rubin
No exec. dir., no office, 150 members
Founded: 1916
Serves: Jewish American girls 9-18 on the
North and Northwest Sides and suburbs
Purpose: To provide a mentoring program
Programs: Provide individual big sisters;
recreational/cultural/religious events; social
service counseling and referrals,
heritage/history
Volunteers: Welcome

Jewish Burial Society
6025 N. Christiana
Chicago, IL 60659
Phone: (773)588-2762
Fax: (773)539-8218
e-mail: info@jewishburial.org
Web: www.jewishburial.org

Pres.: Gary Siegel
Founded: 1975
Serves: Jews in Chicago metro area
Purpose: To obtain traditional Jewish burials at reasonable cost
Programs: Help families obtain dignified, traditional funerals at reasonable cost
Volunteers: Welcome

Jewish Cemeteries Preservation Foundation
1400 S. Des Plaines Ave.
Forest Park, IL 60170
Phone: (708)366-4541
Evenings/weekends: (847)509-9045
Fax: (708)366-4575
Exec. Dir.: Irwin Lapping
Pres.: Dan Roin
Founded: 1990
Serves: Jews in Chicago metro area
Purpose: To renovate and preserve old inactive Jewish cemeteries
Programs: Culture preservation, heritage/history

Jewish Children's Bureau of Chicago
One S. Franklin St.
Chicago, IL 60606
Phone: (312)444-2090
Fax: (312)855-3754
e-mail: bobuc58@aol.com
Exec. Dir.: Dr. Robert B. Bloom
Pres.: Brenda Wolf
Founded: 1893
Serves: Mainly Jewish American, also African Americans, Hispanics and Native Americans, in Chicago and suburbs
Purpose: To provide an intensive multi-service agency for abused, neglected and troubled children
Programs: Special-education school, respite services for developmentally disabled, intensive therapeutic residential placement, foster care, counseling, mental health, referral,autism center
Volunteers: Welcome

Jewish Community Centers of Chicago
1 S. Franklin St.
Chicago, IL 60606
Phone: (312)357-4700
Fax: (312)855-3283
e-mail: MarketTheJ@aol.com
Web: www.jccofchicago.org

Exec. Dir.: Dr. Avrum I. Cohen
Pres.: Melvin L. Hecktman
Founded: 1903
Local chapter of national organization
Serves: Mostly Jewish Americans, any others, in Chicago and suburbs
Purpose: To give leadership and guidance to programs for individuals, families and groups that promote and enhance a rewarding and continuing Jewish life in America
Programs: Children, day care, community center, early childhood education, family, immigrant resettlement and adjustment, recreation, senior citizens, youth; EZRA Multi-Service Center in Uptown (see separate listing)
Additional locations: 3003 W. Touhy Ave., 1100 E. Hyde Park Blvd., 524 W. Melrose, Buffalo Grove, Flossmoor, Northbrook, Skokie
Volunteers: Welcome

Jewish Community Relations Council (Jewish United Fund of Metro Chicago)
1 South Franklin, #703
Chicago, IL 60606
Phone: (312)357-4770
Fax: (312)855-2476
e-mail: jtcath@juf.org
Web: www.juf.org
Exec. Dir.: Jay Tcath
Chr.: Charles F. Kriser
The umbrella body for 39 major Jewish organizations in the Chicago area and community relations arm of the Jewish Federation/Jewish United Fund
Serves: Jewish Americans in the Chicago metro area
Purpose: To be the instrument through which the organized Jewish community collectively makes policy on the shared agenda of its constituent members
Programs: Information resource, advocate, sponsors annual celebrations, coordinates programming, provides assistance

Jewish Council on Urban Affairs
6185 S. Michigan Ave., Suite 700
Chicago, IL 60605
Phone: (312)663-0960
Evening/weekend: same (ans. machine)
Fax: (312)663-5305
e-mail: jcua.org

Web: www.jcua.org
Exec. Dir.: Jane Ramsey
Pres.: Nikki Will Stein
Founded: 1964
Serves: All affected by poverty and injustice in metropolitan Chicago
Purpose: To combat poverty, racism and anti-Semitism in partnership with Chicago's diverse communities
Programs: Technical assistance to low-income and minority community groups, coalition-building with diverse groups, advocacy on issues of poverty and racism, mobilizing Jewish constituency to create a more just city
Volunteers: Welcome

Jewish Family and Community Service
1 S. Franklin, Suite 403
Chicago, IL 60606
Phone: (312)357-4800
Fax: (312)855-3750
Web: (Jewish United Fund)www.juf.org
Pres.: Marla Gordon
Act. Exec. Dir.: Natalie Ross
Founded: 1859
Serves: Families and individuals in Chicago metro area
Purpose: To provide social services
Programs: Individual and family counseling; therapeutic nursery school; child development programs; family-life education; services to the deaf and hearing-impaired, those affected or infected by HIV/AIDS and the Holocaust community; refugee resettlement, bilingual staff speaking Russian and English
Other locations:
Central District
205 W. Randolph, Suite 1100
Chicago, IL 60606-1814
Phone: (312)263-5523
Fax: (312)263-1929
Contact: Marilyn Siegel
Niles Township District
Goldie Bachmann Luftig Building
5150 W. Golf Road
Skokie, IL 60077
Phone: (847)568-5200
Fax: (847)568-5250
TTY: (847)568-5240
Contact: Michael Ostrower
AIDS contact: Judith Gapiel
Keshev program for hearing impaired

North Suburban District
210 Skokie Valley Road
Highland Park, IL 60035
Phone: (847)831-4225
Fax: (847)831-2290
Contact: Beverly Shapiro
Northern District
2710 W. Devon Ave.
Chicago, IL 60659-1778
Contact: Carole Spreitzer
Northwest Suburban Office
Jacob Duman Building
1250 Radcliffe Road, Suite 206
Buffalo Grove, IL 60089-4298
Phone: (847)392-8820
Fax: (847)392-3221
Contact: Ronni Weinbstein
South Suburban Office
3649 W. 183rd St., Suite 123
Hazel Crest, IL 60429-2409
Phone: (708)799-1869
Virginia Frank Development Center
3033 W. Touhy Ave.
Chicago, IL 60645-2833
Phone: (773)761-4550
Fax: (773)761-6426
Contact: Leslie Ripp

**Jewish Federation
of Metropolitan Chicago**
1 S. Franklin St.
Chicago, IL 60606
Phone: (312)346-6700
Fax: (312)444-2086
e-mail: joel-m-carp@compuserve.com
Pres.: Dr. Steven B. Nasatir
Chr.: Manfred Steinfeld
Local chapter of national organization
Founded: 1900
Serves: Mainly Jews but helps African Americans, Latinos, Indochinese and others through grants
Purpose: To plan, coordinate, implement and finance sound programs of social welfare, education and medical benefit to Jewish and general communities.
Programs: Large number of services provided through affiliated organizations, such as abortion counseling, adult education, adult recreation, adoptions, aged, blind and visually handicapped, blood banks, camps, chaplaincy, child development, child welfare, abused children, foster families, institutional care and group homes for

children, youth recreation, social
development and outreach, chronically ill,
community health, campus services,
community centers, community relations,
vocational counseling, family counseling,
crisis intervention, cults counseling, cultural
arts, day care, deaf and hard of hearing,
disability services, drug abuse, early
childhood education, EZRA Hotline, special
education, emergency assistance,
employment training, equal opportunity,
extended care, family planning, financial
assistance, fund raising, grief counseling,
health, health clubs, higher education, home
care, home-delivered meals, housing for
elderly, immigrant services, referral, Israel
programs, Jewish education, leadership
development, learning disabilities, legal aid,
marriage counseling, maternity centers,
mental health clinics and hospitals, nutrition,
occupational therapy, physical therapy, rape
counseling, rehabilitation, research,
runaways, unmarried parents, single parents,
teacher training, transportation, translating
Other offices: Governmental affairs offices
in Springfield, IL, and Washington, D.C.
Volunteers: Welcome

Jewish Genealogical Society
of Illinois
P.O. Box 515
Northbrook, IL 60065-0515
Phone: (312)666-0100
Evening/weekend: (847)679-1995
Fax: (847)679-3268
Pres.: Larry Hamilton
No office, no exec. dir., 225 members
Affiliated with national association
Founded: 1982
Serves: Jewish Americans in Illinois
Purpose: To provide information on how
and where to search for one's family
"roots," as well as networking with other
researchers
Programs: Advice on how to learn about
one's personal heritage and history
Volunteers: Welcome

Jewish Labor Committee
947 Shoreline Rd.
Barrington, IL 60010
Phone: (847)381-1713
e-mail: nsweiler@avenew.com
Exec. Dir.: N. Sue Weiler

Pres.: Michael Perry
Local chapter of national organization
Founded: 1935
Serves: Jews in Illinois
Purpose: To be a liaison between the
Jewish community and labor movement, as
well as other ethnic labor organizations
Programs: Civil rights, heritage/history,
politics, workers rights, labor unions
Volunteers: Welcome
Jewish-Serbian Friendship Society
(see Serbian American)

Jewish United Fund
of Metropolitan Chicago
1 S. Franklin St.
Chicago, IL 60606
Phone: (312)346-6700
Fax: (312)444-2086
Pres.: Dr. Steven Nasatir
Chr.: Manfred Steinfeld
Founded: 1949
Serves: Jews and the greater community in
the Chicago metro area and worldwide
Purpose: To raise and allocate funds to
support local institutions of health and
human welfare, education and identity and
culture in community; and to rescue, resettle
and care for Jews in need throughout the
world
Programs: Philanthropic, Russian
translation services in connection with
citizenship services
Volunteers: Welcome

Jewish Vocational Service
One South Franklin
Chicago, IL 60606
Phone: (312)357-4500
Fax: (312)855-3282
e-mail: jvschicago@juf.org
Exec. V.P.: Alan Goldstein
Pres.: Seth A. Eisner
Founded: More than 100 years ago
Serves: Mostly Caucasians, African
Americans and Hispanics, in Chicago and
suburbs
Purpose: To provide educational and
vocational counseling, job placement,
rehabilitation and skills training services to
more than 11,000 people in Chicago area
Programs: Educational and vocational
counseling, job placement, rehabilitation,
skills training, ESL

Other locations: 328 S. Jefferson, 600 W.
Van Buren, 2020 W. Devon, 6336 N.
Lincoln, 950 E. 61st St., Buffalo Grove and
Skokie
Volunteers: Welcome

**Jewish War Veterans of the USA,
Illinois Department**
2640 W. Touhy Ave.
Chicago, IL 60645
Phone: (773)764-7176
Evening/weekend: (847)676-9794
Commander: Gordon G. Kornblith
Founded: 1939
Local chapter of national organization
Serves: Jewish and other hospitalized
veterans in Illinois
Purpose: To provide service to Jewish
veterans and all hospitalized veterans and
families in need
Programs: Education, financial aid,
social/fraternal, support for students, aid
in claims

Keshet
3210 Dundee Road
Northbrook, IL 60062
Phone: (847)205-0274
Fax: (847)205-1530
e-mail: Keschet2@aol.com
Exec. Dir.: Dave Gendel
Pres.: Gail Metrick and Caryn Zelinger
Founded: 1984
Serves: Mostly Jews, some others, in
Chicago and suburbs
Purpose: To serve needs of disabled Jewish
children and their families
Programs: Day school, Sunday school,
summer day camp and overnight camp for
disabled Jewish children; support groups;
parent education; referral
Other addresses: Bais Yaakov School, 6100
N. California; Ida Crown Jewish Academy,
2828 W. Pratt
Volunteers: Welcome

Labor Zionist Alliance of Chicago
5050 Church St. #204
Skokie, IL 60077
Phone: (847)675-1677
Fax: (847)675-9521
Pres.: Prof. Leonard Robins
Local chapter of national organization
Founded: 1910

Serves: Jewish Americans on the North Side
of Chicago and suburbs
Purpose: To promote support of the Israeli
Labor Government and provide education
about Jewish culture
Programs: Political, educational
Volunteers: Welcome

Magen David Adom
8930 Gross Point, Suite 800
Skokie, IL 60077
Phone: (847)583-0664
Fax: (847)583-8556
e-mail: magendavidadom@hotmail.com
Web: www.magendavidadom.org
Exec. Dir.: Gary Kenzer
Founded: 1950
Serves: Anyone interested in humanitarian
needs in Israel and around the world
Purpose: To raise funds to support Israel's
emergency medical, health, blood and
disaster services
Programs: Fund raising for purchase of
ambulances, mobile intensive care units,
bloodmobiles, blood-bank equipment, first-
aid stations, e-mail updates about Israel,
young leadership events

Mid-West Jewish Council
P.O. Box 59032
Chicago, IL 60659
Phone: (773)274-0570
Pres.: Milton Herst
No exec. dir., no office, 500 members
Serves: Jewish Americans in Chicago and
suburbs
Purpose: To ensure that the
commemoration of the heroic uprising in the
Warsaw ghetto is continued
Programs: Monthly forums on current
events and other subjects

Na'amat USA Greater Chicago Council
5050 W. Church St., Suite 226
Skokie, IL 60077
Phone: (847)675-7275
Fax: (847)329-7174
Exec. Dir.: Barbara Novick
Pres.: Wendy Frankel
Local chapter of international organization
Founded: (USA)1925
Serves: Jewish Americans in Chicago,
suburbs and several Midwest states

Purpose: To enhance the status of women, children and families in Israel and the U.S. as part of a worldwide progressive Jewish women's organization and the Labor Zionist Movement; to support the State of Israel in the quest for a comprehensive and just peace with all its neighbors and guaranteeing full and equal rights to all its citizens irrespective of religion, gender or nationality
Programs: Fund raising to support educational, vocational, social and legal services for women and families in Israel; education on issues
Volunteers: Yes, upon occasion

National Council of Jewish Women
3056 W. Jerome
Chicago, IL 60645
Phone: (773)262-5088
Evening/weekend: same
Pres.: Nancy Liebman
Treas.: Lyn Garrick-Weil
Local chapter of national organization
Founded: 1893
Serves: Jewish Americans in Chicago metro area
Purpose: To work in advocacy and community service to improve the quality of life for women, children and families
Programs: Children, civil rights, community service, education, government, senior citizen, women
Volunteers: Welcome

Olin-Sang-Ruby Union Institute (Union of American Hebrew Congregations)
555 Skokie Blvd., Suite 225
Northbrook, IL 60062
Phone: (847)509-0990
Fax: (847)509-0970
e-mail: gkaye@aol.com, osrinfo@aol.com
Exec. Dir.: Gerard Kaye
Chr.: Michael Lorge
Founded: 1941
Serves: Jewish Americans in Illinois and the Midwest
Purpose: To provide a religious and educational camp and retreat center
Programs: Summer residential camp in Oconomowoc, WI; programs for older adults (elder hostel); retreats for kids, families and adults
Volunteers: Welcome

Russian Senior Center (see Russian)

Spertus Institute of Jewish Studies
618 S. Michigan Ave.
Chicago, IL 60605
Phone: (312)922-9012
Fax: (312)922-6406
e-mail: sijs@spertus.edu
Web: www.spertus.edu
Pres.: Dr. Howard A. Sulkin
Founded: 1924
Serves: Jews and non-Jews of all ages, locally nationally and around the world
Purpose: To preserve and disseminate the intellectual, cultural, social and spiritual legacy of the Jewish past and utilize its wisdom to shape the future
Programs: Spertus Museum (permanent collection of Judaic objects, art and artifacts, exhibitions, Zell Holocaust Memorial, Rosenbaum Children's ARTiFACT Center, groups tours); Spertus College (graduate studies degrees and programs with "distance learning" option, continuing education); Asher Library (Judaic books, periodicals, music and video); Bariff Shop for Judaica (ceremonial objects, art, books, music, gifts).
Volunteers: Welcome

Women's American ORT, Midwest Satellite Office
3701 Commercial Ave., Suite 6
Northbrook, IL 60062
Phone: (847)498-8280
Fax: (847)498-8284
e-mail: WAORT@waort.org
Web: www.waort.org
Midwest Dir.: Lori Rabb
Founded: 1927
Serves: Jewish Americans in Illinois and eight states of Midwest
Purpose: To support a worldwide network of 800 schools and programs in 60 countries, training 260,000 students annually; to strengthen Jewish communities around the world through ORT's program of quality education and innovative distance learning; to unite men and women interested in education, the community and the future of Jews worldwide
Programs: Annual fund-raising activities including an annual Contributors Dinner, Party Planning Showcase, Passport Program,

and financial planning/planned giving seminars; forums on issues of community and educational concern; programs to help thousands of immigrants adapt to a new country, learn new skills and lead productive lives; Zarem/Golde ORT Technical Institute (see below)
Volunteers: Welcome

Women's American ORT
(Suburban Chicago Region)
3400 Dundee Road
Northbrook, IL 60062
Phone: (847)291-0475
Fax: (847)291-7538
e-mail: jsiegal@waort.org
Web: www.waort.org
Pres.: Ronna Heftman
Founded: 1927
Serves: Jewish Americans in suburban Chicago
Purpose: To support a worldwide network of 800 schools and programs in 60 countries, training 260,000 students annually; to strengthen Jewish communities around the world through ORT's program of quality education and innovative distance learning; to unite men and women interested in education, the community and the future of Jews worldwide
Programs: Annual fund-raising activities including an annual Contributors Dinner, Party Planning Showcase, Passport Program, and financial planning/planned giving seminars; young women's outreach programs; forums on issues of community and educational concern; programs to help thousands of immigrants adapt to a new country, learn new skills and lead productive lives; Zarem/Golde ORT Technical Institute\
Volunteers: Welcome

Zarem/Golde ORT Technical Institute
3050 W. Touhy Ave.
Chicago, IL 60645
Phone: (773)761-5900
Fax: (773)761-0969
e-mail: RickReeder@aol.com
Dir.: Arthur Eldar
Operates under the auspices of Women's American ORT and American ORT
Founded: 1990

Serves: Immigrants from all countries. Most of the students are Russian, Bosnian, Korean, Polish and Bulgarian
Purpose: To train students in ESL and technical programs and to provide job-placement assistance
Programs: Classes in computerized accounting, computer-aided drafting and design, and microcomputer technology and networking
Volunteers: Welcome

Zionist Organization of Chicago
5050 W. Church St., Suite 202
Skokie, IL 60077-1292
Phone: (847)568-0244
Evening/weekend: same
Fax: (847)568-1233
Co-Pres.: Harry Berger, Dr. Milton Shulman
Founded: 1897
Serves: People in the Midwest
Purpose: To develop greater understanding between Americans and the people of Israel -- economic, political, cultural, social, trade -- and to further Jewish education and continuing to help in the survival of the Jewish people
Programs: Education, culture and social, lectures, films, public forums
Volunteers: Welcome

Korean American

Center for Seniors
2645 W. Peterson Ave.
Chicago, IL 60659
Phone: (773)275-4989
Fax: (773)275-5545
Exec. Dir.: Jae Kwan Ha
Coord.: Young C. Ha
Founded: 1992
Serves: Korean American senior citizens in Chicago and Illinois
Purpose: To serve medical and social needs of senior citizens
Programs: Adult day care, bilingual services, arts & crafts, meals, transportation, group activities, audio-visual program, outings, exercise classes, medical check-ups, recreation, translation by phone
Volunteers: Welcome if bilingual in English and Korean

**Korean American Association
of Chicago**
5941 N. Lincoln Ave.
Chicago, IL 60659
Phone: (773)878-1900
Fax: (773)878-9075
Exec. Dir.: Woo Park
Pres.: Kyun Hee Park
Founded: 1962
Serves: Korean Americans in Chicago and
suburbs
Purpose: To provide human services for
immigrants adjusting to a new environment
Programs: Naturalization assistance,
counseling, violent crime-victim prevention,
community employment program
Volunteers: Welcome

**Korean American
Chamber of Commerce**
5601 N. Spaulding
Chicago, IL 60659
Phone: (773)583-1700
Fax: (773)583-9724
e-mail: ckacc@aol.com
Exec. Dir.: Joanne Lee
Pres.: Yong Choi
Founded: 1976
Serves: Korean Americans in Chicago and
suburbs
Purpose: To provide assistance to small
businesses owned by Korean Americans
Programs: Business and professional
support, counseling, economic development,
financial aid, referral, technical assistance
Volunteers: Welcome

Korean American Citizens Coalition
2807 W. Montrose Ave.
Chicago, IL 60618
Phone: (773)539-6503
Fax: (773)539-5407
Pres.: So Young Kwon
No exec. dir., no office, 40 members
Founded: 1990
Formerly Korean American Citizens Action
Committee
Serves: Korean Americans in Chicago
Purpose: To promote and protect the
interests of the Korean American
community, so it may fully, fairly and
successfully participate in American life
Programs: Legislation follow-up, voter
registration, voter education, candidate

forums, advocacy, civil rights, career-
planning seminars, information on property
assessments and appeals
Volunteers: Welcome

Korean American Community Services
4300 N. California
Chicago, IL 60618
Phone: (773)583-5501
Fax: (773)583-7009
Exec. Dir.: InChul Choi
Pres.: Jae Bong Lee
Founded: 1972
Serves: Mainly Korean Americans in
Chicago and suburbs
Purpose: To provide services to Korean
Americans and others who are in need of
economic, educational, cultural and social
assistance
Programs: Counseling, community
organizing and development, day care,
immigration and naturalization, technical
assistance to small businesses, senior
housing management, employment services
Volunteers: Welcome

**Korean American Merchants Assn.
of Chicago**
4300 N. California Ave.
Chicago, IL 60618
Phone: (773)583-5501
Fax: (773)583-7009
Exec. Dir.: InChul Choi
Pres.: Han S. Suh
Founded: 1990
Serves: Korean Americans in Chicago
Purpose: To represent, advocate and protect
interests of Korean American merchants; to
promote harmonious and mutually beneficial
relations between merchants and residents;
to provide educational and cultural programs
Programs: Business support, technical
assistance, educational and cultural
programs
Volunteers: Welcome

**Korean American Seniors Association
of Chicagoland**
4740 N. Racine
Chicago, IL 60640
Phone: (773)334-1561
Fax: (773)334-1552
Pres.: Hyo H. Byun
Chr.: Jung Chae Kim

Founded: 1975
Serves: Korean Americans in Chicago and suburbs
Purpose: To represent Korean seniors in every aspect of their needs
Programs: Arts, counseling, citizenship, civil rights, culture preservation, education, history/heritage, immigrant adjustment, language, literacy, social/fraternal, tutoring, translating
Volunteers: Welcome

Korean American Senior Center, Inc.
4750 N. Sheridan Road, Suite 400
Chicago, IL 60640
Phone: (773)878-7272
Fax: (773)878-4461
e-mail: aging@chikasc.org
Web: www.chikasc.org
Exec. Dir.: Paul S. Yun
Pres.: Charlotte C. Kim
Founded: 1987
Serves: Mostly Korean Americans, also Russian Americans, Latinos, African Americans in Uptown and nearby neighborhoods
Purpose: To help elderly strive for dignity and self-sufficiency
Programs: ESL, job training and placement, home care, crime-victim assistance, information, referral, case management, arts & culture, citizenship, health seminars, translating
Volunteers: Welcome

Korean American Women in Need
P.O. Box 59133
Chicago, IL 60659
Phone: (773)583-1392
Fax: (773)583-2454
Pres.: Catalina Shin Hatch
Sec.: Haeyoung Kim
Founded: 1990
Serves: Korean Americans in Chicago, suburbs and Midwest
Purpose: To serve abused Korean American women
Programs: Crisis hotline (773)583-0880; crisis counseling, intervention and interpretation; legal and social advocacy; child care; transportation, referral; community education
Volunteers: Welcome (need 40-hour training)

Korean American Women's Association of Chicago
4300 N. California Ave.
Chicago, IL 60618
Phone: (773)866-1855
Fax: (630)655-2363
Pres.: Young Kim
Chr.: Suhn Yung Ahn
Founded: 1980
Serves: Korean Americans in Chicago and suburbs
Purpose: To offer Korean women a variety of services to assist in building confidence, self-esteem and security
Programs: Women's Corner, a cable TV educational program; Talk Line, telephone counseling; women's chorus and arts; education seminar, translating (on request)
Volunteers: Welcome

Korean Veterans Association, Midwest Region
4120 W. Lawrence
Chicago, IL 60630
Phone: (773)777-9660
Fax: (773)777-9620
Exec. Dir.: Joon Hyung Song
Pres.: Yang H. Song
Founded: 1985
Serves: Korean Americans and some others who were Korean war veterans
Purpose: To promote friendship among Korean war veterans
Programs: Invite 200 Korean war veterans to Korea through Korea Revisit Program; maintain contact with veterans and keep them informed about Korea

Korean YMCA of Chicago
5820 N. Lincoln Ave.
Chicago, IL 60659
Phone: (773)275-0101
Evening/weekend: (847)296-0971
Fax: (773)275-0194
Exec. Dir.: Chang S. Lee
Pres.: Gi Cheol Yun
Local chapter of national organization
Founded: 1969
Serves: Korean Americans and some Chinese and Hispanics in Chicago and suburbs
Purpose: To help new Korean immigrants adjust in the American community

Programs: ESL, foreign language classes (Chinese, Japanese, Spanish, etc.), swimming, winter sports, drug prevention, matchmaking counseling, guest house for tourists and people with family problems, financial and legal instruction, vocational training, cultural classes
Volunteers: Welcome

Metropolitan Chicago Korean YWCA
5941 N. Lincoln Ave.
Chicago, IL 60659
Phone: (773)561-2877
Fax: same
Dir.: Sung Choi
Pres.: Charlotte K. Kim
Founded: 1991
Serves: Korean Americans in Chicago and suburbs
Purpose: To service the vast variety of needs of the Korean community in the Chicago metro area
Programs: Dating, youth, education, counseling for domestic or sexual violence
Volunteers: Welcome

Lao American

Lao American Community Services
4750 N. Sheridan Road
Chicago, IL 60640
Phone: (773)271-0004
Fax: (773)271-1682
Exec. Dir.: Tom Parthong
Pres.: Tom Pharthong
Founded: 1984
Local chapter of national organization
Serves: Mostly Laotians, also Thais and Cambodians
Purpose: To help Laotian refugees adjust to American society
Programs: Citizenship, community center, counseling, culture preservation, immigrant resettlement, senior citizen, women, youth, translating
Volunteers: Welcome

National Association for the Education and Advancement of Cambodian and Laotian Americans (See Cambodian)

Latvian American

Chicago Latvian Association, Inc.
4146 N. Elston Ave.
Chicago, IL 60618
Phone: (773)588-2085
Fax: (773)588-3405
Pres.: Baiba Liepins
Founded: 1935
Serves: Latvian Americans in Chicago metro area
Purpose: To offer a variety of social services for the Latvian community
Programs: Museum, folk art museum, concerts, other arts and cultural activities, community center, support groups, counseling
Volunteers: Must speak Latvian

Liberian American

Liberian Emergency Relief Fund
2230 E. 71st St.
Chicago, IL 60649
Phone: (773)324-5703
Evening/weekend: (773)643-8635
Fax: (773)288-8893
Exec. Dir. & Pres.: Alexander P. Gbayee
Founded: 1990
Serves: Liberians and other Africans in Chicago metro area and in Africa
Purpose: To give charitable assistance to displaced Liberians and Liberian refugees
Programs: Housing, clothing, food, medicine, transportation, public education, translating
Other locations: 7342 S. Bennett
Volunteers: Welcome

Organization of Liberian Communities in Illinois
P.O. Box 377724
Chicago, IL 60637-7724
Phone: (708)922-3719
Evening/weekend: same
Pres.: Christian Amegashie
No office, no exec. dir., 300 members
Founded: 1952
Serves: Liberians in Illinois
Purpose: To promote and enhance public awareness of the culture and history of Liberia; to provide assistance to members in

matters of immigration, employment and housing
Programs: Immigration, employment, community organizing, culture preservation, social/fraternal

Lithuanian American

**Balzekas Museum
of Lithuanian Culture**
6500 S. Pulaski Road
Chicago, IL 60629-5136
Phone (773)582-6500
Evening/weekend: same
Fax: (773)582-5133
Exec. Dir. & Pres.: Stanley Balzekas Jr.
Founded: 1966
Serves: Lithuanian Americans in Chicago metro area, Illinois and USA
Purpose: To preserve posterity and the wealth of material pertaining to Lithuania and Lithuanians, and to serve as a resource and research center for students and scholars
Programs: Lectures, workshops, exhibits, audio-visual programs, seminars in genealogy, resource center, archives, translating
Volunteers: Welcome

**Cultural Council of Lithuanian
American Community, Inc.**
2841 Denton Ct.
Westchester, IL 60154
Phone: (708)262-1448
Evening/weekend: same
Chr.: Marisa Remiene
Founded: 1947
Serves: Lithuanian Americans in USA
Purpose: To maintain Lithuanian cultural heritage
Programs: Culture, education, translating
Volunteers: Welcome

Lithuanian American Council, Inc.
5620 S. Claremont
Chicago, IL 60636
Phone: (773)434-2040
Fax: (773)434-2014
e-mail: lrsc@mcs.net
Bus. Mgr.: Danute Petrulis
Pres.: Dr. John A. Rackauskas
Founded: 1940

Serves: Lithuanian Americans in the Chicago metro area and USA
Purpose: To serve and protect the political rights and interests of the Lithuanian people
Programs: Lobbying in D.C. with Congress to influence decisions affecting Lithuanians and those in other Baltic states, translating
Volunteers: Welcome

**Lithuanian-American Community, Inc.
Human Services Council**
2713 W. 71st St.
Chicago, IL 60629
Phone: (773)476-2655
Fax: (773)436-6909
e-mail: margutis@worldnet.att.net
Chr.: Birute Jasaitis
Arm of national organization
Founded: 1951
Serves: Lithuanians nationwide
Purpose: To help Lithuanian needy people with various social needs
Programs: Meals-on-wheels, Lithuanian Children's Hope, Lithuanian orphan care, aid to newcomers to the USA, senior citizens, letter translation

**Lithuanian Children's Hope
(Lithuanian Human Services Council)**
2711 W. 71st St.
Chicago, IL 60629
Phone: (773)476-0664
Fax: (773)436-6909
e-mail: margutis@worldnet.att.net
Exec. Dir.: Birute Jasaitis
Pres.: Grazina Liautaud
Founded: 1991
Serves: Lithuanians in the USA and Lithuania
Purpose: To provide specialized medical assistance to Lithuania's children who are unable to receive it in their homeland
Programs: Children's health care, translating
Volunteers: Welcome

Lithuanian Foundation, Inc.
14911 127th St.
Lemont, IL 60439
Phone: (630)257-1616
Fax: (630)257-1647
Exec. Dir.: Ale A. Razma
Pres.: Ruta Staniulis
Chr.: Algirdas Ostis

Founded: 1962
Serves: Lithuanians in the USA and elsewhere
Purpose: To support the survival of Lithuanian cultural and educational endeavors in multi-ethnic and multi-cultural USA
Programs: Culture preservation, education, heritage/history, youth scholarships

Lithuanian Human Services Council of the USA, Inc.
2711 West 71st St.
Chicago, IL 60629
Phone: (773)476-2655
Evening/weekend: same
Fax: (773)436-6909
e-mail: margutis@worldnet.att.net
Exec. Dir. & Pres.: Birute Jasaitis
National organization
Founded: 1982
Serves: Lithuanian Americans in the USA
Purpose: To help Lithuanian people
Programs: Counseling, community center, culture preservation, referral, senior citizen, translating
Volunteers: Welcome

Lithuanian Mercy Lift
P.O. Box 88
Palos Heights, IL 60463
Phone: (708)448-6173
Evening/weekend: (708)388-2041
Fax: (708)388-2059
Pres.: George G. Lendraitis
V.P.: Frances M. Slutas
Founded: 1990
Serves: Lithuanians in Lithuania
Purpose: To provide humanitarian (medical) aid to Lithuania
Programs: Sending medical aid and medical education programs to Lithuania
Volunteers: Welcome

Lithuanian Research & Studies Center
5620 S. Claremont Ave.
Chicago, IL 60636
Phone: (773)434-4545
Fax: (773)434-9363
e-mail: lrsc@mcs.net
Pres.: Dr. John A. Rackauskas
Founded: 1982
Serves: Lithuanians throughout the world, also other Americans and foreign scholars

Purpose: To preserve documentation and artifacts of Lithuanian culture and activities of Lithuanian Americans and to meet needs of researchers interested in these subjects
Programs: Arts, culture preservation, education, foreign aid (books), heritage/history, language, research, Lithuanian Historical Society, Lithuanian Institute of Education, Lithuanian Museum of Medicine, translation services

Lithuanian World Center
14911 127th St.
Lemont, IL 60439
Phone: (630)257-8787
Fax: (630)257-6887
Exec. Dir.: Alexander Domanskis
Pres.: Kestlitis Jecius
Founded: 1988
Serves: Lithuanian Americans in Chicago metro area
Purpose: To serve as an exchange center between Lithuania and America's Lithuanian community, and to keep the culture and customs alive
Programs: Montessori school, Saturday school, Catholic mission, art museum, Mercy Lift, halls for cultural and social events, athletic facilities, library for archives and exhibits, rehearsal rooms, office space for Lithuanian organizations
Volunteers: Welcome

Lithuanian World Community
14911 127th St.
Lemont, IL 60439
Phone: (630)257-8217
Evening/weekend: same
Fax: (630)257-5216
e-mail: plbvaldyba@aol.com
Exec. Dir. & Pres.: Vytautas Kamantas (in Michigan)
International organization, federation of 30 Lithuanian communities
Founded: 1949
Serves: Lithuanians in 30 countries around the world
Purpose: To promote Lithuanian heritage outside Lithuania, with emphasis on language, tradition, culture and education
Programs: Publishes The World Lithuanian magazine, arts, citizenship, culture preservation, economic development,

education, heritage/history, language, literature, translating
Additional office: Grand Rapids, MI
Volunteers: Welcome

Lithuanian Youth Center
5620 S. Claremont Ave.
Chicago, IL 60629
Phone: (773)778-7500
Fax: (773)434-9363
Pres.: Maria Utz
Serves: Lithuanian Americans in Marquette Park, Brighton Park, Gage Park neighborhoods, Chicago and suburbs, Illinois and for special events the USA and world
Purpose: To provide a facility for Lithuanian American activity
Programs: Saturday School, cultural and social gatherings, art gallery, museum, archives
Volunteers: Welcome

Mexican American

(See also Hispanic/Latino)

Centro Sin Fronteras
1205 N. Milwaukee Ave.
Chicago, IL 60622
Phone: (773)772-8383
Fax: (773)772-9173
Founded: 1988
Exec. Dir.: Emma Lozano
Pres.: Jacobita Alonso
Serves: Mostly Mexican American, some other Latinos, whites, blacks in Chicago
Purpose: To educate and mobilize to bring needed services to improve the quality of life in our community
Programs: Citizenship classes, workshop on immigrant rights, health-education classes, WIC, housing, legal clinic, education committees with block-by-block structure
Volunteers: Welcome

+League of Young Mexican American Voters of Illinois
4739 S. Avers
Chicago, IL 60632
Phone: (312)807-1970
Evening/weekend: same

Fax: (312)666-2981
President: Thomas Ramos, Jr.
Founded: 1992
No office, no exec. dir., 65 members
Serves: Mexican Americans in Chicago and suburbs
Purpose: Educate, energize young Mexican Americans in voting, civic responsibilities
Programs: Voter registration, scholarship opportunities, jobs, consulting, translating
Volunteers: Welcome

Little Village Chamber of Commerce (see Hispanic/Latino)

Little Village Community Council (see Hispanic/Latino)

Mexican American Chamber of Commerce of Illinois, Inc.
122 S. Michigan Ave., Suite 1449
Chicago, IL 60603
Phone: (312)554-0844
Fax: (312)554-0848
e-mail: macc@maccbusiness.com
Exec. Dir.: Juan A. Ochoa
Pres.: Edward Gomez
Founded: 1990
Serves: Mostly Mexican Americans in Illinois
Purpose: To promote and develop business opportunities for Mexican Americans
Programs: Advocacy, networking, development of business opportunities, certification
Volunteers: Welcome

Mexican American Legal Defense & Educational Fund (see Hispanic/Latino)

Mexican American Police Organization
3418 W. 26th St.
Chicago, IL 60623
Phone: (773)736-6524
Evening/weekend: same
Fax: same
Pres.: Juan Reyes III
V.P.: Linda Flores
No exec. dir., no office, 250 members
Local chapter of national organization
Founded: 1990
Serves: Mostly Mexican Americans, in Chicago and Illinois

Purpose: To encourage hiring and promotion for Mexican American police officers in Chicago; to enhance relations within the community; to promote the benefits of education
Programs: Youth, education, voter registration, citizenship, with other organizations tutoring for promotional exams, encouraging youth to stay in school, speaking in grammar schools

Mexican Civic Committee
3934 W. 26th St.
Chicago, IL 60623
Phone: (773) 521-2700
Fax: (773) 521-7908
Exec. Dir.: Anita Villarreal
Pres.: Loretta Long
Founded: 1940
Serves: Mostly Mexican Americans on the West Side of Chicago
Purpose: To encourage citizenship and to direct people to services
Programs: Counseling, referral, translating and interpreting, health-care information, legal-aid referral, translating
Volunteers: Welcome

Mexican Civic Society of Illinois, Inc.
2130-32 West 21st St.
Chicago, IL 60608
Phone: (773)847-9653
Evening/weekend: same
Fax: (773)521-0641
Dir.: Martha Guitierrez
Pres.: Jaime Arce
1st V.P: Zeferino Ochoa
Founded: 1969
Serves: Mostly Mexican Americans, in Pilsen and Little Village
Purpose: To preserve culture and traditions
Programs: Organize main Mexican Parade in downtown Chicago, civic ceremony of "El Grito" at Petrillo Band Shell, celebrate other important dates in Mexico's history, health fairs, literacy, citizenship, food baskets to needy Thanksgiving and Christmas

Mexican Community Committee
2939 E. 91st St.
Chicago, IL 60617
Phone: (773)978-6441
Fax: (773)978-2376

Exec. Dir.: Henry Martinez
Pres.: Al Juarez
Founded: 1958
Serves: Mostly Latinos, some African Americans, in Chicago and suburbs
Purpose: Multi-purpose organization
Programs: Employment, health care, youth, crime-fighting, translating
Volunteers: Welcome

Mexican Fine Arts Center Museum
1852 W. 19th St.
Chicago, IL 60608
Phone: (312)738-1503
Weekend: same
Fax: (312)738-9740
e-mail: mfacm@mfacmchicago.com
Web: www.mfacmchicago.org
Exec. Dir.: Carlos Tortolero
Chr.: Julie Chavez
Founded: 1982
Serves: The Pilsen/Little Village area and entire metropolitan area
Purpose: To preserve and promote the cultural/artistic expression of the Mexican culture in and outside of Mexico
Programs: Cultural center/museum, events and exhibits, permanent collection of Mexican art, professional development of local Mexican artists, arts education, advocacy

The Resurrection Project
1818 S. Paulina St.
Chicago, IL 60608
Phone: (312)666-1323
Fax: (312)942-1123
Exec. Dir.: Raul I. Raymundo
Pres.: Javier Crespo
Founded: 1990
Serves: Mexicans and Mexican Americans, and other Latinos, European Americans and African Americans, in Pilsen/Little Village
Purpose: To build relationships and challenge people to act on their faith and values to create healthy communities through organizing, education and community development
Programs: Community organizing and development, economic development, housing, family
Volunteers: Welcome

Native American

American Indian Center
1630 W. Wilson Ave.
Chicago, IL 60640
Phone: (773)275-5871
Evening/weekend: same
Fax: (773)275-5874
Exec. Dir.: Maxine Spataro
Founded: 1955
Serves: Native Americans and some others in metro area, mostly in Uptown
Purpose: To preserve culture and provide social services
Programs: Arts, counseling, children, community center, culture preservation, family, heritage/history, senior citizens, veterans, youth

American Indian Health Service
838 W. Irving Park Road
Chicago, IL 60613
Phone: (773)883-9100
Fax: (773)883-0005
e-mail: ahealthser@aol.com
Exec. Dir.: Amelia Ortiz
Founded: 1974
Serves: Native Americans and their spouses in Chicago and suburbs
Purpose: To provide sensitive and holistic health care for Native Americans
Programs: General health care, prevention and intervention, dentistry, substance abuse, mental health, HIV/AIDS prevention, Four Directions after-school study program
Volunteers: Welcome

Anawim Center
4750 N. Sheridan, Suite 255
Chicago, IL 60640
Phone: (773)561-6155
Evening/weekend: same
Fax: same
Exec. Dir.: Sister Toni Harris
Founded: 1982
Serves: Native Americans in Chicago area
Purpose: To provide an interfaith spiritual center for native people in Chicago's urban environment
Programs: Advocacy for indigenous rights, artists cooperative, religious ceremonies (Christian and Traditional Native American), information and referral, youth

Volunteers: Welcome

Chicago Native American Urban Indian Retreat
1819 W. Wilson Ave.
Chicago, IL 60640
Phone: (773)561-1336
Fax: (773)561-1331
Chr.: Joseph Peralez
Founded: 1994
Serves: Mostly Chicago Native American Indian Community in Uptown and surrounding neighborhoods, others in suburbs and Illinois
Purpose: To empower urban Indians in Chicago to maintain/discover spiritual and cultural values and communal lifestyle through educational/spiritual and community gatherings and cultural events
Programs: Culture preservation, family, tutoring/mentoring, referral, substance abuse
Volunteers: Welcome

Mitchell Indian Museum at Kendall College
2600 Central Park
Evanston, IL 60201
Phone: (847)866-1395
Evening/weekend: same
Fax: (847)866-1320
Exec. Dir.: Virginia Heidenreich-Barber
Founded: 1977
Serves: Native Americans, school groups and general public in Chicago metro area
Purpose: To maintain a collection representing native peoples of the USA and Canada
Programs: Reference library includes books, periodicals, videos, audio tapes; gift shop sells Native American pottery, jewelry, fetishes, books; permanent exhibits on hunting and harvesting by peoples of western Great Lakes, buffalo hunters of northern plains, Pueblo farmers and pastoral Navajo

Native American Educational Services College, Chicago Campus
2838 W. Peterson
Chicago, IL 60659
Phone: (773)761-5000
Fax: (773)761-3808
e-mail: DaveNaes@aol.com
Dean: Dr. David Beck

Pres.: Faith Smith
Campus of national college
Founded: 1975
Serves: Mostly Native Americans and
Alaska Natives in Chicago, the suburbs and
Illinois
Purpose: To provide community
development, education and leadership
development
Programs: Bachelor's degree, advanced
study, adult education and Urban Natives of
Chicago
Volunteers: Welcome

**St. Augustine's Center
for American Indians, Inc.**
4512 N. Sheridan Road
Chicago, IL 60640
Phone: (773)784-1050
Evening/weekend: same
Fax: (773)784-1254
Exec. Dir.: Arleen R. Williams
Pres.: The Rt. Rev. James W. Montgomery
Founded: 1958
Serves: American Indians and some others,
in Uptown, Chicago and Illinois
Purpose: To serve the Native American
people in metropolitan Chicago
Programs: Religious and social services,
Indian Child Welfare, Program Excel
(education), alcohol/substance abuse
prevention and rehabilitation
Other locations: 4506 N. Sheridan, 4420 N.
Broadway
Volunteers: Welcome, call first

Nicaraguan American

+Casa Nicaragua
3411 W. Diversey Ave., Suite 6-7
Chicago, IL 60647-1125
Phone: (773)278-8345, -4021
Fax: (773)278-4023
e-mail: Casanic@aol.com
Pres.: Abraham M. Aich-Sandino
Founded: 1976
Serves: Nicaraguans living in Chicago area
and surrounding states
Purpose: To unify and maintain traditions
of fellow Nicaraguans, to support and
educate our people in American society
Programs: Citizenship, community
organizing, culture preservation, education,

employment, referrals, political education,
social/fraternal activities, student exchange,
translation/interpretation
Volunteers: Welcome

Nigerian American

+Nigerian-American Youth Association
P.O. Box 201
Evanston, IL 60204
Phone: (773)761-3498
Fax: same
e-mail: naya4life@hotmail.com
Web: www.geocities.com/Heartland/
Estates/2597/naya.html
Pres. & Exec. Dir.: JoAnne Bolude
Founded: 1996
No office, 100 members
Serves: Nigerians and some other Africans
in Chicago and suburbs
Purpose: To unite the Nigerian community
and create successful leaders
Programs: Economic development for
Nigeria, foreign aid, heritage/history,
recreation, youth, culture, preservation,
community organization
Volunteers: Welcome

Nigerian National Alliance
P.O. Box 60141
Chicago, IL 60626
Phone: (773)743-1186
Evening/weekend: (773)743-1186
Pres.: Yemi Onayemi
V.P.: Dr. Stephen Aghahowa
Founded: 1987
Serves: Mostly Nigerians, other Africans
and African Americans, in Chicago, suburbs
and Illinois
Purpose: To meet the educational, cultural,
social and economic needs of the
community
Programs: Social assistance to Nigerian
community; promote social, cultural,
economic, educational and scientific
knowledge of Nigerian community; promote
positive image of Nigeria; address
discrimination and immigration issues;
promote Nigerian culture
Volunteers: Welcome

+Yoruba People's Congress, Inc.
9418 S. Racine Ave.
Chicago, IL 60620
(773)233-5216
Evening/Weekend: same
Fax: (708)709-3328
Exec. Dir. & Pres.: Tokumbo Ben Macarthy
Founded: 1995
No office, 45 members
Local chapter of national organization
Serves: Yoruba from western Nigeria in
Chicago metro area, including Indiana
Purpose: To foster our cultural heritage, to
be a social organization, to help train and
settle newcomers from home in the Chicago
area
Programs: Professional support,
counseling, citizenship, community center,
community organization, culture
preservation, economic development,
employment, education, family, mentoring,
resettlement and adjustment.

Norwegian American

**Norwegian American
Chamber of Commerce, Inc.,
Midwest-Chicago Chapter**
P.O. Box 964
Arlington Heights, IL 60006
Phone: (312)943-0154
Evening/weekend: (312)266-2642
Fax: (312)943-9112
e-mail: pmaltd@att.net
Pres.: Myrna Pedersen
Chr.: Rolf Hennington
Local chapter of national organization
Founded: 1959
Serves: Norwegian Americans and other
Scandinavians in Chicago and suburbs
Purpose: To promote trade and goodwill
and foster business, financial and
professional interests between Norway and
the USA; to advance common purposes of
members
Programs: Business or professional support
through monthly meetings, field trips to
member companies, networking,
membership directory, social events

**Norwegian National League
of Chicago**
c/o Lynn Maxson
715 Laurel Ave.
Des Plaines, IL 60016
Phone: (847)297-1656
e-mail: somax@chicago.avenew.com
No exec. dir., no office, 32 delegates
Pres.: Lynn Sove Maxson
Corr. Sec.: Nina Cudecki
Founded: 1899
Serves: Norwegian Americans in Chicago
and suburbs
Purpose: To work for perpetuation and
strengthening of interest in Norwegian
traditions and culture; to support Norwegian
and Norwegian-American organizations; to
arrange holiday festivals
Programs: Norway Constitution Day (May
17), Lief Erickson Fest (Oct. 9) and
Christmas Around the World at Museum of
Science and Industry; displays and program
in schools and libraries, translating
Volunteers: Welcome

Pakistani American

+Indus Society of North America
5737 S. Archer
Summit, IL 60501
Phone: (708)496-0511
Evening/weekend: (708)496-8370
Fax: (708)594-8245
Pres.: Dr. Ajaz Alvi
Founded: 1988
Serves: Pakistani Americans in Chicago and
suburbs
Purpose: To promote cultural values, and
social and political interests of the
community
Programs: Celebrating Pakistan Day in
March and Pakistani Independence Day in
August, translation
Volunteers: Welcome

Pakistan Federation of America, Chicago
2323 W. Devon Ave.
Chicago, IL 60659
Phone: (773)338-3492, (773)262-1500
Fax: (773)262-1606
e-mail: pfachicago@aol.com
Chr.: Hameedullah Khan
Pres.: Mohammad Bashir

Community liaison: Saeed Uz Zafar
Founded: 1983
Serves: Pakistani Americans in Illinois
Purpose: To be the leading Pakistani-American community organization for multi-purpose uses
Programs: Arts and cultural activities, business and professional support, citizenship and immigration seminar, employment workshop, recreation, social, translating on request
Volunteers: Welcome

Palestinian American

+Palestinian American Congress, Chicago Chapter
C/o Fadi Zanayed
7905 S. Cicero
Chicago, IL 60652
Phone: (773)735-7755
Fax: (773) 735-8466
e-mail: fzanayed@aol.com
Pres.: Fadi Zanayed
Founded: 1995
No office, 700 members
Local chapter of national organization
Serves: Palestinians, and Arabs in general, in Chicago and suburbs
Purpose: Social, cultural, political
Programs: Community organizing, culture preservation, political, translation

Ramallah Club of Chicago
2700 N. Central Ave.
Chicago, IL 60639
Phone: (773)237-2727
Pres.: Sami Fadayel
Local chapter of national organization
Founded: 1959
Serves: Mostly Palestinian Arabs, others in Arab American community, in Chicago metropolitan area
Purpose: To help a community that traces its origins to the village of Ramallah to maintain its ties
Programs: Arabic school

Polish American

Advocates Society
P.O. Box 641883

Chicago, IL 60664-1833
Phone: (847)298-8900
Fax: (847)298-8930
Pres.: Peter C. Wachowski
No exec. dir., no office, 250 members
Founded: 1931
Serves: Polish Americans in Chicago and suburbs
Purpose: To provide professional, social and ethnic activities that relate to the practice of law and development of legal skills and knowledge
Programs: Legal clinic, scholarships, formal dinner dance, judges reception and annual installation dinner

Alliance of Friends of the Polish Village
7006 W. Henderson
Chicago, IL 60634
Phone: (773)283-2824
Evening/weekend: same
Exec. Dir.: Walter Suchowiejko
Pres.: Boleslaw (Bill) Krakowski
Founded: 1947
Serves: Polish Americans in Chicago and suburbs
Purpose: To propagate Polish folklore and support the Polish Peasant Party
Programs: Traditional artistic Polish Harvest Festival, keep contact with leaders of Polish Peasant Party

Amicus Poloniae Polish Legal Volunteer Services
5711 N. Milwaukee Ave.
Chicago, IL 60646
Phone: (773)763-8520
Evening/weekend: same (ans. machine)
Fax: (773)763-7114
Co-Chrs.: David Pudlo & Lillian Swiader
Sen. Admin.: Marianna Lach
Founded: 1990
Serves: Polish Americans in Chicago and suburbs
Purpose: To provide legal services to Polish-speaking community of Chicago
Programs: General legal advice, legal representation, referrals to attorneys, Saturday a.m. clinic twice monthly
Volunteers: Welcome

Copernicus Foundation
5216 W. Lawrence Ave.

Chicago, IL 60630
Phone: (773)777-8898
Fax: (773)777-6120
e-mail: info@copernicusfdn.com
Web: www.copernicusfdn.com
Exec. Dir.: Sophia Kaspar
Pres.: Donald A. Gutowski
Founded: 1971
Serves: Most Polish Americans, also some Koreans, Hispanics and others, in the Jefferson Park neighborhood, Chicago and suburbs
Purpose: To promote Polish culture, customs and traditions; to serve the community in which it is located; to build understanding with other ethnic groups
Programs: Taste of Polonia, Copernican Awards, culture preservation, community center, education, language, classic silent films, Law Fair
Volunteers: Welcome

Council of Educators in Polonia
7551 W. Palatine
Chicago, IL 60631
Phone: (773)763-5587
Fax: (773)534-3558
e-mail: Ken29Gill@aol.com
Evening/weekend: same
Exec. Dir. & Pres.: Ken Gill
Founded: 1930
Serves: Polish American Educators in Chicago, suburbs, Illinois and USA
Purpose: To help bilingual teachers in the Chicago Public Schools
Programs: Network with other teachers and schools for jobs and information on educational matters and bilingual teaching, translating
Volunteers: Welcome

Gift from the Heart Foundation
2653 N. Narragansett Ave.
Chicago, IL 60639
Phone: (773)237-4800
Fax: (773)237-1221
e-mail: giftfoun@corecomm.net
Web: www.giftfromtheheart.org
Exec. Dir.: Roman Jurewicz
Pres.: Krystyna R. Pasek
Founded: 1988
Serves: Mostly Polish Americans,
Purpose: To help disabled and seriously ill children

Programs: Buy rehab equipment; provide food, lodging, transport and interpreters for children from abroad; learn about available medical care for disabled children
Volunteers: Welcome

International Polka Association (see Multi-ethnic)

Italian-Polish American Unity Organization (see Italian American)

Kosciuszko Foundation, Chicago Chapter
1513 W. Harrison
Chicago, IL 60607
Phone: (312)829-1455
Evening/weekend: same
Fax: (312)829-7125
Pres.: Dr. Ewa Radwanska
Sec.: Danuta Lusinska
No exec. dir., no office, 100 members
Local chapter of national organization
Founded: 1984
Serves: Polish Americans in Chicago, suburbs, Illinois and Midwest
Purpose: Cultural/educational exchange and scholarships
Programs: Polish-language summer scholarships, Polish American cultural events, annual Chopin piano competition, recital
Volunteers: Welcome

The Lira Ensemble
6525 N. Sheridan Rd., #Sky 905
Chicago, IL 60626
Phone: (773)539-4900, (773)508-7040
Evening/weekend: same
Fax: (773)508-7043
Gen. Mgr., Art. Dir.: Lucyna Migala
Chr.: Lewis F. Matuszewich
V. Chr.: Frank A. Cizon
Founded: 1965
Serves: Mostly Polish Americans, also African Americans, Mexican Americans and others in Chicago, USA and Poland
Purpose: To help acquaint Americans with the richness of Poland's thousand-year-old heritage of music and dance, and help Americans learn about and appreciate Polish culture and traditions
Programs: Performances by the Lira Company, consisting of the Lira Singers,

Chamber Chorus, Chamber Orchestra, Children's Chorus and Dancers; artist in residence at University of Chicago; outreach concerts to and with several major ethnic communities in Chicago; recordings
Volunteers: Welcome

Polish American Association
(formerly Polish Welfare Association)
3834 N. Cicero Ave.
Chicago, IL 60641
Phone: (773)282-8206
Fax: (773)282-1324
e-mail: paa@polish.org
Exec. Dir.: Karen Popowski
Chr.: Rev. Edmund Siedlecki
Founded: 1922
Serves: Mostly Polish Americans, some other Eastern Europeans, in Chicago and suburbs
Purpose: To be a comprehensive Polish bilingual and bicultural social-service agency
Programs: Counseling, citizenship, education, employment, food pantry, health screenings, homeless outreach, immigrant adjustment, senior citizen, shelter for homeless men, substance-abuse treatment, vocational training, women, youth, advocacy
Other office: 4327 S. Richmond, 3815 N. Cicero
Volunteers: Welcome

Polish American Congress
5711 N. Milwaukee Ave.
Chicago, IL 60646-6294
Phone: (773)763-9944
Fax: (773)763-7114
e-mail: pacchgo@mindspring.com;
Web: www.polamcon.org
Nat. Exec. Dir.: Les S. Kuczynski
Pres.: Edward J. Moskal
National headquarters of organization
Founded: 1944
Serves: Polish Americans in the U.S.
Purpose: To serve as an umbrella organization of more than 3,000 organizations and clubs and to further knowledge of Polish history, language and culture as well as stimulate Polish American involvement and accomplishments
Programs: Civic, education, culture preservation, fraternal, heritage/history,

veteran, religious, professional; humanitarian aid for Poland through the PAC Charitable Foundation
Volunteers: Welcome

Polish American Congress, Illinois Division
5711 N. Milwaukee Ave.
Chicago, IL 60646
Phone: (773)631-3300
Evening/weekend: same
Fax: (773)774-0022
Web: www.pac-il.org
Exec. Dir. & Pres.: Christopher Kurczaba
1st V.P.: Joseph Sikora
2nd V.P.: Eva Betka
Local chapter of national organization
Founded: 1945
Serves: Polish Americans in Chicago, suburbs and Illinois
Purpose: To stimulate and unify people of Polish descent, and to help people in Poland
Programs: Community services, promotion of Polish heritage and culture

Polish Arts Club of Chicago
2329 W. Walton
Chicago, IL 60622
Phone: (312)421-6073
Evening/weekend: (773)278-7155
Fax: (312)421-6563
Pres.: Jessica Jagielnik
No exec. dir., no office, 200 members
Local chapter of national organization
Founded: 1926
Serves: Polish Americans in Chicago and suburbs
Purpose: Arts appreciation and to promoted interest and knowledge of Polish culture
Programs: Art exhibitions, literary competition, art & book fair, recitals, scholarships based on artistic merit, club for people who appreciate all forms of art, translating (on request)
Volunteers: Welcome

Polish Falcons Alliance of America, Nest 2
c/o John J. Stanclik
2109 Chilmark Ln.
Schaumburg, IL 60193-1061
Phone: (847)524-9113
Evening/weekend: same
Pres.: John J. Stanclik

No exec. dir., no office, 85 members
Local chapter of national organization
Founded: 1887
Serves: Polish Americans and their families in Chicago who have life insurance certificate issued by Polish Falcons of America
Purpose: To support gymnastic development of young members and provide scholarships
Programs: Culture preservation, education, charitable, civic, immigrant, neighborhood, health, financial aid for blind children in Poland, fraternal insurance, track and field meets, scholarships

Polish Genealogical Society of America
984 N. Milwaukee Ave.
Chicago, IL 60622
Phone: (773)776-5551
Evening: (773)776-4969
e-mail: pgsamerica@aol.com
Web: www.pgsa.org
Pres.: Dr. Paul S. Valasek
V.P. : Dr. Gregory Gazda
No exec. dir., no office, 1,700 members
Founded: 1978
Serves: Poles and genealogists around the world
Purpose: Help Poles trace genealogy
Programs: Conferences, workshops, genealogical trips for personal research, publications and books
Volunteers: Welcome

PNA Polish Information Center
5711 N. Milwaukee Ave.
Chicago, IL 60646
Phone: (773)763-8520
Fax: (773)763-7114
Contact: Marianna Lach
Founded: 1975
Serves: Polish Americans in Chicago, suburbs and Illinois
Purpose: To provide address information, referrals and social services
Programs: Social/fraternal, social service, referral

Polish Museum of America
984 N. Milwaukee Ave.
Chicago, IL 60622
Phone: (773)384-3352

Evening/weekend: same
Fax: (773)384-3799
e-mail: PGSAmerica@aol.com
Exec. Dir.: Jan M. Lorys
Pres.: Joann Kosinski
Founded: 1935 (opened 1937)
Serves: All people in Illinois
Purpose: To uphold and promote Polish and Polish American history and culture through programs, lectures and performances
Programs: Arts; culture preservation; education; research; archives with 60,000 volumes, 250 periodicals, Polish and American music collection; translating (limited)
Volunteers: Welcome

Polish National Alliance
6100 N. Cicero
Chicago, IL 60646
Phone: (773)286-0500
Fax: (773)286-3156
Pres.: Edward J. Moskal
Sec.: Frank Spula
National ethnic fraternal insurance benefit society
Founded: 1880
Serves: Members of the PNA, Polish Americans in the USA
Purpose: To provide insurance protection and serve the ethnic community
Programs: Scholarships, education, sports, youth, seniors, cultural (ethnic press, radio, cultural events)

Polish Roman Catholic Union of America
984 N. Milwaukee Ave.
Chicago, IL 60622
Phone: (773)278-3210 or 1-800-772-8632
Fax: (773)278-4595
e-mail: wmozog@prcua.org
Pres.: Wallace M. Ozog
Resident V.P.: Jerry Kucharski
Founded: 1873
Serves: Polish Americans in the USA
Purpose: To strengthen and preserve spiritual values, patriotic zeal, ethnic culture and heritage; and to foster cultural relations between the USA and Poland
Programs: Life insurance, fraternal, sports teams, language classes, crafts, youth festivals, folk dancing, singing, scholarships,

museum patron, archives, art exhibits, awards to outstanding Polish Americans

Polish Women's Alliance of America
205 S. Northwest Highway
Park Ridge, IL 60068
Phone: (847)384-1200
Fax: (847)384-1222
e-mail: pwaa@pwaa.org
Pres.: Virginia Sikora
Founded: 1898
Serves: Polish Americans in the USA
Purpose: To provide fraternal benefit life insurance and promote the Polish culture
Programs: Dance classes, language, youth, assisting immigrants with insurance plans, scholarships, social events

Polish Women's Civic Club, Inc.
1015 Cypress Drive
Arlington Heights, IL 60005
Phone: (847)394-2520
Evening/weekend: same
No exec. dir, no office, 300 members
Chr.: Camille Kopielski
Founded: 1924
Serves: Polish Americans in Chicago and suburbs
Purpose: To provide scholarships to qualified Polish American college students
Programs: Contributions to hospitals, museums, institutions for needy and aged; scholarships

Polish Youth Association in USA
6434 W. Belmont Ave.
Chicago, IL 60634
Phone: (773)481-2718
Fax: (847)298-0553
Exec. Dir.: Elizabeth Ciezkowski
Founded: 1949
Serves: Polish American youth in Chicago area
Purpose: To continue scouting movement that began in Poland; to preserve Polish culture and heritage
Programs: Dance troops, camping, culture preservation/heritage
Volunteers: Welcome

Polish Youth Organization "Rzeszowiacy," John Paul II Catholic Center of Polish Culture
1317 N. Ashland Ave.

Chicago, IL 60622
Phone: (773)276-7171
Fax: (773)276-5479
Exec. Dir.: Most Rev. Bronislaw Wojdyla
Instructor: Andrzej Nowak
Founded: 1979
Serves: Mostly Polish American, and others in Chicago , suburbs and other states
Purpose: To promote Polish cultural traditions among Polish Americans, especially youth. Also to prepare Polish immigrants to adapt to this country and share with American youth their experiences in Poland
Programs: Folk songs, ballet, folk and classical music, and theater; help for new Polish immigrants, especially youth; seasonal English classes, religious education, radio program in Polish, translating (occasionally) and charity work
Volunteers: Welcome

Siberian Society
6930 W. 26th St.
Berwyn, IL 60402
Phone: (708)484-6351, (847)647-0568
Exec. Dir.: Henryk Stankiewicz
Pres.: Henryk C. Scigala
Founded: 1992
Serves: Polish Americans in Chicago, suburbs and the USA
Purpose: To provide help to and information about Polish victims of Stalin's oppression
Programs: Civil rights, culture preservation, immigrant resettlement, senior citizen, veterans, social
Volunteers: Welcome

Puerto Rican

(See also Hispanic/Latino)

Nat. Committee to Free Puerto Rican Prisoners of War & Political Prisoners
2607 W. Division St.
Chicago, IL 60622
Phone: (773)278-0885
Evening/weekend: same
Fax: (773)278-1633
e-mail: alm1998@aol.com
Exec. Dir.: Alejandro Molino
Local chapter of national organization

Founded: 1979
Serves: Puerto Ricans in the Midwest and U.S.
Purpose: Human rights advocacy for Puerto Rican political prisoners
Programs: Education, heritage/history
Volunteers: Yes

Puerto Rican Chamber of Commerce
2436 W. Division St.
Chicago, IL 60622
Phone: (773)486-1331
Fax: (773)486-1340
e-mail: prcc1963@aol.com
Exec. Dir.: Angelo Sanchez
Pres.: Luis E. Cuevas
Founded: 1963
Serves: Puerto Ricans and other Hispanics in Illinois
Purpose: To serve as a clearing house of information and to assist the Hispanic business community
Programs: Networking for business professionals with one another, government agencies, other business organizations and corporate America; continuing education seminars; annual banquet to honor outstanding member; technical assistance; minority business certification
Volunteers: Welcome

Puerto Rican Cultural Center
1671 N. Claremont St.
Chicago, IL 60647
Phone: (773)342-8023
Evening/weekend: same
Fax: (773)342-6609
Exec. Dir.: Jose E. Lopez
Founded: 1972
Serves: Puerto Ricans and other Latinos in West Town, Logan Square and Humboldt Park neighborhoods of Chicago
Purpose: Multi-purpose agency
Programs: Arts, community organizing, culture preservation, day care, economic development, education, health care, heritage/history, research, youth
Volunteers: Welcome

Puertorriquenos Unidos de Chicago
2935 W. 71st St.
Chicago, IL 60629
Phone: (773)436-1159/7078
Evening/weekend: (773)436-2044

Exec. Dir.: Jesse Gomez
Pres.: Paulina Carballo
Founded: 1990
Serves: Mostly people of Puerto Rican descent, in Southwest Chicago (Chicago Lawn)
Purpose: To serve the economically disadvantaged, with emphasis on the Puerto Rican and Latino community, via social services and a scholarship program
Programs: Intake site for Low Income Home Energy Assistance Program (LIHEAP); scholarship fund, health fairs, past participation in Mayor's Office of Employment and Training summer program; toy and food collection during post-holiday season for Three Kings Day tradition
Volunteers: Welcome

El Rincon Community Clinic
1874 N. Milwaukee Ave.
Chicago, IL 60647-4491
Phone: (773)276-0200
Fax: (773)276-4226
Exec. Dir.: Rafael Rios
Chr.: Rolando Correa
Founded: 1972
Serves: Mostly Puerto Ricans, other Hispanics, some African Americans
Purpose: Outpatient narcotics treatment
Program: Narcotics treatment and detox, HIV/AIDS, mental health, health
Volunteers: Welcome

Spanish Action Committee of Chicago
2452 W. Division St.
Chicago, IL 60622
Phone: (773)292-1052
Evening/weekend: same
Fax: (773)292-1073
Contact: Leoncio Vazquez
Pres.: Carmen M. Moreno
Founded: 1966
Serves: Anyone who walks in the door
Purpose: To demonstrate to Chicago's Spanish-speaking residents that they can and must play a major role in determining and directing their destiny
Programs: Advocacy for Puerto Rican civil rights, social service, community organizing,, community development, domestic violence counseling

Romanian American

European American Association (see Multi-ethnic)

Romanian Mission of Chicago
(mailing)1411 W. Farwell
Chicago, IL 60626
6854 N. Glenwood
Chicago, IL 60626
Phone: (773)764-5991
e-mail: rmcisfan@geocities.com
Exec. Dir.: Iosif Isfan
Local chapter of national organization
Founded: 1986
Serves: Mostly Romanian Americans, also some Russian, Croatian, Latvian and Ukrainian Americans, in Chicago
Purpose: To help people in Romania and immigrants in Chicago establish a new life
Programs: Drop-off point to collect food, clothing, furniture, medical supplies, Christian literature to send to Romania; Christian camp in Romania; vehicles for Romanian needy; jail ministry
Volunteers: Welcome

Russian American

Friends of Refugees of Eastern Europe (see Jewish)

Russian Independent Mutual Aid Society
917 N. Wood
Chicago, IL 6062660622
Phone: (312)421-2272
Pres.: Michael Lynch
Local chapter of national organization
Founded: 1912
Serves: Mostly Russian Americans, some Ukrainian and Polish Americans
Purpose: To provide burial insurance
Programs: Occasional donations to those in need in Russia

Russian Senior Center
5959 N. Sheridan Road
Chicago, IL 60660
Phone: (773)784-7449
Fax: (773)761-8835, (773)561-5420
Exec. Dir.: Anna Gurevich

Founded: 1994
Serves: Jews from the former Soviet Union, in Chicago and suburbs
Purpose: To overcome loneliness and isolation of elderly immigrants
Programs: English, classes, Yiddish Club, choir, dancing lessons, parties, lectures, arts, culture preservation
Volunteers: English-speaking volunteers for English-speaking club

Scandinavian American

(see also **Finnish, Swedish, Norwegian**)

Center for Scandinavian Studies
North Park University, 3225 W. Foster Ave.
Chicago, IL 60625
Phone: (773)244-5615
Evening/weekend: (773)588-3591
Fax: (773)583-0858
e-mail: cpeterson@northpark.edu
Exec. Dir.: Charles Peterson
Chr.: Brad Halverson
Founded: 1984
Serves: Scandinavian Americans in the USA
Purpose: To provide educational exchanges and cultural programming
Programs: Student and faculty exchanges with Scandinavia, guest lectures, exhibits and performances, archives, reference and translation services
Volunteers: Welcome

Scottish American

Illinois St. Andrew Society
2800 Des Plaines Ave.
North Riverside, IL 60546
Phone: (708)447-5092
Evening/weekend: (630)665-2947
Fax: (708)447-5269
e-mail: wrethford@aol.com
Pres.: Wayne Rethford
Founded: 1845
Serves: Scottish Americans in Chicago metro area and Illinois
Purpose: To operate Scottish Home for retirement and health care and foster Scottish heritage

Programs: Highland Games, Scottish history club, Scottish genealogy, area receptions
Volunteers: Welcome

Scottish Cultural Society
1104 S. Highland
Oak Park, IL 60304
Phone: (708)383-2138
Exec. Dir.: Donna Sell
Pres.: Judi MacRae
Founded: 1975
Serves: Scottish Americans in Chicago
Purpose: To promote Scottish culture and heritage
Programs: Scottish fair, monthly meetings, translating
Volunteers: Welcome

Senegalese American

Chicago Assn. of Senegalese Immigrants
7306 N. Winchester Ave.
Chicago, IL 60626
Phone: (773)338-2297
Evening/weekend: same
Exec. Dir.: Bassirou Mbszke
Pres.: Badara Diakhate
Founded: 1993
Serves: Senegalese in Chicago and suburbs
Purpose: To teach, provide social services and organize cultural activities
Programs: Culture preservation, immigrant resettlement and adjustment, education, language, civil rights, community organizing, economic development, social, translating

Serbian American

Jewish-Serbian Friendship Society
1872 N. Clybourn
Chicago, IL 60614
Phone: (773)327-8521
Evening/weekend: same
Fax: same
e-mail: betsylalic@aol.com
Rep.: Betsy Lalich
No exec. dir., no office, 100 members
Local chapter of international organization
Founded: 1989

Serves: Serbians and Jews in Illinois and the Midwest
Purpose: To continue the traditional alliance between these two communities
Program: Culture preservation, education, heritage/history, social, Holocaust remembrance

Slovak American

Slovak American Cultural Society of the Midwest
P.O. Box 5398
Naperville, IL 60567
Phone: (815)838-9877
Evening/weekend: same
Fax: (815)838-9877
e-mail: SACSM@IllinoisSlovak.com
Chr.: Thomas Klimek Ward
Rec. Sec.: Rosemary Macko Wisnosky
Founded: 1991
No office, no exec. dir., 746 members
Serves: Slovaks in USA
Purpose: To preserve and promote Slovak American heritage and culture
Programs: Tri-annual Slovak-American Newsletter, annual SlovakFest Midwest celebration of heritage and culture, arts and culture preservation, history

Slovak Catholic Cultural Center and Museum
5900 W. 147th St.
Oak Forest, IL 60452
Phone: (708)687-2877
Evening/weekend: same
Fax:: (708)687-2880
Pres.: Sr. Irene Sebo, OSB
Exec. Dir.: Sr. Methodia Machalica, OSB
Founded: 1978
Serves: Slovaks in Chicago metro area and 3 other states
Purpose: To preserve archives, traditions and culture of Slovak people
Program: Ethnic social gatherings, teaching of Slovak language, culture preservation, archives, library and museum, religious services
Volunteers: Welcome

Slovak World Congress
c/o Martha Mistina Kona
600 Third St.

Wilmette, IL 60091
Phone: (847)251-3514
Fax: (847)251-3514
e-mail: mmkusa@juno.com
Midwest contact: Martha Mistina Kona
Local chapter of national organization
Founded: 1970
Serves: Slovaks in the Midwest
Purpose: To help increase Slovak awareness, spiritual life, socio-economic development, cultural and scientific progress and physical awareness of the people of Slovak origin
Programs: Promote enthusiasm and interest in Slovak identity, heritage/history, culture preservation, social/fraternal, political, youth

Swedish American

Central Swedish Comm. of Chicago
c/o B. Pearson
4646 Larch
Glenview, IL 60025
Phone: (847)824-4366
Weekend/evening: same
No exec. dir., no office, 70-90 reps
Pres.: Barbro Pearson
Founded: 1960 (Incorp. 1971)
Serves: Mostly Swedish Americans and other Scandinavians in Chicago and northern Illinois
Purpose: Representation and continuity in Swedish American community
Programs: Civic/fraternal, cultural/arts, children's groups with traditional ethnic programs, coordination with mayor's and governor's office, Swedish holiday celebrations, calendar of events, coordination with Swedish consulate
Volunteers: Welcome

**Swedish-American
Chamber of Commerce**
150 N. Michigan Ave., Suite 1200
Chicago, IL 60601
Phone: (312)781-6234
Fax: (312)346-0683
e-mail: sacc-chi@sacc-usa.org
Exec. Adm.: Pia Wennerth
Pres.: Annette Gustafsson-Guenther
Founded: 1975

Serves: Mostly Swedes and Swedish Americans, in Chicago, suburbs, Illinois, Wisconsin, Indiana and Ohio
Purpose: To promote trade and commerce between Sweden and Chicago and the Midwest
Programs: Trade shows, cultural events, business exchanges, trade missions to Sweden, golf outing, speakers
Volunteers: Welcome

Swedish-American Historical Society
5125 N. Spaulding Ave.
Chicago, IL 60625
Phone: (773)583-5722
e-mail: kanderson@northpark.edu
Pres.: Philip J. Anderson
Founded: 1948
Serves: Swedes around the world
Purpose: Historical, publications
Programs: Quarterly scholarly journal, programs, lectures, conferences, culture preservation, education, heritage/history, research

Swedish American Museum
5211 N. Clark St.
Chicago, IL 60640
Phone: (773)728-8111
Fax: (773)728-8870
e-mail: museum@samac.org
Web: www.samac.org
Exec. Dir.: Kerstin Lane
Pres.: Margareta Alexander
Founded: 1976
Serves: Mostly Swedish Americans in Chicago, Illinois and the USA and Chicago school children
Purpose: To be a focal point for Swedish and Swedish American activities and the preservation of Swedish heritage
Programs: Permanent exhibit on Swedish immigration to Chicago, temporary exhibits on contemporary Swedish culture, classes, concerts, lectures, celebration of holidays
Volunteers: Welcome

Swedish Cultural Society in America
434 W. Armitage Ave.
Chicago, IL 60614
Phone: (773)472-0942
Evening/weekend: same
Fax: (773)472-0011
e-mail: JanneUSA@aol.com

Imm. Past Pres.: Jan E. Muller
Local chapter of national organization
Founded: 1923
Serves: Swedish Americans in Chicago area and USA
Purpose: To promote Swedish heritage in America
Programs: Arts, concerts, lectures, business and professional support, education, family, heritage/history, immigrant resettlement, language, senior citizen, social/fraternal, translating
Volunteers: Welcome

Thai American

Thai American Southerner Association of Illinois
1968 Jamestown St.
Palatine, IL 60074
Phone: (847)991-9189
e-mail: tunyavngs@aol.com
Pres.: Vinai Tunyawong
Local chapter of national organization
Founded: 1975
Serves: Mostly Thai Americans, also Lao and Chinese, in Illinois
Purpose: To unite and raise money to send help to the southern part of Thailand
Programs: Foreign aid, heritage/history, culture preservation, family, immigrant resettlement, adjustment, legal, philanthropic, translating
Other locations: Palatine, Morton Grove
Volunteers: Welcome

Thai Association of Illinois
955 Bermuda Dunes
Northbrook, IL 60062
Phone: (847)272-6735
Fax: (847)272-6978
Chr.: Dr. Pipit Chiemmongkultip
Pres.: Edward Lin
Founded: 1969
Serves: Thai and other Asian Americans in Illinois
Purpose: To help needy people in the Thai community
Programs: Health education, economics, health fair, counseling and support for the needy, financial help, immigration, translating (limited)
Volunteers: Welcome

Tibetan American

Tibetan Alliance of Chicago
4750 N. Sheridan Road, Suite 469
Chicago, IL 60640
Phone: (773)275-7454
Fax: (773)275-9171
e-mail: sgyatso@aol.com
Exec. Dir.: Sherab Gyatso
Pres.: Nina Nathan Schroeder
Founded: 1992
Serves: Tibetan community in Chicago
Purpose: To help Tibetan community, to empower the community and foster further development, to tell the story of Tibet and gain support for her cause
Programs: Employment, health , information, children's education, cultural education and programs, creating awareness of Tibetan situation, events to promote the cause of Tibet, public talks about Tibet
Volunteers: Welcome

+TIBET Center
P.O. Box 60914
Chicago, IL 60660-0914
Phone: (773)743-2404
Fax: (773)743-7772
e-mail:tibetvcen@aol.com
Web: www.buddhapia.com/tibet/tibetcen
Pres.: Tsering Tashi
Founded: 1999
Serves: Tibetans in the Midwest
Purpose: To preserve and promote the cultural heritage of Tibet and provide a venue for Tibetan and Buddhist studies
Programs: Arts, culture, preservation, translating
Volunteers: Welcome

Ukrainian American

American Ukrainian Youth Association
2457 W. Chicago Ave.
Chicago, IL 60622
Phone: (773)486-4204
Pres.: Chrystya Wereszczak
Founded: 1948
Serves: Ukrainian Americans in the Chicago metropolitan area

Purpose: To provide cultural, sports, social and camping activities for youth of Ukrainian descent
Programs: Dance, choirs, art, theater; soccer, volleyball and softball teams; camping; translating (informally)
Additional location: Palatine
Volunteers: Welcome

School of Ukrainian Studies "Ridna Shkola"
2220 W. Rice St.
Chicago, IL 60622
Phone: (773)276-9088 (Sat. a.m.)
Evening/weekend: (708)687-9263
Fax: (708)687-9357
Exec. Dir.: Nadija Ludmyla Chojnacki
Pres.: Victor Wojtychiw
Local chapter of national organization
Founded: 1978
Serves: Ukrainian Americans in Chicago and suburbs and Illinois
Purpose: To educate about Ukrainian roots
Programs: Ukrainian Saturday School, grades pre-school through 11, teaching language, literature, history, geography, culture and traditions
Volunteers: Welcome

Selfreliance Association of American Ukrainians
2355 W. Chicago Ave.
Chicago, IL 60622
Phone: (773)235-2895
Exec. Dir.: Volodymyr Szczeblowsky
Pres.: Leo Kazaniwskyj
Local chapter of national organization
Founded: 1949
Serves: Ukrainian Americans in Chicago, suburbs and Illinois
Purpose: Multi-purpose organization
Programs: Community organizing, culture preservation, education, family, heritage, immigrant resettlement, legal, youth, recreation, referral, translating
Volunteers: Welcome

Ukrainian American Club
2234 W. Chicago Ave.
Chicago, IL 60622
Phone: (773)252-1417
Evening/weekend: (773)342-4668
Pres.: John J. Horodecki
Founded: 1936

Serves: Ukrainian Americans in USA
Purpose: To disseminate knowledge in English and Ukrainian languages; to encourage study of American Democratic institutions; to aid readjustment of Ukrainians in America; to nurture Ukrainian culture and tradition; to promote moral and financial status of members
Programs: School to teach ESL, annual dinner
Volunteers: Welcome

Ukrainian Congress Committee of America, Illinois Division
2247 W. Chicago Ave.
Chicago, IL 60622
Phone: (847)292-5757
Evening/weekend: (773)252-1228
Fax: (847)825-8617
Web: www.ukmop.com/baranyk
Pres.: Orest Baranyk
Founded: 1940s
Serves: Ukrainian Americans in Illinois
Purpose: Umbrella organization for all civic, religious, cultural, social and youth organizations for Ukrainians in Illinois
Programs: Coordination, Ukrainian Fest sponsor, advocacy, forums and assistance for new immigrants

Ukrainian Institute of Modern Art
2320 W. Chicago Ave.
Chicago, IL 60622
Phone: (773)227-5522
Evening/weekend: (773)878-2442
Web: www.brama.com/uima
Pres.: Oleh Kowerko
Chr.: Lubomyr Krushelnycky
Founded: 1971
Serves: Ukrainian Americans and others in Illinois and nearby states
Purpose: To serve the community as an educational art center
Programs: Permanent art collection, periodic art exhibits, concerts and literary evenings
Volunteers: Welcome

Ukrainian National Aid Association of America
925 N. Western Ave.
Chicago, IL 60622
Phone: (773)342-5102
Fax: (773)342-5370

Pres.: Wolodymyr Okipniuk
Founded: 1914
Serves: Ukrainian Americans in Chicago
metro area, Illinois and USA
Purpose: Fraternal organization that sells
life insurance
Programs: Life insurance, mortgages to
members

Ukrainian National Museum
721 N. Oakley Blvd.
Chicago, IL 60612
Phone: (773)421-8020
Evening/weekend: same
Fax: (773)693-7479
Web: www.urknlmuseum.org
Pres.: Dr. George Hrycelak
Founded: 1952
Serves: Ukrainian Americans in Ukrainian
Village neighborhood
Purpose: To increase ethnic sensitivity in a
changing word, promote Ukrainian history
and culture, and serve as an educational
resource
Programs: Library, archives available for
research, educational programs and speakers
sent to grammar schools throughout Chicago
area
Volunteers: Welcome

Ukrainian Social Service Bureau
2355 W. Chicago Ave.
Chicago, IL 60622
Phone: (773)235-2895
Exec. Dir. & Pres.: Volodymyr
Szczeblowsky
Founded: 1976
Serves: Mostly Ukrainians, also some
Polish, Italian and Slovak Americans, in
Ukrainian Village neighborhood and
Chicago metro area
Purpose: To serve the needs of senior
citizens
Programs: Health care, housing, senior-
citizen shelter, social, recreational, referral,
language, legal, mental health, immigrant
resettlement and adjustment, counseling,
meals on wheels, Golden Diners Club,
translating
Volunteers: Welcome

Vietnamese American

Nghia Sinh International, Inc.
1652 N. Rockwell St.
Chicago, IL 60647
Phone: (773)235-9838
Fax: (773)534-4287
e-mail: nsii@juno.com
Web: www.NghiaSihn.8m.com
Exec. Dir.: Dr. Nguyen-Trung Hieu
Pres.: Luan Nguyen
Founded: 1963
Serves: Mostly Vietnamese Americans, also
Chinese and Cambodian Americans in
Chicago
Purpose: To assist refugees and immigrants
in their adjustment to America
Programs: Cultural, eductional, social
services
Volunteers: Welcome

**Vietnamese American Community
In Illinois**
3849 N. Seeley Ave.
Chicago, IL 60618
(Phone: (773)935-7842
Fax: (773)281-9060
e-mail: Hotran@aol.com
Pres.: Ho L. Tran, M.D.
Founded: 1995
Serves: Vietnamese and some Chinese in
Uptown, Albany Park, Chicago and suburbs
Purpose: Education to promote well-being,,
economic and health
Programs: Cultural events (Vietnamese New
Year, children's festival, Founding Fathers
Day), workshops on political, social and
health issues, health fairs, Vietnamese
cemetery, translation
Volunteers: Welcome

Vietnamese Association of Illinois
5252 N. Broadway, 2nd floor
Chicago, IL 60640
Phone (773)728-3700
Fax: (773)728-0497
e-mail: vietassn@aol.com
Exec. Dir.: Trung Phan
Pres.: Lien Du
Founded: 1976
Serves: Mostly Vietnamese Americans and
some other refugees in Uptown, Albany

Park, the rest of the Chicago metro area and Illinois
Purpose: To provide social services for the Vietnamese community and residents of the North Side of Chicago
Programs: Counseling, citizenship, community center, culture preservation, economic development, employment services, health education, literacy, referral, senior citizens, tutoring, youth, translating
Volunteers: Welcome

Multi-ethnic

American Friends Service Committee
59 E. Van Buren, Suite 1400
Chicago, IL 60605
Phone: (312)427-2533
Fax: (312)427-4171
e-mail: mmcconnell-glr@afsc.org
Exec. dir.: Michael McConnell
Local chapter of national organization
Founded: 1917
Serves: Mostly African Americans and Latinos in Chicago
Purpose: To develop leadership from within the diverse communities of Chicago, and to build a sustainable peace-with-justice movement that reaches beyond the city's borders
Programs: Community organizing; economic development; economic literacy; African American mentorship; Mexican Agenda Project to help unify Mexican leaders, activists and organizations; Palestinian Family Reunification Project.

Biracial Family Network
P.O. Box 3214
Chicago, IL 60654-0214
Phone: (773)288-3644
e-mail: bfnchicago@aol.com
No exec. dir., no office, 80 member families
Pres.: Dorothy Adams
Contact: Irene Carr
Founded: 1980
Serves: Chicago and suburbs, Midwest
Purpose: To provide support and information to interracial couples of all ethnic and racial combinations and biracial children and adults
Programs: Business and professional support, culture preservation, day care,

education, family, heritage/history, mentoring, recreation, research, social support, networking, speakers for conferences and workshops, national newsletter

Catholic Charities/ALAC Immigration, Naturalization and Refugee Settlement
126 N. Des Plaines
Chicago, IL 60661
Phone: (312)427-7078 (Immigrants
 (312)655-7860 (Refugees)
Fax: (312)427-3130
Exec. Dir.: J. Zeferino Ochoa
Local chapter of national organization
Founded: 1954
Serves: Spanish-speaking, also Afghani, Arabs, Assyrians, Bosnians, Haitians, Iraqi, Lao, Somalians, Sudanese, Syrians, Ukrainians, Vietnamese
Purpose: Holistic assistance for newcomers during adjustment to a new environment
Programs: Family reunification petitions, citizenship, adjustment, resettlement, referral
Volunteers: Welcome

Chicago Council on Urban Affairs
11 S. LaSalle St., Suite 3201
Chicago, IL 60602
Phone: (312)782-3511
Fax: (312)782-0748
e-mail: ccua@ccua.org
Web: www.ccua.org
Pres.: Lucretia A. Bailey
Chr.: Mathew Smith
Founded: 1969
Serves: all in Chicago metro area
Purpose: Independent multicultural/multiracial civic organization that works to improve quality of life and equality of opportunity for all
Programs: Educational forums; in-depth study and projects on issues like public policy and race, race and ethnic relations, and crime and justice
Volunteers: Welcome

+Coalition of African, Asian and Latino Immigrants if Illinois (CAALII)
c/o Chinese Mutual Aid Assn.
1016 W. Argyle St.
Chicago, IL 60640
Exec. Dir.: Dale Asis

Phone: (773)784-2900
Fax: (773)784-2984
Evening/weekend: (773)743-8141
e-mail: chinesemutualaid@ameritech.net
Founded: 1996
Serves: Cambodians, Ethiopians, Latinos, Chinese, Koreans and Vietnamese in Chicago
Purpose: To organized member communities through education and leadership development, to advocate for immigrants and refugees and provide direct services
Programs: Education, leadership development, advocacy for immigrants and refugees, citizenship, translating
Volunteers: Welcome

Coalition of Limited English Speaking Elderly
53 W. Jackson Blvd., Suite 1301
Chicago, IL 60604-3702
Phone: (312)461-0812
Fax: (312)461-1466
Exec. Dir.: Rosemary Gemperle
Pres.: Sueylee Chang
V.P.: Agnes Kowalewicz
Founded: 1989
Serves: Limited-English-speaking elderly of any ethnicity
Purpose: To assure that older people who don't speak English have access to the same services as English-speaking elderly
Programs: Technical assistance to home-care providers, health screening, nutrition, information and assistance, citizenship, advocacy

Community Renewal Society
332 S. Michigan Ave., Suite 500
Chicago, IL 60604
Phone: (312)427-4830
Fax: (312)427-6130
Web: www.crs-ucc.org
Exec. Dir.: Rev. Calvin Morris
Pres.: Rev. Elizabeth Bueschel
Founded: 1882
Serves: African Americans, Latinos, Asian Americans and the poor, in Chicago
Purpose: To address issues of race and poverty in order to achieve just and caring communities
Programs: Technical assistance to community-based organizations, workshops and training; anti-violence initiative, choruses, consulting to inner city churches, senior ministry project; publishes The Chicago Reporter and CATALYST
Volunteers: Welcome

Ethnic Cultural Preservation Council
6500 S. Pulaski Road
Chicago, IL 60629-5136
Phone: (773)582-5143
Fax: (773)582-5133
Evening/weekend: same
Pres.: Stanley Balzekas
Founded: 1969
Serves: All ethnic groups in Chicago
Purpose: To facilitate the study, preservation and enhancement of one's own heritage and background
Programs: Disseminates information on artists, art organizations, ethnic customs and traditions, translating (for a fee)
Volunteers: Welcome

European American Association
2827 W. Division St.
Chicago, IL 60622
Phone: (773)342-5868
Fax: (773)342-5533
Exec. Dir.: John Herman
Pres.: Elea Poleuca
Founded: 1991
Serves: Mostly Romanian Americans, also Hispanics, African Americans, Polish Americans, Russian Americans in West Town and Humboldt Park
Purpose: To help people survive today and prepare for tomorrow
Programs: Energy assistance, food distribution, senior-citizen home care, community center, community organizing, culture preservation, employment, housing, immigrant resettlement, language, referral, translating Romanian-English
Volunteers: Welcome

Heartland Alliance for Human Needs and Human Rights
(formerly Travelers & Immigrants Aid)
208 S. LaSalle St., Suite 1818
Chicago, IL 60604
Phone: (312)629-4500
Fax: (312)629-4550
e-mail: moreinfo@heartland-alliance.org
Web: www.heartland-alliance.org

Exec. Dir.: Rev. Sid Mohn
Chr.: William H. Dunbar, Jr.
Founded: 1888
Serves: Homeless and low-income families and individuals, including immigrants and refugees; homeless youth; low-income people with HIV and AIDS; survivors of domestic violence; survivors of torture; seniors and veterans; marginally housed individuals; the chronically mentally ill
Purpose: To provide housing, health care and human services while developing long-term solutions to factors that lead to poverty
Programs: Immigrant and refugee resettlement; immigration and asylum legal assistance; citizenship training; primary, mental and oral health care; health care interpreting and translating; supportive housing; education and employment assistance; women and family services; substance-abuse recovery; HIV education, prevention and treatment; advocacy and public policy research; affordable housing; programs for homeless teens
Additional offices: Century Place Development Corp. (312)629-4500, ext. 3302; Chicago Health Outreach (773)275-2060; Chicago Connections (312)629-4500, ext. 4525; Midwest Immigrant Rights Center (312)629-1960; Neon Street Programs (312)271-NEON
Volunteers: Welcome

Illinois Coalition for Immigrant and Refugee Rights
36 S. Wabash, Suite 1425
Chicago, IL 60603
Phone: (312)441-2990
Fax: (312)441-2999
e-mail: info@icirr.org
Exec. Dir.: Maricela Garcia
Acting Pres.: Susan Gzesh
Founded: 1986
Serves: Immigrants throughout Illinois
Purpose: To promote immigrants' and refugees' rights to participate fully and equally in a diverse society in an increasingly interdependent world
Programs: Outreach and information, referral, advocacy, training and conference coordination
Volunteers: Welcome

Illinois Ethnic Coalition
55 E. Monroe, Suite 2930
Chicago, IL 60603
Phone: (312)368-1155
Fax: (312)251-8815
e-mail: IECChicago@aol.com
Web: www.medill.nwu.edu/IEC
Exec. Dir.: Jeryl Levin
Pres.: Anthony Fornelli
Founded: 1971
Serves: All in the Chicago metropolitan area
Purpose: To educate about the diverse ethnic, racial and cultural groups; to provide and disseminate information on Illinois' ethnic and racial communities
Programs: Resources, publications, demographics, Census 2000 outreach and education, special programs, training, forums, consultation, advocacy
Volunteers: Welcome

Interchurch Refugee & Immigration Ministries
4753 N. Broadway, Suite 401
Chicago, IL 60640
Phone: (773)989-5647
Fax: (773)989-0484
e-mail: irim@irim.org
Web: www.irim.org
Exec. Dir.: May Campbell
Pres.: Mary Beth Jorgensen
Local chapter of national organization
Founded: 1992
Affiliate of Church World Service
Serves: Primarily Albanians from Kosovo, Bosnians, Middle Easterners, Ukrainians, Cubans, Africans and Vietnamese
Purpose: To provide services to help refugees become self-sufficient, help with immigration laws and procedures, advocate for fair and humane treatment of immigrants and refugees; to encourage church support for refugee resettlement
Programs: Reception and placement, English-language training, employment, family adjustment, refugee child and family outreach, immigration services, refugee senior services, vocational training, citizenship application and education, translating
Volunteers: Welcome

**International Polka Association/
Polka Music Hall of Fame**
4145 S. Kedzie Ave.
Chicago, IL 60632
Phone: (773)254-7771
Evening/weekend: (708)352-2109
Fax: (773)254-8111
Pres.: Jerry Wantroba
Local chapter of national organization
Founded: 1968
Serves: Poles, Czechs, Slovenians, Germans
in the U.S., Canada and the world
Purpose: To promote and perpetuate Polka
music
Programs: Culture preservation, education,
heritage/history, research, social/fraternal,
promotion of festivals and other Polka
events, Hall of Fame and annual Polka
music awards, museum, public information,
radio program
Volunteers: Welcome

**International Medical Council
of Illinois**
26 Blue Grass Ct.
Oak Brook, IL 60523
Phone:(630)455-1996
Pres.: Antonio Senat, M.D.
V.P.: Julita Orbeta, M.D.
Local chapter of national organization
Founded: 1983
Serves: Mostly Asians, also Hispanics,
African Americans, European Americans, in
Illinois
Purpose: To protect immigrant physicians
from discrimination in the medical field
Programs: Lobbying and professional
advocacy

**Leadership Council for Metropolitan
Open Communities (see African
American)**

**Legal Services Center for Immigrants
(Legal Assistance Foundation
of Chicago)**
111 W. Jackson, 3rd Floor
Chicago, IL 60604
Phone: (312)341-9617
Fax: (312)341-1041
Supv. Atty.: Lisa J. Palumbo
Founded: 1976
Serves: Low-income immigrants in Illinois

Purpose: To provide low-income
immigrants with affordable legal
representation in removal proceedings and
in abused-spouse or child petitions; to
provide brief legal advice and referral on
other immigration cases
Programs: Legal advice, representation and
referral

**The National Conference
for Community and Justice**
(Formerly National Conference of Christians
and Jews)
17 E. Monroe, 4th Floor
Chicago, IL 60603
Phone: (312)236-9272
Fax: (312)236-0029
e-mail: Chicago@nccj.org
Exec. Dir.: The Rev. Stanley L. Davis, Jr.
Chr.: Michael Hayes
Local chapter of national organization
Founded: 1935
Serves: All ethnic groups in Chicago and
northern Illinois
Purpose: To fight bias, bigotry and racism
and to promote understanding and respect
among all races, religions and cultures
Programs: Training and education for
youth and adults in multicultural awareness,
interfaith relations, leadership development,
team-building, conflict resolution
Volunteers: Welcome

New World Resource Center
2600 W. Fullerton
Chicago, IL 60647
Phone: (773)227-4011
Manager: Alynne Romo
Chr.: Martha Quinn
Founded: 1972
Serves: African Americans, Latinos, Asian
Americans in Chicago and suburbs
Purpose: To provide a bookstore, resource
center and meeting space
Programs: Resource center with materials
on African-American, Latino and Asian-
American studies; economic and cultural
empowerment, labor studies, liberation
struggles, civil rights, community center,
history, community organizing, economic
development, education, health care,
immigrant resettlement and adjustment,
women
Volunteers: Welcome

Office for Ethnic Ministry
Archdiocese of Chicago
155 E. Superior St.
Chicago, IL 60611
Phone: (312)751-8301
Fax: (312)751-5207
Exec. Dir.: Rev. John P. Boivin
Founded: 1990
Serves: Poles, Hispanics, African
Americans and Filipinos plus numerous
European, Asian and Native American
communities in Cook and Lake Counties,
Purpose: To provide worship opportunities,
to strengthen and deepen the spiritual life of
Catholics from other cultures
Programs: Religious

Public Health & Education Association,
Midwest (Was American Refugee
Committee 1978-92)
317 Howard St.
Evanston, IL 60202
Phone: (847)328-1620
Evening/weekend: same
Fax: (847)328-1642
e-mail: pjh@micworld.com
Exec. Dir.: Phyllis J. Handelman
Pres.: Robin Zeldin
Founded: 1993
Serves: Refugees, immigrants and
minorities on North Side of Chicago, Illinois
and Midwest
Purpose: To provide health education and
medical linkages to the target populations,
and cross-cultural training for medical
professionals; to conduct conferences and
meetings in the health field
Programs: Health education, health fairs,
training in cross-cultural health, women's
health issues, adolescent health care,
pregnancy prevention, linkage for Hispanic
population
Volunteers: Need to walk to 2nd floor

Rainbow House/Arco Iris
20 E. Jackson, Suite 1550
Chicago, IL 60604
Phone: (312)935-3430
Evening/weekend: same
Hot line: (773)762-6611
Exec. Dir.: Diedre Cutlisse
Prog. Coord.: Kara Henner
Founded: 1982

Serves: African Americans, Latinos and
Asian Americans in Chicago and suburbs
Purpose: To offer services and assistance to
battered women and their children
Programs: Shelter, counseling, legal
advocacy, nutrition, support groups,
translating
Volunteers: Welcome

The Society for Arts
1112 N. Milwaukee Ave.
Chicago, IL 60622
Phone: (773)486-9612
Evening/weekend: same
Fax: (773)486-9613
e-mail: Socforarts@aol.com
Founded: 1982
Exec. Dir. & Pres.: Christopher Kamyszew
Serves: Europeans in North America
Purpose: To promote and promulgate
European arts and culture in North America
and to enhance artistic and intellectual
exchange between Europe and the states
Programs: Exhibitions of European artists
or American artists of European descent;
workshops in art and film; lectures and
meetings with artists; film festivals
including the Polish Film Festival and
European film festival, translating from
Polish, Russian and French
Volunteers: Welcome

South Central Community Services
8316 S. Ellis Ave.
Chicago, IL 60619
Phone: (773)483-0900
Evening/weekend: same
Fax: (773)483-5701
e-mail: sccsinc@earthlink.net
Pres. & CEO: Dr. Felicia Y. Blasingame
Founded: 1970
Serves: People of all races in
Chatham/Avalon/Burnside/Greater Grand
Crossing/South Shore, Roseland/Englewood
neighborhoods of Chicago and in suburbs
Purpose: To provide for the social,
economic, mental health, cultural
enrichment, educational and recreational
needs of the individuals and families in the
communities it serves
Programs: Child welfare/foster, outpatient,
day treatment, individual and family
counseling, Operation B.E.E., adult
literacy/GED, community center, athletic,

recreation, cultural, food pantry, Head Start, senior citizens, translating, after school As and Bs
Other locations: 1021 E. 83rd St., 7550 S. Phillips, 253 E. 113th St., 8545 S. Cottage Grove, 7101 S. Union Ave., 840 E. 87th St., Joliet
Volunteers: Welcome

Support Center
3811 N. Lawndale, #100
Chicago, IL 60618
Phone: (773)539-4741
Fax: (773)539-4751
e-mail: supportchi@aol.com
Exec. Dir.: Nancy Watkins
Pres.: Jean Joque
Local chapter of national organization
Founded: 1972
Serves: African Americans, Hispanics, Asians and Native Americans in Chicago and the Midwest
Purpose: To provide management and technical assistance
Programs: 300 seminars and workshops on business and human resource topics (open to public), on-site tailored training, long-term consultation services, mobile computer training
Volunteers: Welcome

Travelers & Immigrants Aid
(see Heartland Alliance above)

United Network for Immigrant and Refugee Rights (see Hispanic/Latino)

World Relief
3507 W. Lawrence
Chicago, IL 60625
Phone: (773)583-9191
Fax: (773)583-9410
e-mail: chicago@wr.org
Web: www.wr.org
Dir.: Wayne Anson
Dir. Soc. Svcs.: Dori Dinsmore
Dir. Empl. and Ed.: Michelle McGillivray
Founded: 1979
Local affiliate of national corporation
Serves: Recent immigrants and refugees, primarily Kosovars, Bosnians and Central Americans, but also Iraqis, Cubans, Mexicans, Ukrainians, Somalis, Vietnamese

and others in Chicago, Cook and Lake County suburbs
Purpose: To provide services and support that address the needs of very vulnerable newcomers to this country
Programs: Resettlement, adjustment, employment, social work, mental health services, ESL/education, paralegal counseling, advocacy, translation (limited and for a fee)
Volunteers: Welcome

Government agencies

Chicago Commission
on Human Relations
510 N. Peshtigo Court, Room 608
Chicago, IL 60611
Phone: (312)744-4111
Fax: (312)744-1081
Web: www.ci.chi.il.us
Chr./Comm.: Clarence N. Wood
Man.g. Deputy Comm.: Kenneth Gunn
Founded: 1946
Serves: All ethnic groups in Chicago
Purpose: To combat discrimination, prejudice and bigotry by enforcing the Chicago Human Rights Ordinance
Programs: Investigation and adjudication of complaints about discrimination in employment, housing, public accommodations, credit and bonding; help for hate-crime victims; community crisis intervention and tension reduction; anti-bias workshops
HRC Advisory Councils:
African Affairs: Arnold Romeo, director (312)774-1543
Arab Affairs: Salameh (Sam) Zanayed, director (312)744-4115
Asian Affairs: vacant (312)744-4479
Immigrant & Refugee Affairs: Hayelom Ayele, dir. (312)744-1098
Latino Affairs: vacant (312)744-4119
Volunteers: Welcome

Cook County Commission
on Human Rights
69 W. Washington St., Suite 2900
Chicago, IL 60602
Phone: (312)603-1100
Evening/weekend: same (voice mail)
Fax: (312)603-9988

Exec. Dir.: Jennifer Vidis
Chr.: William B. Kelley
Founded: 1993
Serves: All ethnic groups, in Cook County
Purpose: To enforce ordinance prohibiting discrimination in employment, housing, credit and public accommodations in Cook County
Programs: Civil rights law enforcement, educational programs on preventing harassment and discrimination, civil rights compliance and improving intergroup relations
Volunteers: Welcome

Illinois Dept. of Human Rights
100 W. Randolph St., Suite 10-100
Chicago, IL 60601
Phone: (312)814-6200
Fax: (312)814-6251
Web: www.state.il.us/dhr/
Exec. Dir.: Carlos J. Salazar
Dep. Dir.: Helen Jett
Serves: All residents of Illinois
Purpose To investigate charges alleging discrimination against people based on race, religion, color sex and any other bases that prevent equal rights and opportunities
Programs: Investigation, seminars, speakers, translating
Volunteers: Welcome

Illinois Department of Human Services, Refugee & Immigrant Services
401 S. Clinton
Chicago, IL 60607
Phone: (312)793-7120
Fax: (312)793-2281
e-mail: esilverman@dhs.state.il.us
or erech@dhs.state.il.us
Manager: Edwin B. Silverman
Asst. to Mgr.: Carol Rech
Founded: 1976
Serves: South East Asians, people from the former USSR, Bosnians, Latinos, Ethiopians and others
Purpose: To expedite resettlement and facilitate citizenship
Programs: Counseling, employment, adjustment, instruction, health and mental health

Immigration and Naturalization Service
10 W. Jackson
Chicago, IL 60604
Phone: (312)385-1500
Fax: (312)385-3400
Web: www.insdoj.gov
Dist. Dir.: Brian Perryman
Serves: Immigrants and others in Chicago and Illinois
Purpose: To effectively enforce the Immigration and Nationality Act and to provide responsive service and benefits to the general public
Programs: Processing and adjudication of immigrant and nonimmigrant petitions from aliens residing in the U.S. and relatives abroad; naturalization of lawful permanent residents to U.S. citizenship; facilitation of assimilation of legal immigrants; first line of defense against illegal immigration, including smuggling of aliens, companies that knowingly hire illegal aliens workers, criminal aliens and fraudulent immigration document rings

Ethnic media

African American

African-American Reader
7732 S. Cottage Grove
Chicago, IL 60619
Phone: (773)783-3850
Fax: (773)783-3228
Publisher: Sam Henderson
Editor: Sam Henderson
Started: 1992
Published: Monthly
Circulation: 10,000
Cost: 35 cents
Distributed: Subscription and newsstands on
Southeast Side and suburbs
Editorial focus: Community news
Language: English

Afrique
6167 N. Broadway, Suite 200
Chicago, IL 60660
Phone: (773)743-3200
Fax: (773) 743-3610
Publisher: Andrew Eperi
Editor: Jalyne Strong
Started: 1991
Published: Monthly
Circulation: 75,000
Cost: Free
Distributed: Subscription and
newsstands/Chicago, South Africa,
Caribbean, Detroit, Toronto
Editorial focus: Stories connecting and
empowering people of African descent
Language: English

Austin Voice
5236 W. North Ave.
Chicago, IL 60639
Phone: (773)889-0880
Fax: (773)889-5168
Publisher: Isaac Jones
Assoc. Editor: Brad Cummings
Started: 1985
Published: Twice monthly
Circulation: 30,000
Cost: $36
Distributed: West Humboldt Park, Austin,
East and West Garfield, North Lawndale,
Galewood
Editorial focus: Neighborhood news
Language: English

Chicago Crusader
6429 S. King Drive
Chicago, IL 60637
Phone: (773)752-2500
Fax: (773)752-2817
Publisher: Dorothy Leavell
Editor: Dorothy Leavell
Started: 1937
Published: Weekly
Circulation: 67,000
Cost: 25 cents
Distributed: Newsstands and subscriptions
in South Shore, elsewhere in Chicago
Editorial focus: Black community
Language: English

Chicago Daily Defender
2400 S. Michigan Ave.
Chicago, IL 60616
Phone: (312)225-2400
Fax: (312)225-9231
Publisher: Fredrick Sengstacke
Editor: Leroy Thomas
Started: 1905
Published: 5x/week
Circulation: 22,000 daily; 25,000 weekend
Cost: 35 cents weekdays; 50 cents weekend
Distributed: Chicago, north and south
suburbs
Editorial focus: National and local news of
interest to African American community
Language: English

Chicago Shoreland News
11740 S. Elizabeth
Chicago, IL 60643
Phone: (773)568-7091
Fax: (773)928-6056
Publisher: Albert E. Johnson
Editor: Michael A. Johnson
Started: 1972
Published: Weekly
Circulation: 38,000
Cost: 35cents
Distributed: Local businesses and news
stands in Greater Grand Crossing, South
Shore, Chatham, Roseland, Pullman, West
Pullman, Riverdale and Morgan Park.
Editorial focus: Community news
Language: English

Chicago South Shore Scene
7426 S. Constance Ave. or
P.O. Box 49085

Chicago, IL 60649
Phone: (773)363-0441
Fax: same
Publisher: Dr. Claudette McFarland
Editor: Dr. Claudette McFarland
Started: 1955
Published: Weekly
Circulation: 80,000
Cost: 25 cents
Distributed: Southeast Side of Chicago,
from 47th St. south to city limits, between
Lake Michigan and Dan Ryan
Editorial focus: Chicago news
Language: English

Chicago Standard
615 S. Halsted St.
Chicago Heights, IL 60411
Phone: (708)755-5021
Fax: (708)755-5020
e-mail: standardnews@dejaboo.com
Web: www.standardnewspapers.com
Publisher: Lorenzo Martin
Editor: Lorenzo Martin
Started: 1979
Published: Weekly
Circulation: 40,000
Cost: 20 cents; $30/year
Distributed: Far South Side and suburbs
Editorial focus: Community news
Language: English

Citizen Newspapers
412 E. 87th St.
Chicago, IL 60619
Phone: (773)487-7700
Fax: (773)487-7931
Publisher: William Garth
Editor: Brenda Garth
Started: 1965
Published: Weekly
Circulation: 121,000
Cost: 25 cents; $50/year
Distributed: South Side and other parts of
Chicago
Editorial focus: Community news
Language: English

CopyLine
9026 S. Cregier Ave.
Chicago, IL 60617
Phone: (773)375-8127
Fax: (773)375-7461
e-mail: oneononetv@aol.com

Web: http://users.aol.com/oneonone
Pub.: Juanita Bratcher
Editor: Juanita Bratcher
Started: 1990
Published: Monthly
Circulation: NA
Cost: $2; $12/6 months
Distributed: Newsstands in Chicago and
throughout Illinois
Editorial focus: Political
Language: English

Ebony Magazine
820 S. Michigan Ave.
Chicago, IL 60605
Phone: (312)322-9200
Publisher: John H. Johnson
Editor: Lerone Bennett, Jr.
Started: 1945
Published: Monthly
Circulation: 1.9 million
Cost: $2.50/newsstand; $20/year
Distributed: USA and worldwide
Editorial focus: Pictorial history of
successful black AmericansLanguage:
English

Independent Bulletin
2037 W. 95th St.
Chicago, IL 60643
Phone: (773)783-1040
Fax: None
Publisher: Hurley Green
Editor: Hurley Green
Started: 1958
Published: Weekly
Circulation: 61,000
Cost: $20/year
Distributed: At supermarkets, hospitals, drug
stores, banks, etc. on South Side; and by
subscription throughout Chicago
Editorial focus: Community news
Language: English

Jet Magazine
820 S. Michigan Ave.
Chicago, IL 60605
Phone: (312)322-9200
Fax: (312)322-0951
Publisher: John H. Johnson
Editor: Bob Johnson
Started: 1955
Published: Weekly
Circulation: 900,000

Cost: $1.25/newsstand; $38/year
Distributed: USA and worldwide
Editorial focus: News of importance to black community
Language: English

N'DIGO
401 N. Wabash; Suite 534
Chicago, IL 60611
Phone: (312)822-0202
Fax: (312)822-0288
Publisher: Hermene Hartman
Editor: David Smallwood
Started: 1989
Published: Weekly
Circulation: 500,000
Cost: Free
Distributed: Chicago and suburbs
Editorial focus: African American community
Language: English

New Crusader of Chicago
6429 Martin Luther King Dr.
Chicago, IL 60637
Phone: (773)752-2500
Fax: (773) 752-2817
Publisher: Dorothy Leavell
Editor: Dorothy Leavell
Started: 1940
Circulation: NA
Cost: 25 cents
Distributed: Chicago, Gary
Editorial focus: All news in African American community

New Metro News
501 E. 32nd St., Suite 501
Chicago, IL 60616
Phone: (312)791-0880
Fax: None
Publisher: Nate Clay
Editor: Nate Clay
Started: 1961
Published: Weekly
Circulation: 38,000
Cost: 35 cents; $25/year
Distributed: South Side, West Side, near south suburbs
Editorial focus: General news of interest to black community
Language: English

Tri-City Journal
7115 W. North Ave., Suite 308
Oak Park, IL 60302
Phone: (312)346-8123
Fax: (708)660-0860
Publisher: Gloria Sharrieff
Editor: Gloria Sharrieff
Started: NA
Published: Weekly
Circulation: NA
Cost: Free
Distributed: Chicago's South Side: Kenwood, Oakland, South Shore, Woodlawn
Editorial focus: Black community
Language: English

Westside Journal
16618 S. Hermitage
Markham, IL 60426
Phone: (708)333-2210
Fax: (708)339-8769
Publisher: Heruanita McIlvaine
Editor: Heruanita McIlvaine
Started: 1970
Published: Weekly
Circulation: 27,000
Cost: Free
Distributed: West Side
Editorial Focus: Local African American news
Language: English

Windy City Word
5090 W. Harrison St.
Chicago, IL 60644
Phone: (773)378-0261
Fax: (773)378-2408
Publisher: Mary G. Denson
Editor: LaFlora Fryer
Started: 1991
Published: Weekly
Circulation: 10,000
Cost: Free
Distributed: Austin to Halsted, Cermak to Fullerton
Editorial focus: African American community news and culture
Language: English

WBEE (1570 AM)
15700 Campbell
Harvey, IL 60426
Phone: (708)331-7840

Fax: (708)333-2560
Gen. Mgr.: Shelby Moore
Sales Mgr.: Shelby Moore
Pgm. Dir.: Misty Dotson
Type of programming: Jazz, blues, gospel
On air: 24 hours

WGCI (107.9 FM and 1390 AM)
332 S. Michigan Ave., Suite 600
Chicago, IL 60604
Phone: (312)427-4800
Fax: (312)427-7410
Gen. Sales Mgr.: Launa Thompson
Chicago Sales Mgr.: Bill Ryan
AM Pgm. Dir.: Jacquie Haselrig
FM Pgm. Dir.: Elroy Smith
Pub. Affairs Dir.: Val Landon
Serves: Mostly African Americans, some
Hispanics, Caucasians
Type of programming: Mostly music, news,
weather, talk shows; AM is gospel
On air: 24 hours

WVAZ (102.7 FM)
800 S. Wells St.
Chicago, IL 60607
Phone: (312)360-9000
Fax: (312)360-9070
Gen. Mgr.: Donald Moore
Gen. Sales Mgr.: Kirby Kaden
Pub Affairs Dir.: Wanda Wells
Type of programming: Urban adult
contemporary
On air: 24 hours

WVON (1450 AM)
3550 S. Kedzie Ave.
Chicago, IL 60623
Phone: (773)247-6200
Fax: (773)247-3343
Gen. Mgr.: Melody Spann-Cooper
Sales Consultant: Ken Smikle
Exec. Prod.: Keisha Chavers
Pub. Affairs Dir.: Bridget Goins
Type of programming: News, talk, blues,
international and current issues
On air: midnight -1 p.m.

Arab

Al Bostaan Journal
8301 S. Pulaski Road
Chicago, IL 60652

Phone: (773)581-7777
Fax: (773)581-7847
Editor: Ghassan Barakat
Started: 1986
Published: Twice monthly
Circulation: 9,000
Cost: $1 each; $35/year
Distributed: Chicago & USA
Editorial focus: Social and political news
affecting the Arab and Arab-American
community
Language: Arabic & English

Arab Journal
P.O. Box 5095
Woodridge, IL 60517
Phone: (630)964-8975
Fax: (630)964-8975
Publisher: Ali Baghdadi
Editor: Ali Baghdadi
Started: 1994
Publishes: Monthly
Circulation: 10,000
Cost: $1; $35/year
Distributed: Chicago, Northern Indiana &
Milwaukee
Editorial focus: Muslim & Middle East
news; Arab world politics
Language: English and Arabic

Al Mahjar Newspaper
6000 W. 79th St.
Burbank, IL 60459
Phone: (708)233-1303
Fax: (708)233-1302
Publisher: Khaled Dumisi
Editor: Shafik Khalil
Started: 1993
Published: Every two weeks
Circulation: 30,000
Cost: $1
Distributed: 13 states
Editorial focus: Arab community, local
news, homeland news, cultural, history,
literature
Language: Arabic

Chinese

Chinese American News
2166A S. Archer Ave.
Chicago, IL 60616
Phone: (312)225-5600

Fax: (312)225-8849
e-mail: canews@ameritech.net
Publisher: Peter Chiang
Editor: Lisa Su
Started: 1989
Published: Weekly
Circulation: 10,000
Cost: Free
Distributed: Metro Chicago area
Editorial focus: Chinese American
community
Language: Chinese and English

+China Journal
2112-B S. Archer Ave.
Chicago, IL 60616
Phone: (312)326-3228
Fax: (312)326-3503
e-mail: meizg@pcweb.dpliv.com
Publisher: Sum Yang
Edior: May Zheng
Started: 1991
Published: Weekly
Circulation: 12,000
Cost: Free
Distributed: Chicago metro area
Editorial focus: Chinese American news,
events in China and Taiwan, local Chinese
news
Language: Chinese

+Sing Tao Daily
2134B S. China Place
Chicago, IL 60616
Phone: (312)225-5888
Fax: (312)225-8882
e-mail: rebeccaip18@hotmail.com
Web: www.singtao.com
Publisher: Peter Chiang
Editor: Rebecca Ip
Started: 1978
Published: Daily
Circulation: 5,000
Cost: 60 cents
Distributed: Via retailers in Chinese
communities
Editorial focus: Local, national and
international news
Language: Chinese

Czech

Denni Hlasetel
5906 W. 26th St.
Cicero, IL 60804-3120
Phone: (708)863-1891
Fax: (708)863-1893
Publisher: Josef Kucera, Jr.
Editor: Josef Kucera, Sr.
Started: 1891
Published: Bi-weekly
Circulation: 10,000
Cost: $1.50 each; $50/year
Distributed: Newsstands in Chicago and
western suburbs
Editorial focus: Czech news and
Czech/Slovak American news
Language: Czech and Slovak

+Novy Svet (New World)
3086 N. Milwaukee Ave.
Chicago, IL 60618
Phone: (773)545-8872
Fax (773)545-9250
e-mail: waldemar@surfnetcorp.com
Pub.: Contact CS
Editor: Darek Jakubowski
Started: 1996
Published: biweekly
Circulation: 5,000-7,000
Cost: $1.75
Distributed: Newsstands and by subscription
in Chicago and suburbs
Editorial focus: Immigrants to the U.S. and
their experiences here, general interest,
some stories from home
Languages: Czech and Slovak

Danish

Danish Pioneer
(Den Danske Pioneer)
1582 Glen Lake Rd.
Hoffman Estates, IL 60195-3023
Phone: (847)882-2552
Fax: (847)882-7082
e-mail: info@dendanskepioneer.com
Web: www.dendanskepioneer.com
 www.thedanishpioneer.com
(one Danish, one English)
Publisher: Chris Steffensen
Editor: Chris Steffensen

Started: 1872
Published: 26x/year
Circulation: 3,000
Cost: $27.50/year
Distributed: By subscription only in USA,
Denmark, Canada
Editorial focus: Denmark news and politics,
USA coverage
Language: Danish and English

Filipino

Pilipino Weekly
P.O. Box 68593
Schaumburg, IL 60168
Phone: (847)352-3877
Fax: (847)352-3878
Publisher: Orlando P. Bernardino
Editor: Orlando P. Bernardino
Started: 1984
Published: Weekly
Circulation: 15,000
Distributed: In stores and restaurants in
Chicago area
Editorial focus: News of Philippines and
Chicago's Filipino community
Language: 90% English, 10% Tagalog

+Philippine Time-USA Magazine
P.O. Box 6176
Buffalo Grove, IL 60089
Phone: (847)446-5158
Fax: (847)446-5164
e-mail: philtime@aol.com
Web: www.philtime-usa.com
Publisher: Bart, Jr.,and Yolanda Tubalinal
Editor: Bart SG. Tubalinal, Jr.
Started: 1991
Published: Monthly
Circulation: 38,000
Cost: $1.75; $19.95/year by subscription
Distributed: free circulation in Chicago and
suburbs; by subscription outside
Editorial focus: Events in Philippines and
local Filipino news
Languages English, 2-page Pilipino section

VIA Times
P.O. Box 138155
Chicago, IL 60613
Phone: (773)866-0811
Fax: (773)866-9207
Publisher: Veronica Leighton

Editor: Veronica Leighton
Started: 1984
Published: Monthly
Circulation: 50,000-60,000
Cost: Free
Distributed: Chicago and suburbs
Editorial focus: Filipino-Asian community
Language: Filipino and English

German

Amerika-Woche
4732 N. Lincoln Ave.
Chicago, IL 60625
Phone: (773)275-5054
Fax: (773)275-0596
Publisher: Mario Schiefelbein
Editor: Mario Schiefelbein
Started: 1972
Published: Weekly
Circulation: 25,000
Cost: $1.50
Distributed: In stores and by subscription in
Chicago metro area and other states
Editorial focus: News of Germany and local
German American club news, travel
Language: German

Eintracht
9456 N. Lawler Ave.
Skokie, IL 60077-1290
Phone: (847)677-9456
Fax: (847)677-9471
Publisher: Walter & Klaus Juengling
Editor: Walter & Klaus Juengling
Started: 1923
Published: Weekly
Circulation: 25,000
Cost: $35/year
Distributed: By subscription in Chicago and
suburbs, other states and overseas
Editorial focus: World political news,
sports, happenings in German American
circles
Language: German

German American Journal
4740 N. Western Ave
Chicago, IL 60625
Phone: (773)275-1100
Fax: (773)275-4010
e-mail: ganc@earthlink.net
Web: www.dank.org

Publisher: German American National
Congress
Editor: Ernst Ott
Started: Around 1960
Published: Monthly
Circulation: 18,000
Cost: Free to members
Distributed: Nationwide
Editorial focus: Organization news, news
affecting German Americans, history,
culture
Language: German

Greek

Greek Press
810 W. Jackson Blvd.
Chicago, IL 60607
Phone: (630)766-2955
Fax: (630)766-3069
Publisher: Peter A. Palivos
Editor: Mrs. Aris Angelopoulos
Started: 1911
Published: Twice monthly
Circulation: 13,000
Cost: $20/year
Distributed: By subscription only in Chicago
and suburbs, and surrounding states
Editorial focus: News pertaining to Greek
American community
Language: 99% English, 1% Greek

Greek Star
4710 N. Lincoln Ave.
Chicago, IL 60625
Phone: (773)878-7331
Fax: (773)878-0959
Publisher: UHAC Communications
Editor: Diane Lymberopoulos
Started: 1905
Published: Weekly
Circulation: 7,800
Cost: $30/year
Distributed: By subscription only
Editorial focus: Local Greek American
community
Language: English

Hispanic/Latino

+El Columbiano Newspaper
4765 N. Lincoln Ave.
Chicago, IL 60625
Phone: (773)784-0072
Fax: (773)784-7518
e-mail: alegaceta@aol.com
Publisher: Alvaro Londono
Editor: Alvaro Londono
Started: 1975
Published: Monthly
Circulation: 5,000
Cost: Free
Distributed: Spanish stores in Chicago,
suburbs and part s of Indiana
Editorial focus: Local and national news in
Hispanic communities
Language: Spanish

+El Conquistador
64 E. Downer Pl.
Aurora, IL 60505
Phone: (630)892-9691
Fax: (630)892-9697
e-mail: elconquistador@juno.com
Web: www.conquistadornewspaper.com
Publisher: Laura C. Barth
Editor: Laura C. Barth
Started: 1992
Publishes: Twice monthly
Circulation: 15.000
Distributed: Free through Spanish-speaking
churches, stores, ESL classes, social
services, professional offices and athletic
leagues in Aurora, Joliet and Northwest
suburban areas; also paid subscribers
Editorial focus: Local news involving
Hispanics and news of interest to Hispanic
community
Languages: English and Spanish

El Dia
4818 W. 23rd Place
Cicero, IL 60650
Phone: (708)652-6397
Fax: (708)652-6653
Publisher: Jorge Montes deOca
Editor: Ana Maria Ugalde
Adv. Dir.: Ana Maria Montes deOca
Started: 1984
Published: Weekly
Circulation: 45,000

Cost: 25 cents door-to-door
Distributed: Newsstands and businesses in Chicago and west suburbs
Editorial focus: National and local Hispanic community
Language: 70% Spanish, 30% English

Espectaculos Magazine
2051 W. Cermak Road
Chicago, IL 60608
Phone: (312)523-7356
Fax: (312) 523-8265
Publisher: Ramon DeAnda
Editor: Ramon DeAnda
Started: 1987
Publishes: 4-6x/year
Circulation: 2,500-5,000
Cost: $2.50
Distributed: Businesses in Chicago and suburbs
Editorial focus: Latino community: problems and politics
Language: Spanish

Exito
820 N. Orleans St., Suite 400
Chicago, IL 60610
Phone: (312)654-3004
Fax: (312)654-3029
e-mail: Exito@tribune.com
Publisher: Liza Gross
Editor: Alejandro Escalona
Started: 1993
Publishes: Weekly
Circulation: 85,000
Cost: Free
Distribution: Street boxes in Hispanic neighborhoods in city and suburbs
Coverage: Hispanic local news, entertainment, national news, opinions
Language: Spanish

Extra
3918 W. North Ave.
Chicago, IL 60647
Phone: (773)252-3534
Fax: (773)252-6031
e-mail: Editor@EXTRA.clrs.com
Publisher: Mila Tellez
Assoc. Publisher: Steve Weimer
Editor: Janet Kownacki
Started: 1980
Publishes: Weekly
Circulation: 72,000

Cost: Free
Distributed: Boxes in Chicago, suburbs
Editorial focus: Community news
Language: Spanish and English

El Imparcial
3615 W. 26th St., 2nd Floor
Chicago, IL 60623
Phone: (708)484-1188
Fax: (708) 484-0202
Publisher: Alicia Santelices
Editor: Alicia Santelices
Started: 1986
Publishes: Weekly
Circulation: 30,000
Cost: Free
Distributed: Supermarkets banks, clinics, restaurants and street boxes in Chicago, Berwyn, Cicero, Melrose Park
Editorial focus: Local news, sports, art; national and international news
Language: Spanish

Lawndale News
5416 W. 25th St.
Cicero, IL 60804
Phone: (708)656-6400
Fax: (708)656-2433
Publisher: Linda Nardini
Editor: Daniel Nardini
Started: 1949
Published: Twice a week
Circulation: 270,000
Cost: Free
Distributed: Chicago and suburbs
Editorial focus: Community
Language: English and Spanish

+Nuevo Siglo
3701 S. Paulina
Chicago, IL 60609
Phone: (773)890-1656
Fax: (773)890-2467
e-mail: NuevoSiglo@worldnet.att.net
Publisher: Ezequiel Banda Sifuentes
Editor: León Ramírez
Started: 1996
Publishes:
Circulation: 20,000
Cost: Free in Chicago and nearest suburbs, $30/year for subscription
Distributed: Stores, banks, etc.
Editorial focus: Community issues, local and national news

Language: Spanish

La Opinion
2508 E. East Ave.
Berwyn, IL 60402
Phone: (708)795-1383
Publisher: Felix Caceres
Editor: Felix Caceres
Started: 1978
Publishes: Weekly
Circulation: 15,000-20,000
Cost: Free
Distributed: Chicago and suburbs
Editorial focus: Community news
Language: Spanish and English

+Enlightening the Family
2435 W. Division St.
Chicago, IL 60622
Phone: (773)772-1141
Fax: (773)772-5933
Publisher: Ruth R. Mercado
Editor: Ruth R. Mercado
Started: 1989
Publishes: Monthly
Circulation: 10,000
Cost: Free
Distributed: Chicago and suburbs
Editorial focus: Spanish community news
Language: Spanish

El Pueblo
2408 S. Western Ave.
Chicago, IL 60608
Phone: (773)523-4166/(773)523-7666
Fax: (773) 523-1145
Publisher: Socorro Grajeda
Editor: Socorro Grajeda
Started: 1987
Publishes: Weekly
Circulation: 20,000
Cost: Free
Distributed: Chicago
Editorial focus: Community news
(Pilsen/Little Village)
Language: Spanish and English

La Raza
3909 N. Ashland Ave.
Chicago, IL 60613
Phone: (312)525-1763
Fax: (312)525-7747
e-mail: editorial@laraza.com
Web: www.laraza.com

Publisher: Luis H. Rossi
Editor in Chief: Elbio Rodríguez Barilari
Started: 1971
Publishes: Weekly
Circulation: 175,000
Cost: 25 cents
Distributed: Chicago and suburbs
Editorial focus: Local, nation, international
news; cultural section, including monthly
magazine, Arena Cultural
Language: Spanish & English

Tele Guia de Chicago
3116 S. Austin
Cicero, IL 60804
Phone: (708)656-6666
Fax: (708)656-6679
Publisher: Zeke Montes
Editor: Rose Montes
Started: 1985
Publishes: Weekly
Circulation: 20,000
Cost: 30 cents
Distributed: Chicago and some suburbs
Editorial focus: Spanish entertainment
Language: Spanish

La Voz de Chicago
8624 S. Houston
Chicago, IL 60617
Phone: (773)221-9416
Fax: (773)221-4798
Publisher: Thomas Alvarez
Editor: Thomas Alvarez
Started: 1979
Publishes: Weekly
Circulation: 20,000
Cost: 25 cents
Distributed: Chicago and suburbs
Editorial focus: International news, Spanish-
American community news, and to motivate
the community to become politically active
Language: Spanish and English

WGBO (Ch. 66)
541 N. Fairbanks Ct., Suite 1100
Chicago, IL 60611
Phone: (312)670-1000
Fax: (312)494-6492
V.P., Gen. Mgr.: Bert Medina
Comm. Affairs Dir.: Luisa Echevarria
Language: Spanish,
Type of programming: News, entertainment
On air: 24 hours

WIND (560 AM)
625 N. Michigan Ave., 3rd floor
Chicago, IL 60611
Phone: (312)751-5560
Fax: (312)664-2472
Gen. Mgr.: James Pagliai
Sales Mgr.: Jim Allen
Pgm. Dir.: Juan Silverio Diaz
Pub. Affairs Dir.: Morton Campbell
Language: Spanish
Type of programming: Spanish music
On air: 24 hours

WLEY (107.9 FM)
150 N. Michigan Ave., Suite 1040
Chicago, IL 60601
Phone: (312)920-9500
Fax: (312)920-9515
Gen. Mgr.: Mario Paez
Sales Mgrs. Raul Chavarria, Mark Garry
Pgm. Dir.: Margarita Vazquez
Pub. Affairs Dir.: Sonia Rodriguez
Language: Spanish
Type of programming: Regional Mexican
music
On air: 24 hours

WLXX (1200 AM)
625 Michigan Ave., Suite 300
Chicago, IL 60611
Phone: (312)738-1200
Fax: (312)654-0092
Gen. Mgr.: Jim Pagliai
Sales Mgr.: David Martinez
Pgm. Dir.: Marilyn Santiago
Pub. Affairs Dir.: Marilyn Santiago
Language: Spanish
Type of programming: Spanish music
On air: 24 hours

WOJO (105.1 FM)
625 N. Michigan Ave.
Chicago, IL 60611
Phone: (312)649-0105
Fax: (312)664-2472
Gen. Mgr.: Jim Pagliai
Sales Mgr.: Jim Allen
Pgm. Dir.: Veronica Medina
Language: Spanish
Type of programming: Spanish music
On air: 24 hours

+W0NX Spanish Radio (1590AM)
4357 N. Lincoln Ave.
Chicago, IL 60618-1741
Phone: (773)296-0292
Fax: (773)296-0385
e-mail: Espectaculares@yahoo.com
Gen. Mgr.: Ken Kovas
News Dir.: German Salazar
Pgm. Dir.: Omar Ariza
Pub. Aff.. Dir.: Marychuy Miranda
Language: Spanish
Type of programming: Contemporary
music, news and variety
On air: 24 hours

WSNS-TV (Ch. 44)
430 W. Grant Place
Chicago, IL 60614
Phone: (773)929-1200
Fax: (773)929-8153
Sta. Mgr.: David Cordova
Pgm. Dir.: Martha Muniz
Pub. Affairs Dir.: Martha Muniz
Languages: English and Spanish
Type of programming: News, talk, public
service
On air: 5 a.m.-3:30 a.m.

WRZA (99.9 FM) and
WZCH (103.9 FM)
851 W. Grand Ave.
Chicago, IL 60622
Phone: (312)633-3800
Fax: (312)733-2214
Gen. Mgr.: Ricky Tatum
Sales Mgr.: Felix Villa
Language: Spanish
Type of programming: Regional Mexican
music
On air: 24 hours

Indian

+India Post
2335 W. Devon Ave., #203
Chicago, IL 60659
Phone: (773)973-7394
Fax: (773)973-7396
SRamesh@aol.com
Publisher: Dr. Romesh Japra
Editor: Ramesh Soparawala
Started: 1995
Published: Weekly

Circulation: 35,000
Cost: $25 year
Editorial focus: News of India and Indians in the USA, Info-USA relations, Asian community and minority community
Distributed: By mail/retail in Chicago area and across Midwest
Language: English

India Tribune
3302 W. Peterson Ave.
Chicago, IL 60659
Phone: (773)588-5077
Fax: (773)588-7011
Publisher: Prashant Shah
Editor: Prashant Shah
Started: 1977
Published: Weekly
Circulation: 63,000
Cost: 60 cents/ issue, $26/year
Distributed: USA
Editorial focus: News of India and Indian community in the USA
Language: English

Chitrahar Broadcasting
220 S. State St., Suite 400
Chicago, IL 60604
Phone: (312)986-9000
Fax: (312)431-1310
Web: www.chitrahar.com
Producer/Dir.: Vichitra Nayyar
Exec. Prod.: Anjali Nayyar-Julka
Pub. Rel.: Amrish K. Mahajan
Type of programming: Cultural, educational, news and entertainment from South Asia
Language: English, Hindi, Urdu
On air: Thurs., Sat. and Sun. on different channels in city and suburbs

Irish

Irish American News
503 S. Oak Park Ave., Suite 205
Oak Park, IL 60304
Phone: (708)445-0700
Fax: (708) 445-0784
E-mail: irishnwz@flash.net
Publisher: Cliff Carlson
Editor: Cliff Carlson
Started: 1964
Published: Monthly
Circulation: 10,000

Cost: $1
Distributed: Chicago area 95%
Editorial focus: Local news and current events for the Irish community, poetry, sports, entertainment, history, books
Language: English

Italian

Fra Noi
3800 Division
Stone park, IL 60165
Phone: (708)338-0690
Fax: (708)338-0699
e-mail: franoinews@aol.com
Publisher: Anthony Fornelli
Editor: Paul Basile
Started: 1961
Published: Monthly
Circulation: 10,000
Cost: $18/year, $31/2 years
$42/3 years
Distributed: Metropolitan Chicago
Editorial focus: Italian American accomplishments, news and issues
Language: English and Italian

Japanese

Chicago Shimpo
4670 N. Manor Ave.
Chicago, IL 60625
Phone: (773)478-6170
Fax: (773)478-9360
e-mail: shimpo@mc.net
Publisher: Akiko Sugano
Editor: Akiko Sugano (Japanese)
Started: 1945
Published: Wed. and Fri.
Circulation: 5,000
Cost: 75 cents
Distributed: Stores in Chicago
Editorial focus: Local news and national news affecting the local community, international news from Japan
Language: Japanese and English

Jewish

Chicago Jewish News
2501 W. Peterson
Chicago, IL 60659
Phone: (773)728-3636
Fax: (773)728-3734
e-mail: ChiJewNes@aol.com
Editor/Publisher: Joseph Aaron
Mng. Ed.: Pauline Dubkin Yearwood
Started: 1994
Publishes: Weekly
Circulation: 13,000
Cost: $1/issue; $25/year, $40/2 years
Distributed: Chicago and suburbs
Editorial focus: Jewish community in
Chicago; national and international
Jewish news
Language: English

JUF News
1 S. Franklin St.
Chicago, IL 60606-4694
Phone: (312)357-4848
Fax: (312)855-2470
Publisher: Jewish United Fund
Sr. V.P.: Michael Kotzin
Editor: Aaron B. Cohen
Started: NA
Published: Monthly
Circulation: NA
Cost: Free
Distributed: By mail to those who contribute
$10 to Jewish United Fund
Editorial focus: Chicago's Jewish
community and Israel
Language: English

Chicago Jewish Star
P.O. Box 268
Skokie, IL 60076-0268
Phone: (847)674-STAR
Fax: (847)674-0014
e-mail: chicago-jewish-star@mcimail.com
Publisher: Star Media Group, Inc.
Editor: Douglas Wertheimer
Started: 1990
Published: Every 2 weeks
Circulation: 24,500
Cost: Free
Distributed: Metro Chicago area
Editorial focus: Jewish community news in
Chicago and general international news

Language: English

Korean

Donga Daily News
4635 W. Lawrence Ave.
Chicago, IL 60630
Phone: (773)282-5533
Fax: (773)282-1106
e-mail: chgoilbo@mcs.net
Publisher: Suk Soon Lee
Editor: Kyusuk Chung
Gen. Mgr.: Peter Lee
Started: 1990
Published: Daily Mon.-Sat.
Circulation: 20,000
Cost: 50 cents, $15/month, $140/ year
Distributed: By mail and at newsstands in
Midwest
Editorial focus: Korean American and
Korean news
Language: Korean (Adv. also in Eng.)

Korea Times of Chicago
4447 N. Kedzie Ave.
Chicago, IL 60625
Phone: (773)463-1050
Fax: (773)267-3336
e-mail: Koreatimes@insnet.com
Publisher: Yong W. Kim
Editor: Kwang Dong Jo
Started: 1971
Published: Daily Mon.-Sat.
Circulation: 15,000
Cost: 50 cents, $15/month
Distributed: Midwest
Editorial focus: Korean and American news
Language: Korean

Korea Central Daily News
4546 N. Kedzie
Chicago, IL 60625
Phone: (773)583-2770
Fax: (773)583-9626
Publisher: Gwang-ho Jang
Editor: Yong-Il Kim
Started: NA
Published: Daily Mon.-Sat.
Circulation: 30,000
Cost: $80/6 months, $15/month
$160/year
Distributed: Midwest
Editorial focus: Korean and Korean-

American news
Language: Korean

The Korean Christian Journal
5235 N. Elston Ave.
Chicago, IL 60630
Phone: (773)777-7779
Fax: (773)777-0004
Publisher: Samuel Park
Editor: Samuel Park
Started: 1978
Published: Weekly
Circulation: 5,000
Cost: $50/year
Distributed: USA
Editorial focus: Christian
Language: Korean and English

**+Korean Christian Television
System of Chicago**
4001 W. Devon Ave., #506
Chicago, IL 60646
Phone: (773)202-0495
Fax: (773)202-0497
Prog. Dir.: Jai Ryong Park
Type programming: Christian
Language: Korean
On air: 10-11 p.m. daily on WFDT Ch. 23

Korean News of Chicago
5695 N. Lincoln Ave.
Chicago, IL 60659
Phone: (773)561-0200
Fax: (773)561-2622
Publisher: Won Jeong
Editor: Wonsik Kim
Started: 1986
Published: Weekly
Circulation: 10,000
Cost: $3/month or $32/year
Distributed: Mailed to Chicago and suburbs
Editorial focus: Korean community in USA
Language: Korean

**Chicago Korean Broadcasting, Inc.
(1330 AM)**
4449 N. Kedzie
Chicago, IL 60625
Phone: (773)463-1125
Fax: (773)463-1164
Gen. Mgr.: Jay Kim
News Dir.: Jay Kim
Hours on air: 9 a.m.-5 p.m. Monday
through Friday

Editorial focus: News, pop music,
relationships show
Language: Korean
On air: 9 a.m.-5 p.m. Mon.-Fri.

**Korean Christian Broadcasting System
(103.1 FM KCDS)**
5817 W. Dempster Ave.
Morton Grove, IL 60053
Phone: (847)583-0191
Gen. Mgr.: Peter Choi
Pgm. Dir.: Hyun S. Kim
Focus: Christian Broadcast to Korean people
Language: Korean
Hours on air: 7-9 a.m. daily, 5-8 p.m. Mon.-
Fri.

KBC-TV (WOCH-LP Ch. 28)
5225 N. Kedzie, Suite 200
Chicago, IL 60625
Phone: (773)588-0070
Fax: (773)588-8750
e-mail: kbchami@aol.com
Gen. Mgr.: Myung Hwa Bae
News Dir.: Myng H. Han
Prog. Dir.: Chang R. Choi
Pub. Affairs: Young Hwan Kim
Type of programming: Drama and news
Language: Korean
Hours on air: 12 hours a day

Lithuanian

Draugas
4545 W. 63rd St.
Chicago, IL 60629
Phone: (773)585-9500
Fax: (773)585-8284
Publisher: Lithuanian Catholic Press Society
Editor in Chief: Danute Bindokas
Started: 1909
Published: Daily Tues.-Sat.
Circulation: 6,000
Cost: $100/year
Distributed: Worldwide
Editorial focus: Catholic-oriented, politics,
religion, community in USA and elsewhere
Language: Lithuanian

Sandara
P.O. Box 241
Addison, IL 60101
Phone: (630)543-8198

Fax: same
Publisher: Sandara
Editor: G. J. Lazauskas
Started: 1914
Published: Every other month
Circulation: 1,200
Cost: $10/year
Distributed: USA and Europe
Editorial focus: Worldwide Lithuanian
community
Language: Lithuanian and English

Pakistani

Pakistan Journal of Chicago
c/o Atique Mahmood
3231B W. Lake Ave.
Glenview, IL 60025
Phone: (847)657-7257, (847)778-1721
Fax: (847)657-7257
e-mail: Pakjournal@aol.com
Web:www.coloron.net
Publisher: Atique Mahmood
Editor: Atique Mahmood
Started: 1992
Published: Every two weeks
Circulation: 15,000
Cost: 25 cents
Distributed: Metro Chicago and some
national
Editorial focus: Pakistani community and
general world news
Language: English

The Pakistani
P.O. Box 25870
Chicago, IL 60625
Phone: (630)483-9460
Fax: (630)837-4652
e-mail: thepakistani@ameritech.net
Publisher: Hafiz Mohammad Siddiq Anwar
Editor: Zafar Iqbal
Started: 1984
Published: Daily
Circulation: 9,500
Cost: Free
Distributed: Chicago and surrounding
suburbs,also mailed to USA and Canada
Editorial focus: Pakistani and Muslim
communities
Language: Urdu and English

Urdu Times
6403 N. Oakley
Chicago, IL 60645
Phone: (773)274-3100
Fax: (773)274-9490
Publisher: Mohammad Tariq
Editor: Irshad Hussain
Published: Weekly
Circulation: 30,000
Cost: NA
Distributed: USA
Editorial Focus: Pakistan and Islam
Language: Urdu

Polish

Alfa
4854 W. Addison St.
Chicago, IL 60641
Phone: (773)283-1155
Fax: (773)283-3742
Publisher: Boguslaw Boczarski
Editor: Same
Started: 1988
Publishes: Weekly
Circulation: 17,000
Cost: $2
Distributed: USA, Canada, Germany
Editorial focus: Entertainment news, not
limited to Polish community
Language: Polish

Dziennik Chicagowski
5242 W. Diversey
Chicago, IL 60639
Phone: (773)685-1281
Fax: (773)685-7762
Publisher: Chemigraph Company
Editor: Michael Kuchejda
Started: 1990
Publishes: Daily Mon.-Fri.
Circulation: 40,000 on Friday
Cost: 50 cents/Mon.-Thurs.,
$1/Friday
Distributed: Worldwide
Editorial focus: International Polish
community
Language: Polish

Dziennik Zwiazkowy
(Polish Daily News)
5711 N. Milwaukee Ave.
Chicago, IL 60646
Phone: (773)763-3343
Fax: (773)763-3825
e-mail: polish@popmail.insnet.com
Web: www.polishdailynewes.com
Publisher: Edward J. Moskal
Editor: Wojciech Bialasiewicz
Started: 1908
Published: Daily Mon.-Fri.
Circulation: 25,000
Cost: 50 cents Mon.-Thurs., $1 on Friday,
$80/year
Distributed: Chicago and suburbs and by
subscription worldwide
Editorial focus: General news, editorials,
Polish American community, literature,
history, arts, sports
Inserts: Kalejdoskop, Dziennik Sportowy
Language: Polish

+Monitor
6204 N. Milwaukee Ave.
Chicago, IL 60646
Phone: (773)594-9854
Fax: (773)594-0281
e-mail: monitor@monitorpl.com
Web: www.monitorpl.com
Publisher: Monitor Publishing Co.
Editor: Jacek Zaworski
Started: 1993
Publishes: Monthly
Circulation: 20,000
Cost: Free
Distributed: Chicago and suburbs, Indiana
Editorial focus: Business information and
law advice for Poles living in the U.S.
Language: Polish

Narod Polski
984 Milwaukee Ave.
Chicago, IL 60622
Phone: (773)278-3210
Fax: (773)278-4595
e-mail: KRosypal@prcua.org
Web: www.prcua.org
Publisher: Polish Roman Catholic Union of
America
Editor: Kathryn Rosypal
Started: 1873
Publishes: Twice a month
Circulation: 27,000

Cost: Free for members
Distributed: USA
Editorial focus: Polish community in USA,
Polish traditions, culture, history
Language: Polish and English

Nowe Zycie Magazine
7015 W. Diversey Ave.
Chicago, IL 60607
Phone: (773)637-7312
Fax: (773)637-7430
Publisher: Nowe Zycie Association
Editor: Roman Harmata
Started: 1991
Publishes: Every two weeks
Circulation: 2,000-3,000
Cost: $2
Distributed: Chicago and suburbs; 14 states,
Canada, Poland
Editorial focus: Polish community, religion
Language: Polish and English

Panorama
3104 N. Cicero Ave.
Chicago, IL 60641
Phone: (773)685-0406
Fax: (773)763-0503
Publisher: Stanislaw Pochron
Editor: Stanislaw Pochron
Started: 1982
Published: Weekly
Circulation: 6,000
Cost: $1.25
Distributed: USA
Editorial focus: Polish culture, social events,
Poland and USA Polish community
Language: Polish

Polonia Today
6348 N. Milwaukee Ave., PMB 360
Chicago, IL 60646
Phone: (773)763-1646
Fax: same
e-mail: TRonjh@pipeline.com
Web:www.poloniatoday.com
Publisher: Anglo Pol Corporation
Editor: T. Ron Jasinski-Herbert
Started: 1911
Published: Monthly
Circulation: 17,000
Cost: $1.50/issue, $13.50/year
Distributed: Worldwide (95% in USA)
Editorial focus: Poland and Polish
community worldwide

Language: English

Relax
5242 W. Diversey
Chicago, IL 60639
Phone: (773)685-1281
Fax: (773)685-7762
Publisher: Chemigraph Company
Editor: Michael Kuchejda
Started: 1981
Publishes: Weekly
Circulation: Varies
Cost: $2.20/ issue
Distributed: Worldwide
Editorial focus: Advice, entertainment
Language: Polish

Zgoda Magazine
6100 N. Cicero Ave.
Chicago, IL 60646
Phone: (773)286-0500, ext. 367
Fax: (773)286-0842
Publisher: Polish National Alliance
Editor: Wojciech Wierzewski
Started: 1881
Publishes: Twice a month
Circulation: 65,000
Cost: Free for members
Distributed: Nationwide
Editorial focus: PNA and the Polish
community
Language: English and Polish

WNVR (1030 AM)
4320 Dundee Road
Northbrook, IL 60062
Phone: (847)498-3350
Fax: (847)498-5743
e-mail: pclradio@techinter.com
Web: www.plcradio.com
Gen. Mgr.: Kent Gustafson
Ad. Mgr.: Zofia Oraviec
Pub. Affairs Dir.: Kamila Dworska
Language: Polish
Type of programming: Entertainment and
public issues
On air: 24 hours

Russian

Chicago Pravda
747 Lake Cook Road, Suite 104W
Deerfield, IL 60015

Phone: (847)205-7838
Fax: (847)205-7840
Publisher: Svet Publishing House
Editor: Alexander Etman
Started: NA
Publishes: Biweekly
Circulation: USA
Cost: Free
Editorial focus: Local and foreign news
Language: Russian

Compatriots
2921 W. Devon Ave.
Chicago, IL 60659
Phone: (773)761-0065, (773)267-1387
Fax: same
Publisher: Association Zemliaky
Editor: Irene Polyakova
Founded: 1996
Published: Twice a month
Circulation: 8,000
Cost: Free
Distributed: Mainly in stores, in Chicago
and suburbs
Editorial focus: News from the former
Soviet Union, news about immigrants from
those countries, readers' stories
Language: Russian

For You
2921 W. Devon Ave.
Chicago, IL 60659
Phone: (773)761-0002
Fax: (773)761-0065
Publisher: Valanna Humanity Association
Editor: Valery Kavunovsky
Started: 1993
Published: Monthly
Circulation: 5,000
Cost: $1
Distributed: Chicago and suburbs
Editorial focus: USA news, Russian
community events, world news, Russian
literature
Language: Russian

Obzor
1920 Waukegan Road, Suite 213
Glenview, IL 60060
Phone: (847)724-9870
Fax: (847)724-9860
Publisher: Obraz Publishing Co.
Editor: Igor Tsesarsky
Gen. Mgr.: Gene Kaplan

Started: 1997
Published: Weekly
Circulation: Flexible
Cost: Free
Distributed: Russian network
Editorial focus: News, social life, sports
Language: Russian

Reklama
4868 W. Dempster, 2nd floor
Skokie, IL 60077
Phone: (847)679-6762
Fax: (847)679-6770
Publisher: Vlad Verekin
Editor: Vlad Verekin
Started: 1992
Published: Weekly
Circulation: 45,000
Cost: Free
Distributed: Chicago and suburbs
Editorial focus: Russian community in USA;
world news and sports; Russian literature
and art
Language: Russian

Saturday Plus
747 Lake Cook Road, Suite 104W
Deerfield, IL 60015
Phone: (847)205-7838
Fax: (847)205-7840
Publisher: Svet Publishing House
Editor: Alexander Etman
Started: 1996
Published: Weekly
Circulation: 18,000
Cost: Free
Distributed: USA
Editorial focus: Weekend newspaper with
photo stories on rich and famous here and
abroad; helpful hints on where to go and
what to do around Chicago
Language: Russian

Sport Panorama
474 Lake Cook Road, Suite 104W
Deerfield, IL 60015
Phone: (847)205-7838
Fax: (847)205-7840
Publisher: Svet Publishing. House
Editor: Alexander Etman
Started: 1996
Published: Weekly
Circulation: 5,000
Cost: Free

Distributed: USA
Editorial Focus: Weekly recap of major
sports news in hockey, soccer, basketball,
football, tennis ,etc., focusing on
outstanding Russian athletes
Language: Russian

Svet
747 Lake Cook Road, Suite 104W
Deerfield, IL 60015
Phone: (847)205-7838
Fax: (847)205-7840
Publisher: Svet Publishing House
Editor: Alexander Etman
Started: 1992
Published: Daily
Circulation: 15,000
Cost: Free
Distributed: USA
Editorial focus: General world news
Language: Russian

Vremia
747 Lake Cook Road, Suite 104W
Deerfield, IL 60015
Phone: (847)205-7840
Fax: (847)205-7840
Publisher: Svet Publishing House
Editor: Alexander Etman
Started: NA
Published: Weekly
Circulation: 6,500
Distribution: USA
Editorial focus: Law, taxes and personal
finance
Language: Russian

+WKTA 1330 AM
New Life Russian Radio
310 Melvin Dr.
Northbrook, IL 60062
Phone: (847)498-3400
Fax: (847)498-3488
e-mail: nlbc@attmail.com, or
nlbc@prodigy.net
Web: wwwplcradio.com
Gen. Mgr. Nathan Liberman
Program Dir.: Martha Litas
Public Affairs Dir.: Ellen Ostrov
Ethnic groups served: Russian-speaking
nationalities
Type of programming: news and
information, with special programs for all
ages

Language: Russian
Hours on air: 6 a.m.-11p.m. M-
F, 7 a.m.-2 a.m. Sat., 8 a.m.-4 a.m. Sun.

+WSBC (1240AM)
6600 N. Lincoln, Suite 3012
Lincolnwood, IL 60645
Phone(847)677-1503
Fax: (847)677-2463
News Dir. Michael Smekhov
Program Dir.: Lidya Auerbukh
Pub. Aff.airs Dir.: Lidya Auerbukh
Type of programming: Entertainment, local
news, news of Russia
Language: Russia
On air: 7-9 a.m. Mon.-Fri., 11 a.m.-1 p.m
Sat. & Sun.

Serbian

Sloboda
5782 N. Elston Ave.
Chicago, IL 60646
Phone: (773)775-7772
Fax: (773)775-7779
Publisher: Serbian National Defense Council
Editor: Editorial Board of the Council
Published: Twice a month
Circulation: 1,000
Cost: Free to members with $30/year
membership fee
Distributed: By subscription worldwide
Editorial focus: Serbian community
throughout the world, and Serbian culture,
history, literature
Language: Serbian and English

Vietnamese

+Ban Tin
5252 N. Broadway
Chicago, IL 60640
Phone: (773)728-3700
(773)728-0497
e-mail: vietassn@aol.com
Publisher: Vietnamese Assn. of Illinois
Editor: Trung Phan
Started: 1979
Publishes: Monthly
Circulation: 2,000
Cost: Free

Distributed: By bulk-rate mail, hand and
mail delivery
Editorial focus: News from Vietnam and
local Vietnamese news
Language: Vietnamese, with English section

Multi-ethnic

WCEV (1450 AM)
5356 W. Belmont Ave.
Chicago, IL 60641-4103
Phone: (773)282-6700
Fax: (773)282-5930
Gen. Mgr.: Joseph Migala
Sales Mgr.: Herman Rowe
Pgm. Dir.: Lucyna Migala
Pub. Affairs Dir.: Lucyna Migala
Ethnic groups: Croatians,
Czech/Slovak/Moravians, African
Americans, Irish, Lithuanians, Poles,
Serbians, Ukrainians, Arabs, Bulgarians and
others
Languages: Croatian, Czech, English,
Arabic, Bulgarian, Irish, Lithuanian, Polish,
Serbian, Ukrainian and others
Type of programming: Multi-ethnic
On air: 1-10 p.m. weekdays, 1-8:30 p.m.
Sat., 5 a.m. -10 p.m. Sun.

WFBT (Ch. 23)
26 N. Halsted St.
Chicago, IL 60661
Phone: (312)705-2600
Fax: (312)705-2620
Gen. Mgr. Peter Zomaya
Ad. Dir.: Peter Zomaya
Pub. Affairs Dir.: Laurna Czajka
Ethnic groups: Polish, Chinese, Korean,
Russian, Romanian, Assyrian, Indian,
Bulgarian, Filipino, Pakistani, Hispanic,
Ukrainian, Arab, Greek, Croatian,
Lithuanian
Languages: Polish, Chinese, Korean,
Russian, Romanian, Taiwanese, Pakistani,
Spanish, Ukrainian, Hindi, Greek, Arabic,
Assyrian
Type of programming: News, religious,
entertainment, public affairs
On air: 5:30 a.m.-12 a.m.

WKTA (1330 AM)
4320 Dundee Road
Northbrook, IL 60062

Phone: (847)498-3350
Fax: (847)498-5743
Gen. Mgr.: Kent Gustafson
Ad. Mgr.: Bill Wallace
Pub. Affairs Dir.: Grant Hazen
Ethnic Groups: German, Russian, Korean, Filipino
Languages: same
Type of programming: Entertainment and public issues
On air: 24 hours

WONX (1590 AM)
2100 Lee St.
Evanston, IL 60202
Phone: (847)475-1590
Fax: (773)273-1590
Gen. Mgr.: Ken Kovas
Sales Mgr.:Judy Selby
Pgm. Dir.: James Soisui
Pub. Affairs Dir.: James Soisui
Ethnic groups: Hispanic, Assyrian, Russian, Indian, Haitian, Jewish
Languages: Spanish, Assyrian, Russian, Hindi, Haitian, English
Type of programming: Talk, religion, entertainment, public issues
On air: Mon. 5 a.m.-1 a.m.; Tues., Wed., Thurs.: 5 a.m.-midnight; Fri., Sat., Sun. 5 a.m. to 2 a.m.

WPNA (1490 AM)
408 S. Oak Park Ave.
Oak Park, IL 60302
Phone: (708)848-8980
Fax: (708)848-9220
e-mail: wpna@virtualconduit.com
Web: www.wpnaradio.com
Dir. Comm.: Emily Leszczynski
Sales Mgr.: Jerry Obrecki
Pub. Affairs Dir.: Len Petrulis
Ethnic groups: Polish, Ukrainian, Arabic, Irish, African American

Languages: Polish, Ukrainian, Arabic and English
Type of programming: News, weather, sports, talk, polka, gospel, other music, current public issues
On air: 24 hour

WSBC (1240 AM)
5625 N. Milwaukee Ave.
Chicago, IL 60646
Phone: (773)282-9722
Fax: (773)792-2904
Dir. of Op.: Mark Brantner
Pub. Affairs Dir.: Mark Brantner
Ethnic groups: Hispanic, Polish, Greek, Indian, Irish, Thai, Russian, Latvian, Lithuanian, Ukrainian
Languages: Spanish, Polish, Greek, Hindi, Irish, Thai, English, Russian, Urdu
Type of programming: Music, news, religion, public affairs
On air: 24 hours

Foreign consulates

Argentina
205 N. Michigan Ave., Suite 4209
Chicago, IL 60601
Phone: (312)819-2620
Fax: (312)819-2612
Consul General: Cristina Vallina

Austria
400 N. Michigan Ave., Suite 707
Chicago, IL 60611
Phone: (312)222-1515
Fax: (312)222-4113
Consul General: Christian Krepela

Barbados (Honorary Consulate)
220 S. State St., Suite 2200
Chicago, IL 60604
Phone: (773)667-5963
Honorary Consul Gen.: Andre R. King

Belgium
333 N. Michigan Ave., Suite 2000
Chicago, IL 60601
Phone: (312)263-6624
Fax: (312)263-4805
Consul Gen.: RobertVanDeMeulebroucke

Belize (Honorary Consulate)
1200 Howard Dr.
West Chicago, IL 60185
Phone: (630)293-0010
Fax: (630)293-0463
Honorary Consul Gen.: Edwin Smiling

Bolivia (Honorary Consulate)
1111 W. Superior St., Suite 309
Melrose Park, IL 60160
Phone: (708)343-1234
Fax: (708)34304290
Hon. Consul Gen.: Dr. Jaime R. Escobar

Brazil
401 N. Michigan Ave., Suite 3050
Chicago, IL 60611
Phone: (312)464-0245
Fax: (312)464-0299
Consul Gen.: Alexandre Ador Netto

Burundi (Honorary Consulate)
4250 N. Marine Dr., Suite 1021
Chicago, IL 60613
Phone: (773)929-1012
Hon. Consul Gen.: Dr. Jay H. Schmidt

Canada
Two Prudential Plaza
180 N. Stetson Ave., Suite 2400
Chicago, IL 60601
Phone: (312)616-1860
Fax: (312)616-1877
Consul General: J. Christopher Poole

Chile
875 N. Michigan Ave., Suite 3352
Chicago, IL 60611
Phone: (312)654-8780
Fax: (312)654-8989
Consul General: Alberto Labbe

China
100 W. Erie St.
Chicago, IL 60610
Phone: (312)803-0095
Fax: (312)803-0105
Consul General: Wang Li

Colombia
500 N. Michigan Ave., Suite 2040
Chicago, IL 60611
Phone: (312)923-1196
Fax: (312)923-1197
Consul General: Carlos Alfonso Negrit

Costa Rica
185 N. Wabash, Suite 1123
Chicago, IL 60601
Phone: (312)263-2772
Fax: (312)263-5807
Consul General: Juan Salas

Cyprus (Honorary Consulate)
9301 W. Golf Rd.
Des Plaines, IL 60016
Phone: (847)296-0064
Fax: (847)296-4857
Honorary Consul Gen.: Charles Kanakis

Denmark
875 N. Michigan Ave., Suite 3430
Chicago, IL 60611
Phone: (312)787-8780
Fax: (312)787-8744
Consul General: Bent Kiilerich

Dominican Republic (Honorary)
3228 W. North Ave.
Chicago, IL 60647
Phone: (773)772-6363

Honorary Consul Gen.: Ramon J. Rojas

Ecuador
500 N. Michigan Ave., Suite 1510
Chicago, IL 60611
Phone: (312)329-0266
Fax: (312)329-0359
Consul General: Fernando Chaves

Egypt
500 N. Michigan Ave., Suite 1900
Chicago, IL 60611
Phone: (312)828-9162
Consul General: Ates Anwar

El Salvador
104 S. Michigan Ave., Suite 330
Chicago, IL 60603
Phone: (312)332-1393
Fax: (312)332-4446
Consul General: Alfredo Delgado

Finland (Honorary Consulate)
15 Longcommon Rd.
Riverside, IL 60546
Phone: (708)442-0635
Fax: (708)442-0466
Hon. Consul Gen.: Frederick C. Niemi

France
737 N. Michigan Ave., Suite 2020
Chicago, IL 60611
Phone: (312)787-5359
Fax: (312)664-4196
e-mail: chicago@france-consulat.org
Web: www.france-consulat.org/chicago
Consul General: Jean-RenéGehan

Germany
676 N. Michigan Ave., Suite 3200
Chicago, IL 60611
Phone: (312)580-1199
Fax: (312)580-0099
Consul Gen.: Michael Engelhard

Great Britain
400 N. Michigan Ave., Suite 1300
Chicago, IL 60611
Phone: (312)346-1810
Fax: (312)464-0661
Consul General: Robert Culshaw

Greece
650 N. St. Clair St.
Chicago, IL 60611
Phone: (312)335-3915
Fax: (312)335-3958
Consul General: Dabriel Copsidis

Guatemala
200 N. Michigan Ave., Suite 610
Chicago, IL 60601
Phone: (312)332-1587
Fax: (312)332-4256
Consul General: Rosa María Merida

Haiti
220 S. State St., Suite 2110
Chicago, IL 60604
Phone: (312)922-4004
Fax: (312)922-7122
Consul General: Clausel Rosembert

Honduras
4506 W. Fullerton Ave.
Chicago, IL 60639
Phone: (773)472-8726
Fax: (773)342-8293
Consul General: Sylvia Gonzales

Iceland (Honorary Consulate)
221 N. LaSalle St., Suite 1748
Chicago, IL 60601
Phone: (312)782-6872
Fax: (312)782-0121
Hon. Consul Gen.: Paul Sveinbjorn Johnson

India
NBC Tower
455 N. Cityfront Plaza Dr., Suite 850
Chicago, IL 60611
Phone: (312)595-0410
Fax: (312)595-0417
e-mail: congendia@aol.com
Web: www.chicago.indianconsulate.com
Consul General: J.C. Sharma

Indonesia
72 E. Randolph St.
Chicago, IL 60601
Phone: (312)345-9300
Fax: (312)345-9311
Act. Consul General: Saoma Martini

Ireland
400 N. Michigan Ave., Suite 911
Chicago, IL 60611
Phone: (312)337-1868
Fax: (312)337-1954
Consul General: Eamon Hickey

Israel
111 E. Wacker Dr., Suite 1308
Chicago, IL 60601
Phone: (312)565-3300

Jamaica (Honorary Consulate)
28 E. Jackson Blvd., Suite 1009
Chicago, IL 60604
Phone: (312)663-0023
Fax: (312)663-4247
Honorary Consul Gen.: Lloyd L. Hyde

Japan
737 N. Michigan Ave., Suite 1100
Chicago, IL 60611
Phone: (312)280-0400
Fax: (312)280-9568
Consul General: Mitoji Yabunaka

Korea, Republic of
455 N. Cityfront Plaza Dr., Suite 2700
Chicago, IL 60611
Phone: (312)822-9485
Fax: (312)822-9849
Consul General: Jong Kyou Byun

Latvia (Honorary Consulate)
3239 Arnold Lane
Northbrook, IL 60062
Phone (847)498-4525
Fax: (847)498-4526
Honorary Consul Gen.: Norbert Klaucens

Liberia (Honorary Consulate)
7342 S. Bennett
Chicago, IL 60649
Phone: (773)643-8635
Fax: (773)288-8893
Hon. Consul Gen.: Alexander Poley Gbayee

Lithuania
6500 S. Pulaski Rd.
Chicago, IL 60629
Phone: (312)397-0382
Fax: (312)397-0385
Consul Genera;l: Giedrius Apuokas

Fax: (312)565-3871
Consul General: Tzipora Rimon

Italy
500 N. Michigan Ave., Suite 1850
Chicago, IL 60611
Phone: (312)467-1550 or -1556
Fax: (312)297-4855
e-mail: consul@consitchicago.org
Consul General: Enrico Granara

Luxembourg (Honorary Consulate)
1417 Braeburn Court
Wheeling, IL 60090
Phone: (847)520-5995
Fax: (847)520-0842
e-mail: luxconcul@aol.com
Hon. Consul Gen.: Donald John Hansen

Mexico
300 N. Michigan Ave., 4th Floor
Chicago, IL 60601
Phone: (312)855-1380
Fax: (312)855-9257
Consul Gen.: Heriberto M. Galindo
Honorary Consul: Robert L. Steiner

Nepal (Honorary Consulate)
1500 N. Lake Shore Dr.
Chicago, IL 60610
Phone: (312)787-9199
Fax: (312)235-6807
Honorary Consul Gen.: Mary G. Sethness

The Netherlands
303 E. Wacker Dr., Suite 410
Chicago, IL 60601
Phone: (312)856-0110
Fax: (312)856-9218
Consul Gen.: Gilbert Monod de Froideville

New Zealand (Honorary Consulate)
6250 N. River Rd., Suite 9000
Rosemont, IL 60018
Phone: (847)384-5400
Fax: (847)318-4628
Hon. Consul Gen.: Edward A. Burkhardt

Norway (Honorary Consulate)
900 Lively Blvd.
Elk Grove Village, IL 60007
Phone: (847)956-6969
Fax: (847)956-6969

Honorary Consul Gen.: Per Bye Ohrstrom

Peru
180 N. Michigan Ave., Suite 1830
Chicago, IL 60601
Phone: (312)853-6174
Fax: (312)704-6969
Consul General: Manuel Boza

Philippines
30 N. Michigan Ave., Suite 2100
Chicago, IL 60602
Phone: (312)332-6458
Fax: (312)332-3657
Consul General: Emelinda Lee-Bineda

Poland
1530 N. Lake Shore Dr.
Chicago, IL 60610-1695
Phone: (312)337-8166
Fax: (312)337-7841
e-mail: polcon@interaccess.com
Consul General: Ryszard Sarkowicz

Portugal (Honorary Consulate)
1955 N. New England Ave.
Elmwood Park, IL 60707
Phone: (773)889-7405
Hon. Consul Gen.: Dr. Albano D. Coelho

Slovak Republic (Hon. Consulate)
131 W. Jefferson Ave.
Naperville, IL 60540
Phone: (630)548-1944
Fax: (815)838-9877
Honorary Consul: Thomas Klimek Ward

South Africa
200 S. Michigan Ave., Suite 600
Chicago, IL 60604
Phone: (312)939-7929
Fax: (312)939-2588
Consul General: Bella Harrison

Spain
180 N. Michigan Ave., Suite 1500
Chicago, IL 60601
Phone: (312)782-4588
Fax: (312)782-1635
Consul General: Aguirre De Carcer

Sweden (Honorary Consulate)
150 N. Michigan Ave., Suite 1250
Chicago, IL 60601
Phone: (312)781-6262
Fax: (312)781-1816
Honorary Consul Gen.: Thomas R. Bolling

Switzerland
737 N. Michigan Ave., Suite 2301
Chicago, IL 60611-2615
Phone: (312)915-0061
Fax: (312)915-0388
Consul General: Edward Jaun

Thailand
700 N. Rush St.
Chicago, IL 60611
Phone: (312)664-3129
Fax: (3112)664-3230
e-mail: thaichi@interaccess.com
Consul General: Kasivat Paruggamanont

Turkey
360 N. Michigan Ave., Suite 1405
Chicago, IL 60601
Phone: (312)263-0644
Fax: (312)263-1449
Consul General: Yavuz Aktas

Ukraine
10 E. Huron St.
Chicago, IL 60601
Phone: (312)642-4388
Fax: (312)642-4385
Consul General: Victor Kyryk

Uruguay
875 N. Michigan Ave.
Chicago, IL 60611
Phone: (312)642-3430
Fax: (312)642-4470
Consul General: Graziella Reyes

Venezuela
20 N. Wacker Dr., Suite 1925
Chicago, IL 60606
Consul General: Bertha Cabella
Phone: (312)236-9655
Fax: (312)580-1010

Ethnic studies programs
and scholars

American Studies

Chicago State University. African American Studies, Bartley McSwine, chr. (773)995-2487

Columbia College. Center for Black Music Research, Samuel Floyd, dir. (312)663-1600

Loyola University Chicago. Black World Studies, Ayana Karanja, chr. (773)508-3674

Northern Illinois University. Center for Black Studies, LaVerne Gyant, acting dir. (815)753-1709

Northwestern University. African American Studies, Phil Bowman, chr. (847)491-5122

University Of Illinois-Chicago. African American Studies, Sharon Collins, chr. (312)996-2952

Roosevelt University. St. Clair Drake Center for African and African American Studies, Christopher Reed, dir. (312)341-3817

University of Chicago, African and African American Studies, Kenneth Warren and Ralph Austen, co-chrs. (773)702-8344 or -9761, kwarren@midway. uchicago.edu

Asian American Studies

Loyola University Chicago. Asian and Asian American Studies, Yvonne Lau, chr. (773)508-8997

Korean Studies

North Park University. Center for Korean Studies, Ho-Youn Kwon, chr. (773)244-6200

Latino Studies

DePaul University. Center for Latino Research, Félix Masud-Piloto, dir. (773)325-7472

Northern Illinois University. Center for Latino and Latin American Studies, Michael Gonzales, chr. (815)753-1532

Northwestern University. Latin American-Caribbean Studies, Martin Mueller, chr. (847)491-8249, martinmueller@nwu.edu

University Of Illinois-Chicago. Latin American Studies, Rafael Nuñez-Cedeño, chr. (312)996-2445

Native American Studies

Native American Educational Services (NAES) College. Native American Community Studies, David Beck, chr. (773)761-5000

Newberry Library. D'Arcy McNickle Center for American Indian History, Craig Howe, dir. (312)943-9090

Scandinavian Studies

North Park University. Center for Scandinavian Studies, Charles Peterson, dir. (773)244-5619, cip@northpark.edu

Augustana College. Swenson Swedish Immigration Research Center, Dag Blanck, dir. (309)794-7221

Other Programs

Northeastern Illinois University. Center for Inner City Studies, Jacob Carruthers, dir. (773)268-7500

University of Chicago. Center for Study of Race, Politics and Culture, Michael Dawson, dir., Roland Murray, exec. dir. (773)702-806

African American

Wallace Best. African American religious culture, black urban church. Lecturer and doctoral candidate in history at Northwestern University and researcher at Newberry Library. Wrote "The Chicago Defender and the Realignment of Black Chicago," "Passionately Human, No Less Divine: Racial Ideology and Religious Culture in the Black Churches of Chicago, 1915-1955," " Richard Allen and the Rise of the A.M.E. Church in America." (312)255-3571, (773)262-2652, wallaceb@nwu.edu

Timuel Black. History of African Americans in Chicago. Adj. Prof. of African and African American Studies at Roosevelt University, Prof. Emeritus of City Colleges of Chicago. Wrote chapter on African Americans in *The Ethnic Handbook: A Guide to the Cultures and Traditions of Chicago's Diverse Communities.* Forthcoming: *Bridges of Memory* (three generations of African Americans in Chicago). (773)373-3972.

Dr. James Bowman. Genetics, pathology, medicine, medical ethics, sickle cell, malaria. Prof. Emeritus, Depts. of Pathology and Medicine at University of Chicago, and Dir. of Black History Project at U of C. Co-wrote *Genetic Variation and Disorders in Peoples of African Origin;* wrote "Genetics and Racial Minorities," "The Plight of Poor African-Americans: Public Policy on Sickle Hemoglobins and AIDS," "On the Physical and Intellectual Development of Black Children With and Without Sickle Cell Trait," "The Pathology of Starvation and Malnutrition in North Korean and Chinese Communist Prisoners of War." (773)702-1485

Dr. Charles Branham. African American history, comparative ethnicity. Senior Historian at DuSable Museum and Prof. at Indiana University. Wrote: "Black

Great Migration" in *Ethnic Chicago,* "Albert B. George: The First Black Judge, 1924-1930," *A Bibliography of the Black Community in Chicago* and *The Transformation of Black Political Leadership.* (773)947-0600 and (219)980-6781.

Dr. Johann Buis. Africans, African Americans, music. Center for Black Music Research at Columbia College. Wrote "African Slave Descendants in an American Community," "Should Bach Survive in a Post-Apartheid South Africa?" "Africans and the Blues,"
"Africa, the Blues and Apartheid." (312)344-7573

Dr. Jacob Carruthers. Africans, Caribbeans, African Americans. Prof. and Dir. of Inner City Studies, Northeastern Illinois University. Wrote *African or American: A Question of Intellectual Allegiance* and "The Irritated Genie: An Essay on the Haitian Revolution"; co-edited *Kemet and the African Worldview.* (773)268-7500.

Dr. Sharon Collins. Labor market, black managers. Interim Chr., African American Studies at University of Illinois-Chicago. Wrote *Black Corporate Executives: The Making and Breaking of a Black Middle Class,* "Black Mobility in White Corporations: Up the Ladder But Out on a Limb," "The Making of The Black Middle Class"; co-wrote "Retreat From Equal Opportunity? The Case of Affirmative Action." (312)996-6140, scollins@uic.edu

Dr. Samuel A. Floyd Jr. Black music. Dir. of Center for Black Music Research at Columbia College. Wrote *Black Music in the United States: An Annotated Bibliography of Selected Reference and Research Materials, Black Music Biography: An Annotated Bibliography, Black Music in the Harlem Renaissance* and *The Power of Black Music.* (312)344-7559, cbmr@popmail.colu.edu

Dr. Glennon Graham. African American history. Prof. of History at Columbia College. Wrote *From Slavery to Serfdom: Black Agriculturalists in South Carolina, 1865-1900*, did video interviews for "Looking Backwards to Move Forward: A Project to Recover Westside Black History, 1984-1992." (312)344-7294, glennon620@aol.com,

Dr. James Grossman. African American history, urban history, Chicago. Research Center Dir. of Family and Community History at Newberry Library. Wrote *Land of Hope: Chicago, Black Southerners, and the Great Migration, "A Chance to Make Good": African Americans 1900-1930*, "Chicago and the Great Migration," "Citizenship Rights on the Home Front During World War I: The Great Migration and the New Negro," "The White Man's Union: The Great Migration and the Resonance of Race and Class." (312)255-3568, grossmanj@newberry.org

Dr. LaVerne Gyant. Black experience. Acting Dir. of Center for Black Studies at Northern Illinois University. (815)753-1709, lgyant@niu.edu

Dr. Ayana Karanja. African and African American literature and culture, cultural criticism. Asst. Prof. and Chr. of Black World Studies, Loyola University Chicago. Wrote *Zora Neale Hurston: Dialogue in Spirit and in Truth*. (312)508-3674, akaranj@luc.edu

Dr. Howard O. Lindsey. African American urban history. Assoc. Prof. of History at DePaul University. Wrote *A History of Black America*. (773)325-7000 x1560, hlindsey@wwpost.depaul.edu

Dr. Bartley L. McSwine. Multicultural and African-centered education. Chr. of African American Studies at Chicago State University. Wrote "John Dewey and Race," "The Educational Philosophy of W.E.B. DuBois," "Reconciling the Pragmatism of W.E.B. DuBois and Cornel West." (773)995-2487.

Dr. Salikoko S. Mufwene. Development of African American English, of other North American varieties of English, and of Creole. Prof. of Linguistics at University of Chicago. Edited *Africanisms in Afro-American Language Varieties;* co-edited *African American English: Structure, History and Usage*. (773)702-8531, s-mufwene@uchicago.edu

Dr. Dolores G. Norton. Early child development and families. Prof. in School of Social Service Admin. at University of Chicago. Wrote "Understanding the Early Experience of Black Children in High Risk Environments: Culturally and Ecologically Relevant Research," "Early Linguistic Interaction and School Achievement: An Ethnographical, Ecological Perspective," "Diversity, Early Socialization and Temporal Development: The Dual Perspective Revisited," and *Plurality and Ecology: Beyond the Dual Perspective* (due out in 1998). (773)702-1170, d-norton@uchicago.edu

Dr. Barbara Ransby. African American history, African American women, comparative cultures. Asst. Prof. of African American Studies and History at University of Illinois-Chicago. Wrote *Ella Baker and the Hidden Tradition of Black Women's Organizing* (forthcoming), "The Black Poor and the Politics of Expendability," "The Criminalization of Black, Single Mothers," "A Righteous Rage: African American Women in Defense of Ourselves and Black Women's Response to the Hill-Thomas Hearings," and "Columbus and the Making of Historical Myth." (312)996-2961

Dr. Gary Smith (see African American)

Dempsey Travis. African Americans in Chicago and the USA. Pres. of Urban Research Press and Trustee at Roosevelt University. Wrote *An Autobiography of Black Chicago, An Autobiography of Black Politics, Harold: The People's Mayor, Racism American Style: A Corporate Gift, View from the Back of the Bus During World War II and Beyond*, and *Autobiography of Black Jazz*. (773)994-7200

Dr. Kenneth Warren. African American and American literature. Assoc. Prof. of English and Co-chair of African and African American Studies at University of Chicago. Wrote *Black & White Strangers: Race & American Literary Realism* and "Appeals for (Mis)recognition: Theorizing the Diaspora." (773)702-9761, kwarren@midway.uchicago.edu

Dr. Reggie Young. African American literature. Asst. Prof. of English, Wheaton College. Wrote "Literacy, Literature and Liberation," "Concrete Rituals," "Empowering Literacies." (630)752-5780, Reggie.Young@Wheaton.edu

Dr. Admansu Zike. African Americans. Asst. Provost at Northern Illinois University. (815)753-9175

Arab American

Dr. Hassan Addad. Arabs around the world. Prof. Emeritus of History at St. Xavier University. Wrote *The Arab World: A Handbook.* (708)636-0874.

Louise Cainkar. History of immigrants, discrimination, Arab immigration. Research Assoc. Prof. at Great Cities Institute, University Of Illinois-Chicago. Wrote "Palestinian-American Muslim Women: Living on the Margins of Two Worlds," "Social Class as a Determinant of Adaptation and Identity Among Immigrant Palestinian Women," "The Deteriorating Ethnic Safety Net Among Arab Immigrants in Chicago," and "Changes in the Arab Family: A By-Product of the Changing Social and Economic Contest for Arab Immigrants in Chicago." Book in progress: *Gender, Culture and Politics Among Palestinian Immigrants in the U.S.* (773)561-7260.

Dr. Rashid Khalidi. Middle East history. Prof. of Middle East History and Dir. of Center for International Studies at University of Chicago. Wrote *Palestinian Identity: The Construction of National Consciousness;* co-edited *Palestine and the Gulf* and *The Origins of Arab*

Nationalism. (773)7092-7721, r-khalid@uchicago.edu

Dr. Ghada Kalhani. Arabs and Africans. D.K Pearson Professor of Politics at Lake Forest College. Wrote *The Islamic Mobilization of Women in Egypt,* "The Muslim African Experience," "Palestinian Women: The Case for Political Liberation," "The Human Rights of Women in Islam," and "The Concept of Jihad in Islam." (847)735-5135.

Rev. Don Wagner. Arabs in Chicago, Arab Christians in the Middle East, Christian-Muslim relations. Prof. of Religion and Dir. of Center for Middle Eastern Studies, North Park University. Wrote "The Future of Christianity in the Middle East," "Arabs in Chicago" and *Anxious for Armageddon.* (773)244-5785, dwagner@northpark.edu

Asian American

Dr. Joan Erdman (see Indian)

Dr. Ann Harrington (see Japanese)

Dr. Tong-He Koh (see Korean)

Dr. Ho-Youn Kwon (see Korean)
Dr. Yvonne Lau. Asian Americans education, work and community development. Dir. of Asian and Asian American Studies Program in Sociology Dept. at Loyola University Chicago. Wrote "Asian Americans on College Campuses: Profiles & Trends," "Asian American Women Entrepreneurs," "Political Participation Among Chicago Asian Americans," "Asian American Professionals: Alternative Career Strategies," "Institutionalizing Asian American Studies" and the Chinese American chapter in *The Ethnic Handbook.* (773)508-8997, ylau@luc.edu

Dr. Barbara Posadas (see Filipino)

Dr. Padma Rangaswamy (see Indian)

Assyrian American

Daniel Wolk. Assyrians in the U.S. and Chicago. Doctoral candidate, University of Chicago. Chapter on Assyrian Americans in *The Ethnic Handbook.* (773)508-0827, Wolk@ mcs.net.

Caribbean American

William Leslie Balan-Gaubert. Haitians, Haitian Americans. Scholar in Residence at University of Chicago. Wrote chapter on Haitian Americans in *The Ethnic Handbook.* (773)702-2301

Dr. Vilna Bashi. West Indian immigration. Asst. Prof. of Sociology at Northwestern University. Wrote "A Theory of Immigration and Racial Stratification," "We Don't Have That Back Home: Race, Racism and the Social Networks of West Indian Immigrants"; co-wrote "Globalization and Residential Segregation." (847)491-3718, v-bashi@nwu.edu
Dr. Jacob Carruthers (see African American)

Dr. Mirza Gonzalez (see Cuban)
Dr. Félix Masud-Piloto (see Cuban)

Dr. Marc Zimmerman (see Latino)

Chinese American

Dr. Yvonne Lau (see Asian American)

Croatian American

Ljubo Krasic. Croatian Americans in the U.S. and Canada. Dir. of Croatian Ethnic Institute. Wrote chapter on Croatian Americans in *The Ethnic Handbook,* "Adjustment and Religious Profile Among Croatians in the USA and Canada," "Sociological Investigations on Migration." (773)373-4670

Cuban American

Dr. Mirza Gonzalez. Cuban, Cuban American and Caribbean literature. Prof. of Modern Languages, DePaul University. Wrote "Passage to Hope and Freedom: Luna Park," *Literatura Revolucionaria Hispanoamerican.* (773)325-7000 x1873, mgonzale@wppost.depaul.edu

Dr. Félix Masud-Piloto. Contemporary Caribbean, Latin America and Cuban immigration. Assoc. Prof. of History and Dir. of Center for Latino Research at DePaul University. Wrote *With Open Arms: Cuban Migration to the United States* and *From Welcomed Exiles to Illegal Immigrants: Cuban Migration to the U.S., 1959-1995.* (773)325-7472, Fmasud-P @wppost.depaul.edu

Dr. Jorge Rodriguez-Florido. Cuban Americans, Afro-Hispanic culture and literature. Prof. of Spanish at Chicago State University. Wrote chapter on Cuban Americans in *The Ethnic Handbook,* "Afro-Hispanic History and Culture," "A Chronology from Columbus to the End of the 19th Century," "A Chronology of Afro-Hispanic Poetry and Fiction." (773)995-3991

Ethiopian American

Dr. Erku Yimer. Ethiopians in America. Exec. Dir. of Ethiopian Community Assn. Wrote chapter on Ethiopian Americans in *The Ethnic Handbook* and "From Ethiopia to the USA: Cultural Issues Concerning Refugees." (773)728-0303.

Filipino American

Dr. Barbara Posadas. Filipino Americans in Chicago, American social, ethnic and immigration history. Assoc. Prof. of History at University of Northern Illinois. Co-edited *Refracting America: Gender, Race,*

Ethnicity and Environmental American History to 1877; wrote "Aspiration and Reality: Occupational and Educational Choice Among Filipino Migrants to Chicago, 1900-1935," "Crossed Boundaries in Interracial Chicago: Pilipino American Families Since 1925," "Mestiza Girlhood: Interracial Families in Chicago's Filipino American Community Since 1930." (815)753-6697

German American

Dr. Kathleen Conzen (see multi-ethnic)

Greek American

Dr. Fotios (Frank) Litsas. Greek and Mediterranean studies, Greek Americans. Dir. of Greek Education for Greek Orthodox Diocese of Chicago. Wrote *Greek Immigration* and *Greek Americans, A Companion to the Greek Orthodox Church,* "Greek Education in America," and "Greek Studies in American Universities." (773)465-5048

Dr. Andrew Kopan. Greeks in Chicago, education. Prof. Emeritus of Education at DePaul University. Wrote *Education and Greek Immigrants in Chicago, 1892-1973* and chapters on Greek Americans in *Ethnic Chicago* and *The Ethnic Handbook."* (773)325-7000, x1168.

Dr. Charles Moskos. Greek Americans. Prof. of Sociology at Northwestern University. Wrote *Greek Americans: Struggle and Success,* "The Modern Greek Orthodox Church in America," "The Greeks in the United States," and "The Greeks" chapter in *American Immigrant Cultures.* (847)491-2705, c-moskos@nwu.edu

Dr. Elaine Thomopoulos. Greek Americans, Greek-American women and families. Clinical psychologist. Project director of "Greek American Women in Illinois." (630)655-2077.

Dr. Anthony Xidix. Multilingual/ multicultural/bilingual (Greek) education. Prof. of Greek and Dir. of Institute of Greek Language and Culture. Wrote *The Impact of Greek Bilingual Programs on the Academic Performance, Language Preservation and Ethnicity of Greek American Students: A Case Study of Chicago,* "Bilingual Education in Chicago: A Case Study" and "Issues of Bilingualism and Instructional Strategies for Mainstream Classroom Teachers." (773)775-6504, 534-3220

Indian American

Dr. Padma Rangaswamy. Indian immigrants in Chicago and the USA. Instructor at University of Illinois-Chicago. Wrote *The Imperatives of Choice and Change: Post-1965 Immigrants from India in Metropolitan Chicago* and the chapters on Asian Indians in *Ethnic Chicago* and *The Ethnic Handbook.* (630)654-0168

Dr. Joan Erdman. Indian Americans, India, dance, cultural policy. Prof. of Liberal Education at Columbia College and Research Assoc. for Committee on Southern Asian Studies, University of Chicago. Wrote *Meals from India: An INDIAkit,* "Today and the Good Old Days: South Asian Music and Dance Performances in Chicago," "Preservation and Heritage of the Performing Arts of India." (312)663-1600 x7530, jerdman@popmail.colum.edu

Irish American

Dr. Paul M. Green. Irish in Chicago, politics, government. Dir. of Institute for Public Policy and Administration at Governors State University. Wrote chapter on Irish in *Ethnic Chicago.* (708)534-4999.

Dr. Lawrence McCaffrey. Irish America. Prof. Emeritus of History at Loyola University Chicago. Wrote *Textures of Irish America* and *The Irish Catholic Diaspora in America;* co-wrote *The Irish in Chicago* (847)475-7693.

Dr. Eileen McMahon. Irish Americans, immigration, ethnicity. Adj. Prof. of History at Loyola University. Wrote *What Parish Are You From: The Irish Parish Community and Race Relations, 1956-1970* and the chapter on Irish Americans in *The Ethnic Handbook.* (708)923-1858.

Ellen Skerrett. Irish in Chicago. Independent scholar. Co-wrote *Chicago: City of Neighborhoods, The Irish in Chicago,* and *Catholicism, Chicago Style;* edited *At the Crossroads: Old St. Patrick's and the Chicago Irish.* (773)445-6279. SkerrettE@aol.com

Italian American

Michael Bacarella (see multi-ethnic)

Dr. Dominic Candeloro. Italian Americans in Chicago. Adjunct Prof. of History at Governors State University. Wrote chapter on Italian Americans in *Ethnic Chicago.* Co-wrote chapter on Italian Americans in *The Ethnic Handbook.* (708)756-5315

Dr. Fred Gardaphe. Italian Americans, ethnic literature. Prof. of English at Columbia College. Wrote *Italian Signs, American Streets: The Evolution of Italian American Narrative*, and *Dagoes Read: Tradition and the Italian/American Writer;* wrote two plays, "Vinegar and Oil" and "Imported from Italy."fgardaphe@aol.com

Dr. Paolo Giordano. Italian Americans. Prof. of Modern Languages and Literature at Loyola University Chicago. Wrote *From the Margin: Writings in Italian Americana* and *Beyond the Margin: Writings in Italian Americana.* (773)508-2869, pgiorda@luc.edu

Japanese American

Dr. Ann Harrington. Japanese Americans. Assoc. Prof. of History at Loyola University Chicago. Wrote "Immigration Act of 1995," "Japanese Christianity," and (forthcoming) "Chiyo Murakami." (773)508-8486, aharri1@orion.it.luc.edu

Jewish American

Dr. Barry Chiswick (see multi-ethnic)

Dr. Irving Cutler. Jews of Chicago, Chicago's ethnic neighborhoods. Prof. Emeritus of Geography at Chicago State University. Wrote *The Jews of Chicago: From Shtetl to Suburb* and *Chicago: Metropolis of the Mid-continent.* Contributed to *Ethnic Chicago* and *The Sentinel's History of Chicago Jewry.* (847)251-8927.

Dr. Elliot Lefkovitz. Jewish Americans, Jews. Rabbi, Adj. Prof. of History at Loyola University and Adj. Prof. of Holocaust Studies at Spertus Institute of Jewish Studies. Wrote study guides for Holocaust videos, "A History of Anshe Emet Synagogue" (Chicago), and "A History of Temple Shalom" (Chicago). (847)446-7216

Donald McKay (see multi-ethnic)

Dr. Victor Mirelman. Latin American Jewry, U.S. Jewry. Rabbi and Prof. of History at Spertus Institute. Wrote *Sephardim in Latin America Since Independence, The Jewish Community Versus Crime, Latin American Jewry.* (708)366-9000

Dr. Linda Waite. Family. Prof. of Sociology at University of Chicago. Co-wrote "The Impact of Religious Upbringing and Marriage Markets on Jewish Intermarriage." (773)256-6333, l-waite@uchicago.edu

Korean American

Dr. Tong-He Koh. Asian American (especially Korean) culture and mental health. Clinical psychologist. Wrote "Ethnic Identity: The Impact of Two Cultures on the Psychological Development of Korean American Adolescents," "Ethnic Identity in First, 1.5 and Second-Generation Korean Americans," and "Cognitive and Affective Adaptation of Korean American School Children: Service and Research Priorities." (773)907-9344, tonghekoh@aol.com.

Dr. Ho-Youn Kwon. Korean immigrants, family. Exec. Dir. of Korean Studies at North Park University. Co-edited *The Emerging Generation of Korean Americans;* edited *Korean American Conflict and Harmony, Korean Cultural Roots: Religion and Social Thought,* and *Contemporary Korea.* (773)244-5650, hyk@northpark.edu

Latino

Dr. Beatriz Badikian. Ethnic literature of Chicago and the U.S., popular culture, with emphasis on Latinos. Lecturer in English at Roosevelt University. Wrote: "I Hear You, Sister: Black and Latino Women Speak" and "Food and Sex: That's All We're Good For: Latinas in Film." (312)867-1805, badgart@aol.com.

Mario Castillo (see multi-ethnic)

Dr. Barry Chiswick (see multi-ethnic)

Dr. Wilfredo Cruz. Latinos in Chicago. Faculty member in Liberal Education at Columbia College. Wrote "Police Brutality in Latino and African American Communities," "Anti-Immigrant Attitudes Hurting Chicago's Mexican American Community," "All Politics is Local: A Furor Over Puerto Rican Nationalism Masks the Real Issues at Stake in Chicago School Reform" and "Washburn's Legacy of Exclusion Solidly Built." (312)663-1600 x5533

Dr. Antonio Delgado. Public policy as it impacts Latinos in the U.S., Mexican immigration to the Midwest, Mexicans in Chicago, Latino politics. Adj. Prof. in History and Planning at University of Illinois-Chicago. Wrote *The Under-use of Lincoln Park* by *Blacks, Latinos and Asians* and *Chicago's Early Mexican Settlements, 1910-1960.* (312)409-1840, (773)376-4105

Dr. Renny Golden. Salvadorans and Guatemalans, here and in Central America. Assoc. Prof. of Criminology, Sociology and Social Work at Northeastern Illinois University. Co-wrote *Sanctuary: The New Underground Railroad* and *Dangerous Memories of Invasion and Resistance Since 1492;* wrote *The Hour of the Poor, the Hour of Women: Salvadoran Women Speak.* (773)794-2553.

Dr. Nilda Flores-Gonzalez. Latinos, Puerto Ricans, Native Americans. Asst. Prof. of Sociology and Latin American Studies at University of Illinois-Chicago. (312)996-6886, Nilda@uic.edu

Dr. Michael Gonzales. Mexican immigration to the U.S., Asian immigration to Peru, Latin American history. Dir. of Center for Latino and Latin American Studies at Northern Illinois University. Wrote *Plantation Agriculture and Social Control in Northern Peru 1875-1933* and "Chinese Plantation Workers and Social Conflict in Peru in the Late 19th Century." (815)753-1531, gonzales@niu.edu

Dr. John Hobgood (see Native American)

Dr. Louise Año Nuevo Kerr (see Mexican)

Dr. Isidro Lucas. Hispanics, Puerto Ricans in Chicago and the USA. Dir. of Office of Hispanic Programs at Chicago State University. Wrote "Puerto Rican Politics in Chicago," "Chicago Hispanic Businesses: A Demographic Profile," "Bilingual Education and the Melting Pot: Getting Burned," "The Spanish Speaking in Aurora, Illinois," and the chapter on Puerto Ricans in *The Ethnic Handbook.* (773)995-2526

Dr. Felix Masud-Piloto (see Cuban)

Dr. William McCready (see multi-ethnic)

Dr. RoseAnna Mueller. Latin America, cross-cultural training. Humanities Co-ord. for Liberal Education at Columbia College. Writings and presentations include "Teaching Culturally Diverse Students in the Community College," "Cultural Literacy," and "Gender, Space and Identity in the Writings of Latin American Women." (312)344-7532, RoseAnna.Mueller@mail.colum.edu

Dr. Alvaro Nieves (see multi-ethnic)

Dr. Rafael Nuñez-Cedeño. Hispanic linguistics, bilingualism. Prof. and Dir. of Latin American Studies at University of Illinois-Chicago. Wrote *Studies in Romance Languages*, "The Afro-Hispanic Abakua: a Study of Linguistic Pidginization," "The Abakua Secret Society in Cuba: Language and Culture." (312)996-2445.

Dr. Victor Ortiz (see Mexican)

Dr. Jorge Rodriguez-Florido (see Cuban)

Dr. Peter Sanchez. Latino political participation, Latin America. Asst. Prof. of Political Science at Loyola University. Co-wrote "Latino Electoral and Nonelectoral Political Participation: Findings from the 1996 Chicago Latino Registered Voter Survey." (773)508-8658, psanche@luc.edu

Dr. Maria de los Angeles Torres. Latinos in the U.S., multiculturalism and democracy. Assoc. Prof. of Political Science at DePaul University. Co-edited *Borderless Borders: Latinos and Latin Americans and the Paradoxes of Interdependence.* (773)325-7000 x1984, mtorres@wwpost.depaul.edu

Dr. Marc Zimmerman. Latin American, Central American, Caribbean and U.S. Latino culture. Prof. of Latin American Studies at University of Illinois-Chicago. Wrote "Transplanting Roots and Taking Off: Latino Writers in Illinois," "Los Latinos en los Estados Unidos y en Chicago: Dimensiones Culturales," and "Chicago Culture in the Context of Latino Cultural

Studies"; co-wrote "The Impact of Mexican Immigration." (312)996-2445, Marczim@uic.edu

Lithuanian American

Dr. Antanas J. Van Reenan. Lithuanians in the U.S. and around the world. Adjunct Prof. at Columbia College, St. Xavier University and Vandercook College of Music. Wrote *Lithuanian Diaspora: Königsberg to Chicago,* "Lithuanians Americans," "What Can East Central Europe Offer America: A Spiritual Gift," "Nations and the Global Village: Reflections on Global Culture"; co-wrote chapter on Lithuanian Americans in *The Ethnic Handbook.* (708)423-2364

Dr. Violeta Kelertas. Lithuanian and Lithuanian American literature. Assoc. Prof. of Slavic and Baltic Languages and Literatures at University of Illinois-Chicago. Edited (as Violeta Kelertiene) *Gone Never to Return: Marius Katiliskis in His Life and Work* and wrote chapter for same book "On the Narrative Technique of 'Autumn Comes Through the Forest.'" Wrote "Between History and Responsibility." (312)996-7856, Kelertas@uicvm.uic.edu

Mexican American

Dr. Michael Gonzales (see Latino)

Dr. Antonio Delgado (see Latino)

Dr. Marcia Farr. Mexicans in Chicago and Mexico. Prof. of English and Linguistics at University of Illinois-Chicago. Wrote "Language, Culture and Literacy in a Transitional Community: Old Traditions in New Settings" and "En los dos Idiomas: Literacy Practices Among Mexican Families in Chicago." 413-2231, mfarr@vic.edu

Dr. Louise Año Nuevo Kerr. Mexican Americans and Latinos in the USA, Chicago. Assoc. Prof. of History at University Of Illinois-Chicago. Wrote

Mexicans in the United States, "Chicanos in the Great Depression," "Ethnic Chicago," and chapters on Mexican Americans in *The Ethnic Handbook* and *Ethnic Chicago,* (312)996-3141, lkerr@uic.edu

Dr. Victor Ortiz. Mexican Americans/Chicanos/Latinos, NAFTA. Asst. Prof. of Latin American Studies at University of Illinois-Chicago. Wrote "NAFTA, Time & Space on the Border," "NAFTA, the Border and the Community Beyond." (312)996-7270, vmortiz@uic.edu

Native American

Dr. David Beck. Native American history. Dean of Native American Educational Services (NAES) College. Wrote *The Chicago American Indian Community 1893-1988: Annotated Bibliography and Guide to Sources in Chicago,* "The Chicago American Indian Community, An 'Invisible' Minority," and the chapter on Native Americans in *The Ethnic Handbook,* (773)761-5000, davenaes@aol.com

Dr. Nilda Flores-Gonzalez (see Latino)
Dr. John Hobgood. Native Americans in the Midwest, Meti of the Midwest, Mexican culture and Mexican Americans. Prof. of Anthropology at Chicago State University. Wrote "Métis People in the Midwest," "On Defining Goans and Their Culture." Co-wrote "Meso-Americans as Cultural Brokers in Northern New Spain." (773)995-2333

Dr. Craig Howe. American Indian history and architecture, Sioux Indians, Plains Indians. Dir. of D'Arcy McNickle Center for American Indian History at Newberry Library. Wrote "Mapping the (Un)Settling of America," "American Indian Perspectives on Time and Space," "Hypermedia Tribal Histories," "Architectural Tribalism in the Native American New World." (312)255-3575, howec@newberry.org

Dr. Frederick E. Hoxie. American Indian history. V.P. of Research and Education at the Newberry Library and Adj. Prof. of History at Northwestern University. Wrote *A*

Final Promise: The Campaign to Assimilation of the Indians, 1880-1920; Parading Through History: The Making of the Crow Nation in America, 1805-1935; edited *Indians in American History* and *The Encyclopedia of The American Indians;* co-edited *Discovering America: Essays on the Search for an Identity.* (312)255-3535

Patrick R. Jennings. American Indians. Curator of Mitchell Museum of the American Indian at Kendall College and Instructor at Barat College. Wrote "Cultural Dilemma at an Ethical Crossroads." (847)492-8520.

Rosalyn Rae LaPier. Native Americans. Instructor at Native American Educational Services (NAES) College. Wrote "Between Hay and Grass: A Brief History of Two Metis Communities in Central Montana," *Native Peoples and Philanthropy: An Update for the Years 1991, 1992 and 1993,* "My Grandmother's Grandmother," "Blackfeet Women and Spiritual Power," and "Urban Indians in Chicago During the 1920s and '30s." (847)475-8621, rrlapier@aol.com

Clovia Malatare (Afraid of the Bear). Native American culture, language and issues. Instructor at NAES College. (312)793-8681, malatare@aol.com

Harvey Markowitz. Lakota history, cultural and religious identity. Assoc. Dir. of D'Arcy McNickle Center for American Indian History at Newberry Library. Wrote *Ready Reference: American Indian* and *Native American: An Annotated Bibliography.* (312)255-3563

Dr. A. LaVonne Brown Ruoff. Native American literatures. Prof. Emerita of English at University of Illinois-Chicago. Wrote *American Indian Literatures: An Introduction, Bibliographic Review and Selected Bibliography; Literatures of the American Indian;* and *Redefining American Literary History.* (708)848-9292, lruoff@uic.edu

Dr. Helen Hornbeck Tanner. American Indian history, Latin American history. Senior Research Fellow at Newberry Library. Edited *Atlas of Great Lakes Indian History* and *The Settling of North America*; wrote "Indians of the Western Great Lakes--They are Still Here," "Cherokees in the Ohio Country," and "Pipesmoke and Muskets, Florida Indian Intrigue in the Revolutionary Era."
(312)255-3537, hhtanner@aol.com

Dr. Mary Ann Weston. Native American images in the news media, cross-cultural journalism. Assoc. Prof. at Medill School of Journalism, Northwestern University. Wrote *Native Americans in the News*, co-edited *U.S. News Coverage of Racial Minorities: A Sourcebook* and co-wrote chapter on Native Americans in that book. (847)491-4635, m-a-weston@nwu.edu

Nigerian American

Dr. Sam Enyia. Nigerians in the USA and Chicago. Dir. of Broadcast Program and Prof. of Communications at Lewis University. Wrote chapter on Nigerian Americans in *The Ethnic Handbook.* (815)838-0500 x5238.

Palestinian American

Dr. Louise Cainkar (see Arab American)

Dr. Rashid Khalidi (see Arab American)

Polish American

Dr. William Galush. Polish American history. Assoc. Prof. of History at Loyola University Chicago. Wrote "Purity and Power: Chicago Polonian Feminist Leaders: 1880-1914," "Polish Americans and Religion" and "Movers and Shakers: Fraternalism and Community in Utica, N.Y." (773)508-2230

Dr. Helena Znaniecka Lopata. Polish Americans, women. Prof. of Sociology at Loyola University. Wrote *Polish Americans: Status Competition in an Ethnic Community,"* "The Polish American Family," "The Polish Immigrants and their Descendants in the American Labor Force," "Widowhood in Polonia." (773)508-3465

Dr. Dominic Pacyga. Chicago history, ethnicity, Poles in Chicago. Prof. of Liberal Education at Columbia College. Wrote *Polish Immigrants and Industrial Chicago: Workers on the South Side, 1880-1922* and the chapter on Polish Americans in *Ethnic Chicago.* (312)344-7531, dxpøøø@dns.colum.edu

Dr. Barbara Ann Strassberg. Sociology of culture, Polish Americans and religion. Assoc. Prof. of Sociology at Aurora University. Wrote *The Church in the Process of Assimilation of Polish Americans* (in Polish); "Polish Jewish Immigration to the U.S.," "Polish Baptist Churches in the U.S.," and "Religious Institutions and Assimilation." (630)844-5408, bstrass@admin.aurora.edu

Paul Valasek (see Multi-ethnic)

Puerto Rican

Dr. Isidro Lucas (see Latino)

Swedish American

Dr. Philip J. Anderson. Swedish Immigration to the USA. Prof. of Church History at North Park Theological Seminary. Co-edited *Swedish-American Life in Chicago, Cultural and Urban Aspects of an Immigrant People 1850-1930,* and *Scandinavian Immigrants and Education in North America.* (773)244-6218, panders@npcts.edu

Dr. Dag Blanck. Swedish American History. Dir. of Swenson Swedish Immigration Research Center, Augustana

College, Rock Island. Co-edited *Swedish-American Life in Chicago: Cultural and Urban Aspects of an Immigrant People, 1850-1930;* wrote *Becoming Swedish-American: The Construction of an Ethnic Identity in the Augustana Synod, 1860-1917* and "Swedish-Americans and the 1893 Columbian Exposition." (309)794-7221, swblanck@augustana.edu

Tim Johnson. Swedish Americans. Dir. of Archives at North Park University and Theological Seminary. Wrote chapter on Swedish Americans in *The Ethnic Handbook* and "Independent Order of the Svithiod." (773)244-6224, tjohnso1@northpark.edu

Dr. Charles Peterson. Scandinavian organizations in Chicago and the U.S., Scandinavia. Exec. Dir. of Center for Scandinavian Studies at North Park University. (773)244-5615, cip@northpark.edu

Serbian American

Dr. Biljana Sljivic-Simsic. Serbo-Croatian language, Serbians in Chicago. Prof. of Slavic Languages and Literature at University of Illinois-Chicago. Wrote *Serbo-Croatian-English Dictionary* and *Serbo-Croatian Just for You,* and chapter on Serbian Americans in *The Ethnic Handbook.* Co-wrote *Judeo-Spanish Ballads from Bosnia.* (312)996-4412, bibi@uic.edu

Slovak American

Dr. Ladislav Bolchazy. Slovak academic publishing. Prof. of Classics at Loyola University Chicago. Published English-Slovak dictionary and many Slovak and Greek titles. Pres., Bolchazy-Carducci Publishers. (847)526-4344, Slovak@Bolchazy.com

Marta Mistina Kona. Slovak studies. Former Library Sciences instructor and librarian at University of Illinois Rush -

University. Wrote *Ph.D. Dissertations in Slovakiana in the Western World -- Bibliography* and *Slovak Americans and Canadians in American Catholic Who's Who 1911-1981* and *Slovak Ethnicity.* (847)251-3514

Ukrainian American

Dr. Myron Kuropas. Ukrainians in USA, Chicago. Adj. Prof. at Northern Illinois University. Wrote *Ukrainian Americans: Roots and Aspirations 1884-1954,* "Ukrainian American Citadel: The First Hundred Years of the Ukrainian National Association, 1894-1994," and the chapters on Ukrainians in *Ethnic Chicago* and *The Ethnic Handbook.* (815)758-6897

Dr. Daria Markus. Ukrainians, theory of ethnicity. Asst. Editor of *Encyclopedia of Ukrainian Diaspora,* former teacher at DePaul University and University of Indiana. Wrote *Education of Ethnic Leadership: A Case Study of Ukrainians in the USA, Ukrainians in Chicago and Illinois,* and "The Ukrainian Saturday Schools." (773)478-3587, markusdar@msn.com

Dr. Vasyl Markus. Ethnic relations, politics, religion under Communism. Senior Prof. of Political Science at Loyola University Chicago. Wrote *Encyclopedia of Ukrainian Diaspora* and *Status of Churches and Religion in Ukraine.* (773)489-1339

Multi-ethnic

Michael Bacarella. Italian Americans in American history, Hispanics and Hungarians in the Civil War, Italian American actors. Independent scholar and Chr. of Italian American Actors Committee of the Screen Actors Guild. Wrote *Lincoln's Foreign Legion* and *Ital-Actor* (an encyclopedia of 7,000 Italian American actors). (847)318-0313

Joan Beaudoin. Cultural diversity and media stereotypes. Prof. of Television at Columbia College. Papers and presentations include "Culture, Race and the Media," "Just Like Us on TV: Analyzing Stereotypes as a Common-Ground Approach to Diversity," and "American Commitments in a Diverse Democracy." (312)344-7448, beaubelle@aol.com.

Mario Castillo. Multi-cultural murals, Latino art. Art teacher at Columbia College. (312)663-1600 x7590.

Dr. Barry Chiswick. Immigration, ethnicity, Hispanic immigrants, American Jews, immigrants and the workplace. Research Prof. of Economics at University of Illinois-Chicago. Wrote *Illegal Aliens: Their Employment and Employers*, *The Employment of Immigrants in the United States*, "An Economic Analysis of the Employers of Illegal Aliens: The Case of Chicago," "The Economic Status of American Jews: Analysis of the 1990 National Jewish Population Survey," "The Labor Market Status of Hispanic Men," "The Performance of Immigrants in the United States Labor Market;" co-wrote *The Dilemma of American Immigration: Beyond the Golden Door;* (312)996-2684, brchis@uic.edu

Dr. Kathleen Neils Conzen. U.S. immigration history, German and Luxembourg immigrants. Prof. and Chr. of History at University of Chicago. Wrote *The Stories Immigrants Tell, Ethnic Patterns in American Cities, Ethnicity as Festive Culture: German America on Parade;* co-wrote *The Invention of Ethnicity*. (773)702-8394, k-conzen@uchicago.edu

Dr. Melvin Holli. Ethnicity, urban history, politics. Prof. of History at University of Illinois-Chicago. Co-edited *Ethnic Chicago: A Multicultural Portrait* (four editions) and *The Ethnic Frontier*. (312)996-3141.

Dr. Peter d'A. Jones. Ethnicity in America, American and European economic history. Prof. of History at University of Illinois-Chicago. Wrote *Since Columbus: Pluralism and Poverty in the Americas*. Co-edited *Ethnic Chicago: A Multicultural Portrait* (four editions) . (312)996-2165.

Dr. Paul Kleppner. Race and ethnic relations, racial and ethnic voting patters. Dir. of Office for Social Policy Research at University of Northern Illinois. Wrote *The Cross of Culture: A Social Analysis of Midwestern Politics 1850-1900, The Third Electoral System: Parties, Votes and Political Cultures*, and *Chicago Divided: The Making of a Black Mayor.* (815)758-0780, Kleppner@niu.edu.

Cynthia Linton. Ethnic groups in Chicago, media coverage of ethnicity. Adj. Prof. at Medill School of Journalism, Northwestern University. Edited *The Ethnic Handbook: A Guide to the Cultures and Traditions of Chicago's Diverse Communities, The Directory of Chicago Ethnic Organizations*, and *Ethnic Media Guide for Chicago;* wrote "Immigration and Immigrants: How They're Covered by the Chicago Sun-Times and Chicago Tribune." (847)491-5661, CLinton914@aol.com

Dr. Lowell Livezey. Religions of most ethnic groups. Dir. of Religion in Urban America Program at University of Illinois-Chicago. Edited and co-wrote *Religious Organizations and Structural Change in Metropolitan Chicago*. (312)413-4117, Livezey@uic.edu

Ed Marciniak. Neighborhoods and ethnicity, community organization. Pres. of Institute of Urban Life at Loyola University Chicago. Wrote *Historic Chinatown and Bridgeport: A New Synergism, Reviving an Inner City Community: The Drama of Urban Change in Chicago's East Humboldt Park, Reclaiming the Inner City: Chicago's Near North Revitalization Confronts Cabrini-Green*, and *Mainstreaming the Urban Poor: Enabling Non-public Schools to Survive in Inner-City Neighborhoods*. (312)915-6666.

Dr. William McCready. Urban and ethnic sociology. Dir. of Public Opinion Laboratory and Asst. Prof. of Sociology at Northern Illinois University. Co-wrote "Hispanics in the United States," "Ethnic

Dr. William McCready. Urban and ethnic sociology. Dir. of Public Opinion Laboratory and Asst. Prof. of Sociology at Northern Illinois University. Co-wrote "Hispanics in the United States," "Ethnic Drinking Subcultures," "Ethnicity and Nationality in Alcoholism." (815)753-0039, mccready@niu.edu

Dr. Donald McKay. Immigration history, cross-cultural communication, Soviet Jews, Poles. Dir. of Educational Services at Spanish Coalition for Jobs. Wrote *Soviet Jewish Emigration to Chicago.* (773)247-0707 x230, EngPlus@aol.com

Dr. Alvaro L. Nieves. Race and ethnic relations. Prof. of Sociology at Wheaton College. Wrote "Race, Region and Risk: An Examination of Minority Proximity to Noxious Facilities" and "Minority Issues in the Justice System;" co-edited *Ethnic Minorities and Evangelical Christian Colleges*; co-wrote "Regional Differences in the Potential Exposure of U.S. Minority Populations to Hazardous Facilities." (630)752-5038, nieves@Wheaton.edu

Dr. Dominic Pacyga (see Poles)
Dr. Gary Smith. African American, Native American and multi-ethnic literature. Assoc. Prof. of English at DePaul University. Wrote "Multiculturalism and the Underground Railroad in Black Children's Literature" and *Songs for My Fathers.* Edited *A Life Distilled: Gwendolyn Brooks, Her Poetry and Fiction.* (773)325-7000 x1794, gsimth@wppost.depaul.edu

Paul Valasek. Polish genealogy, immigrant steamships, migration of all ethnic groups from Europe, Czech and Slovak genealogy. Pres. of Polish Genealogical Society of America and founding member and editor for Czech and Slovak American Genealogy Society of Illinois. (773)776-5551, paval56@aol.com

Dr. R. Stephen Warner. Religions of immigrant groups. Prof. of Sociology at University of Illinois-Chicago. Wrote "Religion, Boundaries, and Bridges;" co-edited *Gatherings in Diaspora: Religious Communities and the New Immigration* (due out in 1998). (312)996-0990

Calendar of ethnic holidays

January

1 Japanese New Year.

1 Korean Lunar New Year.

1 Haitian. Independence Day.
Celebrates independence from France in 1804.

6 Fiesta de Reyes. (Epiphany)
religious holiday for Latinos when children receive presents from the Three Wise Men.

7 Christmas. Religious holiday celebrating the birth of Christ for those in most Eastern Orthodox Churches, including Ethiopians, Romanians, Russians and Serbians.

13 Serbian New Year.

15 Martin Luther King Jr.'s birthday. State holiday celebrated on closest Monday.

19 Epiphany. A religious holiday for members of Eastern Orthodox Churches, celebrating the baptism of Christ. An important holiday for Ethiopians.

27 St. Sava's Day. Serbian. Celebrated for the most important Serbian saint, the patron saint of education.

28 Birth of Jose Marti.
Cuban. Commemorates patriot in Spanish Civil War and leader in exile who was killed when he returned to Cuba.

Eid-ul-Fitr. Feast commemorating end of Ramadan for Muslims. Date varies. Will be and Jan. 8, 2000, then backs up into December for three years.
Chinese Lunar New Year. In January or February, depending on lunar calendar. Parades in Chinatown and North Side Chinatown.
Pan-Asian Lunar New Year. Celebrated in Chicago with a banquet, sometimes preceded by a conference. (January or February).

TET/Lunar New Year. Vietnamese. Time of renewal and new start. First day of first lunar month, in late January or early February.

February

16 Independence Feb. 16, 1918.
Lithuanian. Marks independence after 130 years of Russian occupation.

Black History Month.
Trung Sisters Anniversary. Vietnamese. Pays tribute to heroines who in 39 A.D. drove Chinese out of Vietnam after 247 years of domination.

March

1 Martisorul. Romanian.
Celebrates coming of spring.

2 Adwa Victory. Ethiopian. Celebrates victory over colonial army of Italy in 1896.

4 St. Casimir's Day. Celebrates Patron Saint of Lithuania with St. Casimir's Fair on nearest Sunday.

11 Independence March 11, 1990.
Lithuanian. Marks independence after 50 years of Soviet occupation.

15 Revolution of 1848. Hungarian.

17 St. Patrick's Day. Irish. Two parades, downtown and in Beverly Hills.

19 St. Joseph's Day. Celebration for people named Joseph. Important holiday for some Christians, including Czechs and Italians.

23 Declaration of Independence.
Pakistani.

25 Greek Independence Day. Marks independence from Ottoman Empire in 1821.

25 Bielarusian Independence Day. Celebrated on closest weekend at Cultural Center, 3107 W. Fullerton.

Ancestor Day. Vietnamese. Anniversary of death of King Hung Vuong, founder of Vietnamese nation. (March or April)

Casimir Pulaski Day. Polish. Official Illinois holiday commemorating Polish count who fought and died in American Revolution. First Monday in March. Weekend parade.

Eid-ul-Adha. Muslim holiday, the feast of sacrifice, marking when Abraham sacrificed a lamb in place of Ishmael. Marks end of pilgrimage to Mecca during Ramadan. Date varies with sun and moon. Will fall on April 7, 1998, March 28, 1999, March 16 or 17, 2000, and March 6, 2001.

Good Friday and Easter Sunday. Religious holidays for Roman Catholics and Protestants commemorating crucifixion and resurrection of Jesus Christ. Very important holiday for many ethnic groups, including Assyrians, Czechs, Cubans, Filipinos, Germans, Guatemalans, Hungarians, Irish, Italians, Lithuanians, Mexicans, Poles and Slovaks. In March or April, depending on lunar calendar.

Greek Easter. Commemorates crucifixion and resurrection of Jesus. Celebrated between March 21-May 5, on the first Sunday following the first full moon after the vernal equinox, provided Passover has taken place.

Passover. Jewish religious holiday marking exodus of Jews from Egypt. In March or April.

April

1 Kha B'Nissan. Assyrian New Year. Parade on King Sargon Blvd. (Western Avenue)

14 Cambodian New Year. Start of three-day observance.

Chingming/Ghost Festival. Chinese. Marks coming of spring and honors those who have passed away. (Usually April)

Yom Ha'atzmaut. Jewish. Celebrates birth of modern Israel. (April or May)

Yom HaShoah. Jewish. Commemorates those killed in the Holocaust. (April or May)

May

1 Guatemalan Labor Day. Celebrates labor laws that created 8-hour work day.

3 Polish Constitution Day. Celebrates Polish Constitution of 1791, which was never put into practice because of partition of Poland by Prussia, Russia and Austria. Observed with parade.

5 Cinco de Mayo. Mexican. Marks expulsion of French from Mexico in 1867.

10 Mother's Day. Important holiday for Guatemalans.

17 Norwegian Constitution Day. Festival held on closest weekend

18 Flag Day. Haitian.

20 Birth of Cuban Republic.

22 Eritran Independence Day

30 Croatian Independence Day. Marks freedom from Communism and Yugoslavia in 1990.

Asian American Heritage Month.

Flores de Mayo. Filipino religious holiday, a month-long celebration dedicated to the Virgin Mary.

Visakh Boja. Cambodian religious holiday. Celebrates birth, enlightenment and death of Buddha, all of which occurred at the full moon in Visakh (May).

June

6 Swedish Flag Day. Celebrates Sweden and the Swedish people.

1 0 Lidice. Czech. Commemorates annihilation of town of Lidice in 1942 by Nazis. Service in Crest   Hill on closest Saturday.

1 2 Philippine Week. Marks date in 1898 when Philippines won independence from Spain.

1 5 Day of Sorrow. Lithuanian. Marks 1940 occupation of Lithuania by Soviet Union and start of killings and deportations.

1 7 Father's Day. Important day for Guatemalans.

2 3 Midsummer. Swedish. Celebrates longest day of the year, with festivals in Chicago parks.

2 4 Feast of San Juan. Puerto Rican. Honors Patron Saint of the Island.

2 8 Vidovdan. Commemorates Serbians who died in battle against the Ottoman Turks on the Field of Kossovo in 1389.

Juneteenth. African American. Marks signing of Emancipation Proclamation.
Puerto Rican Parade. Accompanied by festival in Humboldt Park. Early June.
Natsu Matsuri. Japanese Summer Festival held last weekend in June at Buddhist Temple, 1151 W. Leland.

July

23 Egyptian Independence Day.

2 5 Constitution Day. Puerto Rican. Observes compact between Island and U.S. and first constitution for the Commonwealth.

2 5 Liberian Independence Day.

29 Fiesta del Sol. Neighborhood Pilsen Festival. Celebration of Latino culture.

August

7 Assyrian Martyrs' Day. Instituted to mark 1933 massacre by Iraqi army, now commemorates martyrdom of Assyrians through long history of persecution.

1 4 Pakistani Independence Day. Commemorates independence from Great Britain in 1947. Celebrated on nearby weekend.

1 5 Assumption Day. Croatian religious holiday with procession   through the streets at St. Jerome's on South Side.

1 5 Chusuk. Korean. Harvest Day celebrated with parade on Lawrence Avenue.

1 5 Indian Independence Day. Celebrates independence from Great Britain in 1947. Parade on Devon Avenue.

2 0 Hungarian Constitution Day. Also called St. Stephen's Day.

2 4 Ukrainian Independence Day. Marking independence   from Soviets in 1991.

August Moon Festival. Chinese. Celebrates harvest and full moon of eighth lunar month.
Bud Billiken Day. African American. Celebrates mythical figure who   protects children. Parade. Second Saturday.
Janmashtami. Indian Hindu religious holiday celebrating birth of Lord Krishna.
Ginza Holiday. Japanese Cultural Festival,usually held third weekend at Midwest Buddhist Temple, 435 W. Menomonee.

September

7 Fiesta Bonica. Puerto Rican festival.

8 Feast of Our Lady of Charity. Cuban religious holiday celebrating patroness of Cuba.

11 Ethiopian New Year. (Sept. 12 in leap year.)

15 Central American Independence Day. Celebrates independence for all of Central America except Panama.

16 El Grito. Mexican. Marks beginning of revolution against Spain in 1810.

15 Guatemalan Independence Day Parade.

28 St. Wenceslaus. Feast of Patron Saint of Czech people.

American Indian Day. State designation. Fourth Friday.

Bon Phchum Bend. Cambodian Ancestor Festival for 15 days.

Mid-Autumn Festival. Vietnamese. Children's festival, usually held during full moon.

Steuben Parade. German. Commemorates Gen. Friedrich von Steuben's achievements in American Revolution. Followed by weekend Germanfest. (A Saturday in September).

Rosh Hashanah. Jewish New Year. Religious holiday in September or October. The 10 days between it and Yom Kippur are devoted to praying for forgiveness of sins and for a good year.

Yom Kippur. Jewish religious holiday. Holiest day of year, the Day of Atonement, marked by 24 hours of fasting. (In September or October.)

Sukkoth. Jewish. Feast of Booths or Harvest Festival. Commemorates 40 years of Jewish wandering in desert on way to Promised Land. (September or October).

October

1 Nigerian Independence Day. Marks independence from British in 1960.

1 Day of the Harvest. Romanian.

6 German American Day. Celebrates first organized immigration of Germans to U.S.

9 Leif Erickson Day. Norwegian. Festival on closest weekend.

12 Columbus Day. Italian. Parade.

23 Revolution of 1956. Hungarian.

26 Day of the Revolution. Guatemalan. Commemorates 10 years of Democracy that ended in 1954.

28 Czechoslovak Independence Day. Celebrates founding of Czechoslovak Republic in 1918.

Divali. Indian Hindu religious holiday, festival of lights, celebrating return of Lord Rama from 14-year exile. (October or November)

Durga Puja. Indian Hindu religious holiday with a 10-day festival celebrating triumph of good over evil. (October or November)

Octoberfest. Cultural and social event Germans brought to U.S. (Date varies.)

November

2 Dia de los Muertos (Day of the Dead). Mexican religious holiday of remembrance, melding ancient Aztec ritual with Christian sentiment.

9 **Birthday of the poet Iqbal,** a founder of Pakistan.

1 1 **Karneval.** German. Mardi Gras-type cultural and social event.

2 2 **Lebanese Independence Day.**

24 **Harvest Festival.** Laotian.

Arab American Heritage Month.

December

1 **Romanian National Day.**

4 **Feast of St. Barbara.** Religious holiday celebrated by Cubans who practice Santeria.

1 3 **St. Lucia Day.** Swedish. Celebrates the Catholic saint who represents light in the darkest of winter.

1 7 **Feast of St. Lazarus.** Religious holiday for Cubans who practice Santeria.

24, 2 5 **Christmas Eve and Christmas Day.** Celebrates the birth of Jesus. Major religious holidays for Roman Catholics and Protestants, including Assyrians, Croatians, Cubans, Filipinos, Germans, Guatemalans, Hungarians, Irish, Italians, Lithuanians, Mexicans, Poles, Puerto Ricans, Slovaks and Swedes.

2 5 **Birthday of Mohammad Ali Jinnah,** founding father of Pakistan.

26 **Kwanzaa.** African American. Festival of life. Continues through Jan. 1.

3 0 **Rizal Day.** Filipino. Marks 1896 execution of Dr. Jose P. Rizal, national hero who focused world attention on Spanish misrule.

Chanukah. (also spelled Hannukah).Jewish religious holiday,festival of lights, marks the heroic battle of the Maccabees. (Usually in December.)

Ramadan. Start of 30 days of fasting for Muslims, to renew piety. Varies, depending on lunar calendar, backing up about 10 days each year. Will fall on Dec. 10, 1999, then moves into November for three years.